French Regional Planning

Indiana University International Studies

FRENCH
REGIONAL PLANNING

Niles M. Hansen 1968

Indiana University Press
Bloomington   London

Published in Canada by Fitzhenry & Whiteside Limited,
Scarborough, Ontario

Library of Congress catalog card number: 68-14603
Manufactured in the United States of America

To my father, Kristian Hansen

CONTENTS

vii

LIST OF FIGURES AND TABLES

xi

Preface

Since the Great Depression there has been a striking revolution in the degree of rational control which governments have exercised over aggregate economic variables. Successful application of essentially Keynesian policy measures has all but removed the old fear of recurrent and lengthy periods of high unemployment and generally depressed economic activity. As problems of full employment and economic growth have been solved there has been a shift of interest toward the regional distribution of national wealth. Thus, in one country after another regional policies have been adopted to aid economically lagging areas and, in some instances, to curb the growth of areas which have become, or are in danger of becoming, overconcentrated in terms of population and economic activity. In the United States, for example, legislation on behalf of lagging regions has included the Area Redevelopment Act of 1961, the Appalachian Regional Development Act of 1965, and the Public Works and Economic Development Act of 1965. In England public policy measures have been designed to restrict industrial expansion in the Southeast in favor of areas with relatively high unemployment rates. Experts from the Common Market countries have met on numerous occasions to discuss regional economic problems within their respective countries and in the European Economic Community as a whole. Perhaps the best known European case is that of Italy, where efforts to encourage development of the Mezzogiorno have received particular attention from American scholars.

On the other hand, the most comprehensive national system of regional planning, that which has evolved in France during the last two decades, heretofore has not been subject to extended examination by English-speaking scholars. The present volume therefore seeks to trace the evolution of French policy for readers not familiar with the relevant French literature, as well as to analyze critically its main

xiii

features in terms which may be useful both to French readers and to others concerned with general issues of spatial resource allocation. An attempt is made not only to describe, but to suggest improvements which might be made in present French policies. Moreover, an effort is made to derive general policy implications from French experience and to apply them to a number of broad issues of immediate concern in the United States. It is hoped, therefore, that this study will be useful to economists, geographers, planners, and others concerned with regional policy, and that the questions raised may enable them to correct or improve whatever deficiencies remain in the policy responses proposed here.

Austin, Texas   N. M. H.
April 19, 1967

Acknowledgments

Parts of Chapter 1 have appeared in articles published in *The Southern Economic Journal*, XXXII (October, 1965), and *The Western Economic Journal*, IV (Fall, 1965). Portions of Chapter 5 have appeared in *Kyklos*, XX (Fasc. 3, 1967). Part of Chapter 7 was published in *The Southern Economic Journal*, XXXIV (July, 1967). Chapter 12 draws heavily on articles previously published in *Land Economics*, XLII (February, 1966), and XLIII (November, 1967).

My research in France during 1965–66 was made possible by a grant from the National Science Foundation. The University of Texas extended to me the financial help required for its terminal stages; Carey Thompson and Stephen McDonald of the Department of Economics and W. Gordon Whaley, Dean of the Graduate School, were particularly helpful in securing this assistance.

I am indebted to numerous French and American colleagues and friends for their invaluable support in the preparation of this study. Indeed, I regret that owing to their great number it is not possible to acknowledge each individual's efforts. Mention must be made, however, of Professor André Vlerick of the University of Ghent (Belgium) and Professor Maurice Byé of the University of Paris for their cooperation in arranging for my research position at the University of Paris. Professor Byé's continuous aid while I was in France deserves special recognition; it was a privilege to be associated with this eminent and humane scholar. I also am grateful to Professor Jacques Boudeville of the University of Paris; as France's most prominent specialist in regional economics his frequent assistance was particularly welcome. This study similarly benefited from conversations which I had in Paris with Professor Lloyd Rodwin, Chairman of the Faculty Committee of the M.I.T.-Harvard Joint Center for Urban Studies. Professor Rodwin also provided valuable criticism of my preliminary manuscript. In addition, I wish to express my appreciation for the cooperation extended by numerous officials and staff members of the General Planning Commission, the Délégation à l'Aménagement du Territoire et à l'Action Régionale, the District de la Région de Paris, the Institut de Science Economique Appliquée, and the European Economic Community Study Center of the University of Paris, and in particular to M. Charles Frappart, M. Jovan Pavlevski, and Mlle. Germaine Ganiayre. In the preparation of my final manuscript I received valuable assistance from Mrs. Donald F. Gaines. Although the merits of this book owe much to these individuals the responsibility for any deficiencies is mine.

My greatest debt, however, is to my wife, who somehow managed to provide me with an ideal working atmosphere while coping with household management, two small children, and the marvelously diverse but arduous task of shopping in a French town. Finally, we both are grateful to the many friends and neighbors who did so much to make our stay in St.-Leu-La-Forêt, where most of this book was written, such a rewarding experience in both scholarly and human terms.

French Regional Planning

1

Resource Allocation in a Regional Context

Like many other countries, the United States is facing numerous major problems related to the location of economic activity. These difficulties fall into two principal categories: those of large urban agglomerations; and those arising from regional disparities in income and economic opportunity. Most metropolitan area problems—slums, public transportation deficiencies, air pollution, lack of parks and recreation facilities, traffic tie-ups—are a consequence of urban congestion. On the other hand, regions characterized by economic stagnation tend to be outside the influence spheres of large cities.

An unfortunate tendency has long been to judge an economy almost solely from the viewpoint of national production and consumption aggregates, without reference to the geographic division of economic activity. However, as John Friedmann and William Alonso have emphasized, the "decision of *where* to locate a new project is as important as the decision to invest in it. The questions of social justice in the distributions of the fruits of economic development are as important and as difficult in terms of regions as in terms of social classes." [1] Thus increasing pressure has been brought to bear on central governments to render assistance to both crowded agglomerations and relatively underdeveloped areas. "But the conceptual structure necessary for the intelligent making of policy is in its infancy. The social sciences, principally economics and sociology, have been laggard in taking notice of space; while geography, which has always dealt with space, has lacked analytic power." [2]

Nevertheless, from an opportunity cost viewpoint it is apparent that government aid programs such as those for metropolitan areas and the Appalachian region have significant consequences for the nature and location of economic activity in general. While it is highly desirable, therefore, that urban and regional development be considered within a unified framework of analysis, American experience has been characterized by a pronounced tendency for specialists in these disciplines to work independently of each other. "Two different professions, two different vocabularies have grown up. Communication between them has become exceedingly difficult, and on the level of practical action there appears to be little coordination between schemes of regional and urban development." [3]

Similarly, the relevance of both the market mechanism and government action should be integrated into any attempt to deal systematically with the problem of spatially optimal resource allocation. Here, too, theory and practice in the United States leave much to be desired concerning the nature and consequences of the various interactions between the public and private sectors of the economy.

The postwar development of indicative planning in France, on the other hand, has served to focus attention in a highly systematic manner on the nature and functions of the modern state in an essentially capitalistic economy. France's nonmandatory planning scheme aims for the most part at achieving the maximum possible rate of growth consistent with stability. With the aid of input-output techniques the General Planning Commission (Commissariat Général du Plan) prepares a four-year plan in association with the Ministry of Finance. The plan is based on information furnished by government agencies, public enterprises, and private firms. Although tentative investment decisions reflected in the plan are not binding, a network of reciprocal expectations is established. Participants generally do act in accord with the plan, because when everyone cooperates uncertainties about future market conditions are reduced considerably for all concerned. As the Hacketts have indicated, "Whatever may be the virtues or shortcomings of the French system of planning . . . it is the most advanced example of such a system in an industrially developed economy whose essential structure remains capitalistic." [4] Similarly, Oxenfeldt and Holubnychy have emphasized that "France has undoubtedly gone farther today than any other middle-way capitalistic economy toward developing novel arrangements and methods for the solution of basic economic problems." [5] Among these basic problems is that of spatial resource allocation, and "until now France is the only European state which has undertaken to establish regional institutions on an economic basis." [6]

The principal task of this book is to describe and evaluate the achievements, shortcomings, and prospects of this unique attempt to deal rationally with spatial resource allocation in both theoretical and practical terms. At the outset this requires an attempt at clarification of the basic notion which animates French thought and policy along these lines, namely, that of *aménagement du territoire*. This term, which has no exact equivalent in English, is by no means a precise concept even in French. To illustrate, it is only necessary to consider a few of the many definitions which have appeared in the relevant French literature.

For Philippe Lamour the basic problem posed by *aménagement du territoire* in France is "the management of a country, in great part insufficiently developed, in such a manner as to bring it to the level of the European countries with which it is associated." [7] Still more vague is the conception of Philippe Laurent, for whom it means "the introduction of rationality in place of only natural determinisms or uncoordinated individual desires." [8] A recent government publication contains a definition which is frankly antieconomic in its implications for factor mobility: "the object of *aménagement du territoire* is to develop each region in a fashion which permits its population to live as well as it could elsewhere through a better utilization of the means available to it." [9] For the group associated with the influential review *Economie et Humanisme,* on the other hand, the basic issue is at once geographic, economic, and human:

"Aménagement" is the technique of enhancement and development in the framework of more or less large natural or political territorial divisions. It presupposes deliberate intervention in order to assure rational enhancement and harmonious development which aim at optimal utilization of resources and the humane elevation of the relevant populations.[10]

In fact, however, these and numerous similar definitions add little to a statement made in 1950 by Eugène Claudius-Petit, one of the earliest persons to press seriously for rational and coordinated research into the spatial aspects of France's economic development. In his view, *"aménagement du territoire* has as its goal the pursuit of a better distribution of the population in relation to natural resources and economic activities; this search, however, is oriented not toward purely economic goals, but more toward the welfare and full development of the potentialities of the population." [11]

Whatever the conceptual difficulties, it is evident that concern in France for *aménagement du territoire,* a term scarcely twenty years old, reflects a genuine need to transcend particular preoccupations such as geographic planning, urbanism, rural planning, and regional economic development. *Aménagement* aims at comprehensiveness and consistency without denying the importance of any of these particular manifestations of concern for rational resource distribution in terms of human satisfactions. The emphasis of a decade ago in France on the theme of "industrial decentralization," with its implicit opposition of Paris and the provinces, has gradually diminished in favor of a policy of *aménagement du territoire,* which has undertaken to emphasize the complementarities of interests hitherto opposed or at best uncoordinated.

In brief, the principal virtue of the French approach lies in its effort to deal comprehensively and systematically with problems of spatial resource allocation,[12] difficulties that have tended to receive only bifurcated and uncoordinated treatment in other countries, including the United States. On the other hand, the effort must be judged according to the extent to which its goals reflect actual social preferences, and to the extent to which its concrete policy measures in fact facilitate achievement of the goals. In these regards, highly generalized definitional statements of the objectives of *aménagement du territoire* are obviously not sufficient. One must elaborate a model which takes into account the nature of different types of regions and of differing types of public and private investment policies, and the relevance of certain investment activities and of their location to social preferences. Such a model should not only be useful in describing present relations but should be capable of indicating how present relations might be altered so as to be more in harmony with social preferences. This implies that both the market mechanism and public policy measures should be examined in the light of cost-benefit considerations, with special attention to opportunity costs.

In the remainder of this chapter I will construct a general model of this type based on both empirical and theoretical considerations. In succeeding chapters the circumstances which have given rise to the evolution of French regional policies are compared with the assumptions of this basic model. The methods and aims of these programs are described in detail and evaluated in terms of their correspondence to prevailing social preferences and rational utilization of economic resources. Attention is given to the basic theoretical notions that have animated French thought concerning regional and urban development, as well as to concrete measures which have been undertaken or which are envisaged for the future. On the basis of these considerations an effort is made to formulate a number of generalizations regarding the potential strengths and difficulties of regional economic policy-making in a mixed economy, and a number of operationally feasible proposals are set forth for dealing with the difficulties. In the concluding chapter the lessons of French experience are applied critically to American regional development policy.

Balanced and Unbalanced Growth in a Regional Setting

In recent years considerable attention has been given to the problem of whether economic development might be best accelerated by "balanced growth" under government direction or by government provocation of imbalances, whereby disequilibria produce positive responses which in turn produce other disequilibria and so on in the manner of a chain reaction.

The balanced growth argument for developing lagging areas involves initiating a large number of interdependent projects simultaneously.[13] The principal justification for such action is based on the phenomenon of external economies. Nurkse,[14] for example, has pointed out that the marginal product of capital may be greater in underdeveloped areas than in those already industrialized, but not necessarily in terms of private profit; individual projects in underdeveloped areas encounter a high degree of uncertainty concerning a market for their products. This disincentive would be overcome if numerous projects were undertaken simultaneously; investments which would not be profitable in isolation become so for the ensemble as a result of mutually favorable external economies.[15]

The applicability of this general approach to problems of underdeveloped countries has been the target of numerous criticisms,[16] some of which are particularly applicable to problems of lagging regions in mature economies. Specifically, "in practice any implementation of the 'big push' proposals would mean a large public sector. . . . Even if the government were to subsidize private firms, instead of operating public concerns, the extent of regulation would be enormous." [17] In most industrialized western economies, institutional patterns would not be compatible with such an approach to developing poorer regions. Moreover, the balanced growth argument implies a closed economy; but "one way a country can have balanced consumption without balanced production, if it can make or grow or mine anything the world wants, is to import goods it cannot afford to produce." [18] This is especially applicable to regional cases, where free interregional trade makes it relatively (to the international case) easy to avoid many of the difficulties posed by capital lumpiness.

In some instances, on the other hand, the thesis of balanced growth via the big push might be more relevant to regional than to national cases. One of the principal arguments against its applicability in underdeveloped countries is that "the resources required for carrying out the policy . . . are of such an order of magnitude that a country disposing of them would in fact not be underdeveloped." [19] But the poverty that characterizes most underdeveloped countries should not be confused with that in lagging regions of industrialized nations. The availability of productive resources in the latter often is not comparable to that in the former. Labor often is anxious to find employment and savings frequently are considerable, though they often flow to expanding regions rather than to local projects. In such conditions the balanced growth doctrine is not without value for public policy.

The unbalanced growth approach has been developed for the most part by A. O. Hirschman and by François Perroux and the French school of economic thought oriented toward regional problems. Hirschman has emphasized that investment strategy should concentrate on a few sectors rather than on widely dispersed projects; the key sectors would be determined by measuring backward and forward linkage effects in terms of input-output maxima.[20] Similarly, Perroux has emphasized that growth does not appear simultaneously and uniformly throughout an economy; rather, it is concentrated, with varying intensity, in certain development poles or propulsive industries.[21] Detailed consideration of the contributions of Perroux and the French school is reserved for Chapter 5.

Even though interregional growth is always unbalanced in geographic terms, it still requires special analytic consideration, for "while the regional setting reveals unbalanced growth at its most obvious, it perhaps does not show it at its best" because successive growth points may all "fall within the same privileged growth space." [22] Thus, in the subsequent analysis primary attention is given to unbalanced growth since this is the characteristic pattern of development in fact followed by mature economies, and since it generally is still the most feasible approach for an institutional point of view. More important, under certain conditions it is also the most rational approach from a purely economic point of view. Before examining this proposition in detail it is necessary to define the variables and clarify the terms to be employed.

Types of Investment
and Regional Prototypes

Discussions concerning optimal investment allocation frequently distinguish between investment in directly productive activities (DPA) and that in public overhead capital (OC). For present purposes, private investment and investment in DPA are treated as synonymous. OC, however, is divided into two components: social (SOC) and economic (EOC). Projects of the latter type are primarily oriented toward supporting DPA or toward the movement of economic resources and include roads, bridges, harbors, power installations, and similar undertakings. SOC projects, on the other hand, are more concerned with the provision of satisfactions which have generally been regarded as noneconomic in nature. Although they may also increase productivity, the manner in which they do so is much less direct than in the case of EOC. Thus SOC would include such activities as education, cultural projects, health programs, and welfare. Investment in SOC may be regarded, therefore, as equivalent to investment in human resources.[23] The reader will note that the use of SOC here differs from that in most of the relevant literature, where it has tended to be synonymous with our OC. However, the usefulness of disaggregating public overhead capital has been acknowledged. Hirschman, for example, distinguishes between "wide" and "narrow" definitions. The latter corresponds closely to our EOC, although Hirschman's criteria are different.[24]

Another refinement concerns the analytic regions to be used. Regional problems often are treated in terms of a two-fold distinction between developed and underdeveloped regions, the familiar North-South problem which characterizes so many mature national economies of the Northern Hemisphere. Here, however, regions are classified into three types: congested, intermediate, and lagging.

Congested regions are those which contain very high concentrations of population and of industrial and commercial activity. Examples would include the London and Paris agglomerations and much of the megalopolis which extends along the northeastern seaboard of the United States. These regions have reached a point where the marginal social costs (private costs plus external, or spillover, effects) of further expansion are equal to, or probably even more than, the concomitant marginal social benefits.[25]

Intermediate regions, on the other hand, are those which offer significant advantages—raw materials, qualified labor, cheap power, etc. —to private firms, and where entry of new firms or expansion of existing firms would result in marginal social benefits substantially in excess of concomitant social costs. In general, expansion of economic activity in these areas to take advantage of unexploited potentials will result in a marginal net social product significantly greater than that which would accrue in congested regions.

Finally, lagging regions present few, if any, attributes which would tend to attract new economic activity. They are generally areas characterized by small-scale agriculture or stagnant or declining industries.

Of course, there often may be some overlap between the intermediate and lagging categories in the case of regions which have long been industrialized but whose dominant industries are experiencing long-run difficulties, for example, the coal sector in large parts of Appalachia, the textile sector in New England, and coal and textiles in the North of France. A distinction must be made between cases of this type and lagging regions which have never been industrialized, since the former generally are characterized by relatively large stocks of private and public capital, a population accustomed to factory work, and a managerial class whose abilities might be adapted to the needs of expanding sectors of the economy. However, it might also be argued that this heritage from the past is more of a liability than an asset to a region.

Professor Krier for example, maintains, contrary to most a priori arguments on the subject, that the attractiveness of regions which already possess industries is sometimes less than that of predominantly agricultural regions. In reality, he maintains, when new enterprises are implanted in a region, what already exists is often an obstacle to them. In the first place, expanding industries usually seek well-equipped, open spaces where buildings can be constructed and arranged in the most rational manner. Such conditions are not likely to be found in older industrial regions, where old buildings predominate and where their arrangement, frequently in the center of cities, is the product of anarchy rather than planning. Entrepreneurs may also seek to avoid conflicts with labor unions by establishing new operations in areas with agricultural traditions. Moreover, the labor force in relatively stagnant industrial areas often is relatively old and can be adapted to new activities only with great difficulty. Finally, in older industries in difficulty, productivity and the rhythm of work have often fallen to a relatively low level. Such conditions are known to more dynamic entrepreneurs, who consequently seek younger and more dynamic workers in agricultural regions.[26] In brief, Krier's arguments assume that reconversion of industry in distressed areas generally is unfeasible because of rigidities which preclude adaptation of existing resources to the needs of expanding sectors. Whether or not these rigidities in fact more than outweigh the acquired advantages of these areas must be determined on the basis of careful empirical study of particular regions.

Unbalanced Growth
and Regional Disparities

Congested regions are the product of unbalanced growth. For the most part, their development begins spontaneously as a result of favorable circumstances such as proximity to principal transportation routes or raw materials. Expansion of private investment increases the need for transportation facilities, water, housing, and power.[27] However, Hirschman has argued that after some time public investment requirements will decline relative to private investment and that earnings from prior investments can be used to finance a higher share of public investment. This process, he finds, "is implicit in the term 'social *overhead* capital.'" Thus, public funds are freed for use in other regions and in the long run will contribute toward diminishing regional differences. However, he also notes the "purely 'permissive' character of the inducement mechanisms set in motion by these investments." In consequence, it also is necessary to endow poorer regions "with some ongoing and actively inducing economic activity of its own, in industry, agriculture, or services." [28]

North has argued even more vigorously that regional differences tend to disappear in the long run. In his view, regional growth is tied to the development of an export base. The growth of new exports is fostered by such factors as the development of transportation, growth in income and demand in other regions, technological innovations, and the provision of public overhead capital. Initially, the export base and service industries benefit from capital investment from the outside. As local population and income increases, regional savings are utilized to broaden the export base. Thus as the region matures the staple base becomes relatively less important as production becomes more varied. "We may expect, therefore, that the differences between regions will become less marked, that secondary industry will tend to be more equalized, and indeed in economic terms that regionalism will tend to disappear." [29]

The position taken here, on the other hand, is that there is no automatic mechanism which may be relied on to check the growth of congested regions or to eliminate interregional differences in income and economic opportunity. Although public policy measures may be useful in attaining these ends, careful attention must be given to the allocation of different types of public investment (EOC, SOC) to different types of regions (congested, intermediate, lagging); otherwise, public action may not only be irrational from a strictly economic point of view but may even fail to achieve ends based on social justice.

Congested Regions

Systematic study of the effects of congested living conditions on human satisfactions is still in its early stages, but available evidence suggests that these effects are in large measure adverse, and that there is more to the discomforts of highly concentrated urban living than incurable rural nostalgia in the mind of the city dweller. For example, Dr. Thomas S. Langner recently reported to the American Psychopathological Association on a study of 1,660 residents in a better middle-class neighborhood of New York City. Examining their backgrounds, the researchers determined that the more stress to which a person was subjected, the more he was inclined toward mental disorder. Langner summarized the situation as "the more the unmerrier." [30]

More recently, a *New York Times* article reported on "what seems to be mounting evidence" that overcrowding, if not checked, "may end not in starvation but in mass psychosis and psychological collapse." This speculation is based on the results of numerous investigations into the effects of crowding on the mental and psychical well-being of living creatures in the laboratory as well as in the wild state. However, Dr. John Christian of Philadelphia's Albert Einstein Medical Center stated that "Although our experiments have been with animals we believe the same mechanism, with certain variations, of course, might be at work in human populations." Some support was given to this view by Dr. W. Horsley Gant of Johns Hopkins University. Dr. Gant said that he had found "indications of increased mental disturbance" in persons who had lived under crowded conditions in Russia.[31]

If urban life under congested conditions is so unaccommodating, why is it that in countries everywhere an increasing proportion of the total population lives in large urban agglomerations? Do individuals in fact prefer to live in these locations? Very little research has been done on this subject in the United States, probably because it is assumed on the basis of the prima facie evidence that because an individual has "chosen" to live in a given location he therefore has revealed his preference for it. But this may not be the case; indeed, it is quite possible that a large urban area may continue to grow even though a substantial number of persons within and without the area would prefer not to live there. How might this come about?

One of the major conclusions derivable from the assumptions of economic theory is that factor mobility will equalize returns to various classes of homogeneous inputs, *ceteris paribus*. Space, however, is not homogeneous. Because clustering results in a wide variety of external economies to both industrial and commercial firms, purely market forces tend to concentrate economic activity in a few focal areas. These economies include relative abundance of public overhead capital, close proximity to buyers and sellers, the presence of numerous auxiliary business services (banking, brokerage, insurance), educational facilities, and a relatively well-trained labor force.[32] "All in all," writes Benjamin Chinitz, "the forces pulling manufacturing employment into the metropolitan areas seem to be increasing rather than diminishing in strength," although there are forces working in the opposite direction, for example higher wages and higher costs for space.[33] Further evidence in this regard is supplied by George Borts, who has shown that demand plays a determining role in attracting capital. This movement also is accompanied by a rise in costs, particularly wages. However, these increased costs are not a determining influence since they are offset by increases in productivity.[34]

In general, then, attraction of investment to already congested areas tends to raise the marginal product of labor in these areas, thereby inducing immigration. Growth of a relatively skilled labor force, induced public overhead investment, and other induced economic activities further enhance the attractiveness of such areas for private investment. This cumulative process results in ever greater concentration of economic activity and population; however, it also entails numerous social costs, including overcrowded streets, clogged intersections, inadequate parks and recreation facilities, slum neighborhoods, natural beauty marred by buildings, highways, and billboards, and air pollution.[35] Moreover, there is nothing in the nature of things to halt this process because the external diseconomies of congestion are usually not internalized costs for private producers; or, if they are internalized, they are not sufficient to balance the external economies of agglomeration. It is this disparity between social and private costs which creates the problem of choice versus preference.

It may be argued that individuals will increase their welfare by

moving into concentrated areas so long as their marginal private gains
in income outweigh their own marginal increase in diseconomies associated with the social costs of congestion. But this does not imply an
increase in social welfare in a Pareto-optimal sense, since such action,
by increasing concentration, results in greater diseconomies to previous
residents. Some previously inframarginal residents might then prefer to
leave the agglomeration. This would be the case where marginal private
income loss from out-migration is less than the increase in marginal
disutility arising from increased congestion. On the other hand, social
and economic rigidities (habituation to neighbors and surroundings,
transport cost, etc.) will cause many of these persons to refrain from
moving, i.e., they will not minimize their welfare loss unless increased
disutility in the agglomeration is substantially greater than private loss
in relocating.

The failure of the free market to check the growth of congested
regions suggests that public policy measures might be employed to slow
down the expansion of congested regions and prevent the expansion
of other regions to a point where they become congested. Taxation and
credit policy and land-use controls could be used to limit the expansion of DPA in congested regions, whereas economic growth in alternative regions could be encouraged by similar devices as well as by
provision of public overhead capital. In fact, governments have rarely
carried out such joint measures in any systematic fashion. Moreover,
there seems to be little evidence of any process, such as that suggested
by Hirschman, whereby public overhead funds tend to be shifted from
regions which have experienced the greatest degree of growth in the
past to relatively less developed regions. This does not deny that less
developed regions may receive more public overhead capital than in
the past, but it is doubtful whether this capital is sufficient to overcome
the attractiveness of that available in "mature" regions.

My own studies based on highly standardized Belgian data show
that while per capita EOC outlays are directly related to growth factors, those for SOC are directly related to absolute population size,
population density, and degree of industrial and commercial importance. The data indicate that even if the growth of an expanding
area, and consequently its EOC requirements, should begin to level
off, there is no guarantee that public investment as a whole will
diminish. In fact, because of increased SOC requirements, areas of

concentrated population and economic activity had significantly higher public investment needs than other areas.[36] Of course, to the extent that the former areas are still expanding, EOC expenditures also will remain relatively high despite a shift in the structure of total investment toward a greater proportion of SOC. Although these results concern "local" investment requirements, the expenditures in question were financed in large part either directly or indirectly by the central government.[37]

It must be recognized that even if a central government should decide to favor less developed regions in the choice of locations for its projects, the investment of local and state (or the foreign equivalent) governments may offset the advantages accruing to the less developed regions. This would be most likely to occur in a nation with strong federal traditions, such as the United States.

The United States data presented in Table 1.1 show that per capita municipal operating expenditures are directly related to population size, implying a direct relationship between per capita capital stock and population. However, there is also a strong direct relationship between capital expenditures (per capita) and population size. Thus current public investment of this type is greatest in areas which have had most investment in the past.[38] Similarly, analysis of census data on direct expenditures of state governments in 1962 shows a strong direct relationship between per capita current operating outlays and per capita capital expenditures. The correlation coefficient relating these two variables is .731, highly significant at the 99 per cent level.[39] These results indicate that even if central government investment policy were to be consciously directed toward favoring lagging regions, it is doubtful whether public investment at all levels of government would, on balance, eliminate regional differences in income or in investment and employment opportunities.

The foregoing discussion may be summarized by reference to Figure 1.1. Along any given isoproduct curve, X_1, $\Delta X = f_s \Delta S + f_e \Delta E + f_d \Delta D = O$. Here X = total net social product, S = SOC, E = EOC, $E + S = P$ (public overhead investment), D = private investment in directly productive activities, and f_j = the marginal product of investment j. Thus, the cost in terms of D of producing X_1 increases if there is less P to help. At the far right of Figure 1.1, increments to relatively plentiful P do not give any significant decline in D. At the

Table 1.1

Average per capita expenditures

of municipal governments in the United States, 1962

(by population size class)

Population size class	Capital outlay	Other	Total
Less than 2,500	$ 9.43	$ 32.48	$ 41.91
2,500–4,999	10.05	42.24	52.28
5,000–9,999	13.63	47.09	60.72
10,000–24,999	17.26	55.17	72.43
25,000–49,999	20.66	75.41	96.08
50,000–99,999	23.79	87.66	111.46
100,000–299,999	30.36	93.76	124.12
300,000–499,999	32.48	91.56	124.04
500,000–999,999	41.27	125.23	166.51
1,000,000 or more	46.80	172.31	219.12

Source: Finances of Municipalities and Townships Governments, U. S. Bureau of the Census, Census of Governments, 1962, Vol. IV, No. 3 (Washington, D.C., 1964), p. 34.
Note: Capital and other outlays may not add to totals because of rounding.

far left, X_1 eventually becomes vertical since any given D requires a minimum level of P. It is assumed that D can be varied continuously but that P is supplied in discrete quanta (for example A, B, and C) so that it is not possible to move from m to n (or from n to o) via a process of directly and continuously balanced growth of D and P. In the initial phase of growth a region which is now congested was at, say, m. Factors favorable to private investment result in a gradual movement from m to m'. Urgent demands for public investment then induce a delayed, discontinuous lump of P and a discrete move to n. This forms the basis for a similar movement from n to o. As the growth of the region continues there is a relative shift in the composition of P; the share accounted for by E (indicated by the dotted portions of segments m' n and n'' o) declines relative to that accounted for by S (the solid portions).

Furthermore, assuming that X_0 is the level of output at which average returns to scale momentarily become constant, there is nothing in the nature of things that will eventually halt this process at some point after $X_1 > X_0$, since the relevant net social product function is not linearly homogeneous. Rather, it will have the form (for example) $X = [2\theta DP - \lambda(D^2) - \beta(P^2)]^{1/2} + [\rho(\alpha D - D^2) - \gamma]$, where θ, λ, β, ρ, α, and γ are constants greater than zero.[40] The last

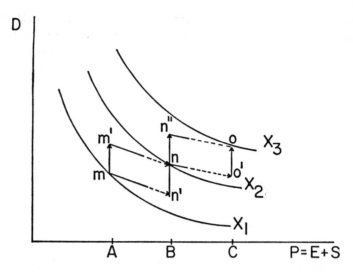

Figure 1.1 Unbalanced growth of public (P) and private (D) investment

term in brackets gives the effects of external economies of agglomeration and external diseconomies of congestion. During the initial phase of the region's growth the former produce increasing average returns to scale. Eventually, however, the effects of external diseconomies become dominant and the bracketed term becomes negative, i.e. X increases less than proportionally with inputs. But since the external diseconomies in question are in large measure not internalized costs for private firms, growth will still continue indefinitely, at least in the absence of public-policy measures.

Intermediate Regions

Decongestion of highly concentrated urban areas and development of poorer regions are complementary aspects of the more general problem of achieving over-all spatially optimal resource allocation. But checking the growth of congested areas by means of taxation policy, land-use controls, or other similar devices would not in itself guarantee more rational allocation. For example, new plants might merely tend to cluster around the restricted area, giving rise to an extension of already congested conditions; or they might tend to cause overexpansion of regions which were previously highly developed but as yet uncongested. In any event, mere prohibition of expansion in congested

areas cannot be expected necessarily to stimulate growth in alternative
regions. It is perhaps in recognition of this that government action has
frequently been proposed to attract new industry directly to such
regions.[41] Too often, however, such suggestions have ignored the question of opportunity cost.

Consider, for example, transportation facilities, or, more specifically,
roads. A new or improved road provides numerous direct and indirect
benefits to a region.[42] From a short-run cost-benefit viewpoint, a
given length and type of road generally will cost more to build, *ceteris
paribus,* in a congested area, say A, than in a less congested area B,
especially if it involves construction requiring land purchase. But marginal direct benefits generally will be proportionally more marked in A,
so that A's ratio of marginal product to marginal cost probably will be
greater. However, the long-run consequences of such investment in A
are not desirable if short-run improvements merely contribute to external effects which reduce private costs and increase industrial concentration. This would result in a long-run situation where more people
merely live under the same state of congestion and social costs as
prevailed before the project was undertaken. On the other hand, the
construction of a new road in B would not in itself guarantee the attraction of new industry. For the long-run net benefits of such public infrastructure investment in less developed regions to outweigh the cost of
foregone opportunities elsewhere (from a social viewpoint), the region
should offer advantages to the private sector in addition to those relating to infrastructure. These might include raw materials, a sufficient
quantity of labor with necessary skills and training, and cheap power.
Of course, these advantages will most likely be found in regions already advanced beyond an underdeveloped state, unless one allows for
fortuitous circumstances such as the discovery of gas or oil.

In brief, long-run cost-benefit considerations may favor concentrating public infrastructure investment in less developed regions, even
though an opposite course of action might be indicated from the long-
and short-run private (firm) viewpoints as well as the short-run social
view-point. The principal beneficiaries of this investment should be intermediate regions which already tend to attract private firms on comparative costs grounds. Such development should, however, insofar as
possible, avoid creating conditions conducive to eventual congestion.

In the regions where these circumstances exist it is reasonable to assume that unbalanced growth will be generated by excess EOC capacity. In terms of Figure 1.1, the development process begins with a discrete increment of E (mn'), followed by a gradual expansion of induced D, which moves the regional economy from n' to n. In this case the production function assumes the form $X = [2\theta DP - \lambda (D^2) - \beta(P^2)]^{1/2} + [\rho(\alpha P - P^2) - \lambda]$, because now net external effects are induced by P.[43] It also should be emphasized that P may continue to induce expansion of D even after E reaches optimum capacity, for, as I have noted, regions which have had large amounts of EOC investment tend to spend heavily on SOC once EOC demand has been largely satisfied.

Lagging Regions

Whatever the weight of political pressures, it is not economically rational to attempt to induce economic growth in lagging regions by means of excess EOC capacity so long as better alternatives exist in intermediate regions. These regions are left, therefore, with two basic alternatives: out-migration; or the development of local resources to a point where they can, in combination with public infrastructure investment, provide a realistic competitive basis for industrial location. However, there is a great deal of empirical evidence that out-migration from lagging regions cannot be relied upon to eliminate interregional differences in income.[44] While interregional wage differences may result in some migration if full employment prevails in the more advanced regions and if net capital formation in such regions represents extensive investment, the effects of capital deepening on employment opportunities will depend both on how it affects the marginal product of labor and on the nature of relevant product markets. Nor will capital flows tend to reduce significantly regional disparities, since, as has been pointed out, new investment tends to flow to already advanced regions; and, in any event, many industries are capital intensive, and labor-intensive industries may not be growing rapidly enough. Since, therefore, most of these regions will not be fortunate enough to benefit from natural resource discoveries, the burden of creating development preconditions falls on public policy—but not primarily along EOC lines. Rather, what is called for in lagging regions is concentrated investment in SOC.

Only in recent years have economists tended to move away from explaining growth almost exclusively in terms of increasing the supply of inputs or shifts in the production function caused by technological innovation, toward emphasis on changes in the quality of the inputs, and especially the quality of the human input. On the one hand, this shift of emphasis has resulted from the evidence provided by numerous empirical studies that only a small part of output growth can be imputed to increases in capital and labor inputs.[45] Consequent attempts to explain the nature of the "residual factor" have led, on the other hand, to greater interest in the role of investment in human resources (SOC) as a source of economic development. Thus, T. W. Schultz has maintained that direct expenditures on education, health, and other activities aimed at improving the "quality of human effort" account "for most of the impressive rise in real earnings per worker."[46]

Edward Denison's remarkable effort to break down the residual into its component parts, although open to certain criticisms, is particularly instructive in this regard. His calculations indicate that improvement in the quality of the labor force through additional education contributed significantly to United States growth rates in the 1929–57 period, equal to 23 per cent of the growth rate of total real national income and 42 per cent of the growth rate of real national income per person employed.[47] The latter growth rate was 1.60, of which .67 percentage points were attributed to increase in education per worker and only .15 percentage points to the increase in the quantity of capital per person employed.

In response to those who have considered his estimate of education's contribution too high, Denison notes four ways in which education contributes to productivity. First, he says, a better educated person will do a better job than a less educated one within a given occupation. Second, additional education makes individuals more receptive to new ideas and more aware of better ways of doing things. Third, it gives an individual a wider range of choice and appreciation of alternative occupations. Finally, there has been a shift "from occupations requiring little education to those requiring more."[48]

It should also be noted that increased education, in addition to being "one of the largest sources of past and prospective economic growth," is also "among the elements most subject to conscious social decision."[49] Moreover, it is possible to develop objective criteria for planning education (and possibly other types of SOC investment) for productive purposes in terms of "how much" and "what kind," as the work of Eckaus has shown.[50]

In the light of recent stress on the benefits of investment in human resources, it is especially important to realize that while the SOC needs of lagging regions are relatively great, their SOC equipment is generally the least well developed. European experience, for example, indicates,

> For a wide range of industries, the skills required of the bulk of the labour force can be easily developed once training facilities are available. But the present distribution of technical schools is very uneven. The figures suggest that the insufficiency or complete lack of facilities for industrial training in less industrialized or under-developed regions is an important factor tending to project the existing distribution of industry into the future.[51]

Furthermore, I have demonstrated that differences in per capita SOC investment between areas of industrial and commercial importance and areas lacking such importance are much greater than differences in per capita EOC outlays.[52] Thus, social opportunity cost considerations would favor concentrating public investments in SOC in lagging regions, where the corresponding marginal products (short- and long-run) generally will be greater than in regions already well equipped along these lines.

Of course, it might be argued that provision of SOC facilities in lagging regions should be primarily a local task. Hoover notes that a region's success in holding and attracting employment is determined more and more by considerations such as standards of education, technical training for new entrants to the labor force, retraining of those already in the labor force, and the region's attractiveness as a place to live, and less and less by locational factors such as transportation and availability of materials and power. He further contends that urban renewal and the education task with respect to manpower resources are "something that can be accomplished in and by the region itself. This kind of policy could not possibly be accomplished, in fact, in any other way." [53] However, while it may be possible for some areas (Pittsburgh, for example) to provide the needed facilities entirely on their own, and while local concern and cooperation certainly are necessary in any attempt at regional development, it is not feasible to expect that most lagging regions will be able to provide sufficient SOC for themselves. A clear indication of this is provided by American experience in state financing of higher education. Seymour Harris has pointed out that "unfortunately, states are not equally capable of financing a higher education programme. What happens is that the poor states spend a larger part of the income of their people on higher education and receive a smaller product than the rich states." In general, the richer states have lower burdens (lower percentage of population in the college age group), higher capacity, and higher achievement, and must make a smaller effort." [54]

Of course, availability of SOC, even if provided in large measure directly or indirectly by the central government, will not in itself necessarily induce immediate growth in lagging regions. It is increasingly apparent that economic opportunities exist primarily for those with the skills and training to take advantage of them. Since skills and training are largely a result of SOC investment, it is quite likely that the development of SOC facilities in lagging regions will result in the out-migration of persons seeking higher wages.

In the long run, out-migration may be expected to decline. Many persons who benefit from initial concentration on SOC will choose to remain in the lagging region, despite the economic disadvantages, because of attachment to family, friends, and surroundings. These persons eventually will constitute a body of qualified labor sufficient to permit greater emphasis on other policy measures. Here the balanced growth doctrine appears more realistic than it might within the context of less developed nations. After an initial emphasis on providing SOC (though not, of course, to the exclusion of EOC), there should be a longer-run shift in SOC-EOC composition in favor of EOC. Then external economies resulting from balanced growth of SOC and EOC may attract significant private investment. In particular, regional savings, which are often considerable in lagging regions of mature economies, should be directed toward local investment. Furthermore, the central government may promote growth directly by transferring some of the activities of its own agencies from congested to lagging regions, or by locating new activities in lagging regions, assuming in either case that such measures would be economically feasible.

Finally, it should also be noted that an increase in out-migration from lagging regions as a result of SOC investment does not imply that EOC investment would not have this result as well, particularly if it is in the form of improved transportation facilities. Those who advocate developing lagging regions by making them more accessible often forget the other side of the coin; since higher wages in other regions become more accessible, labor mobility may increase substantially. Although public investment in a lagging region will tend to result in out-migration regardless of its EOC-SOC composition, SOC projects do have one important advantage. Since the benefits accruing from such investment generally do not become dramatically evident in the short run, a more gradual adaption of regional population to regional resources occurs than would generally be the case for EOC investment. In any event, out-migration should be viewed as a social gain rather than a cause for alarm, at least insofar as regional policy aims at increasing individual welfare rather than maintaining or expanding the number of persons resident in a given area.

Summary and Conclusions

Table 1.2 summarizes the foregoing discussion. Initially, EOC investment is induced by expansion of DPA, which in turn is a function of those costs and revenues entering into internal calculations of private firms. From the social point of view public and private investment is overconcentrated in congested regions to the detriment of other re-

Table 1.2

Regional growth under conditions of induced
public investment (phase I) and excess capacity
of public overhead capital (phases II and III)

Phase	Type of region	Nature of public and private investment activity
I	Congested	Overexpanded OC and DPA
	Intermediate	Deficient EOC
	Lagging	Deficient SOC
II	Congested	Public constraints on expansion of DPA and concomitant OC
	Intermediate	Excess EOC capacity
	Lagging	Excess SOC capacity
III	Congested	Public control on expansion of DPA and concomitant OC
	Intermediate	EOC and DPA approach optimal levels, inducing SOC expansion
	Lagging	Balanced growth of SOC, EOC, and DPA

gions. This happens because private costs do not reflect social costs, including many external diseconomies resulting from congestion, and because of the induced role of public investment.

In phases II and III (Table 1.2) public policy imposes constraints—by tax and credit devices and/or land-use controls—on further expansion in congested regions. The passive role of public investment in phase I is superseded in phase II by projects intended to induce DPA in intermediate and lagging regions. In phase III, EOC and induced DPA have reached a point in intermediate regions where changing tastes and needs induce expansion of SOC; as these regions approach optimal concentration the focus of public policy would shift to the balanced growth of lagging regions, whose populations would have been prepared for development opportunities by the SOC investment of phase II. Throughout both phase II and phase III, though especially in the former, migration should be encouraged (or at least not discouraged) from lagging to intermediate regions.

Interregional equilibrium would be attained when the social marginal product (SMP) associated with a given investment is the same for all types of investment (DPA, SOC, or EOC) and for all regions. For any given investment project i in region j, $SMP_i^j = \dfrac{X-C}{K}$, where $X =$ net social product, including external effects, $C =$ cost of materials, labor, and overhead, and $K =$ capital outlay.[55] X/K expresses output per unit investment, and C/K expresses the value of foregone alternative uses of noncapital inputs. It is assumed that prices are rational and that cost and output streams are discounted to the present. Strictly speaking, an interest rate should be included in $C;$ however, it would not affect relative SMP rankings.

The problems and prospects raised by these general considerations are well illustrated by recent French experience, which will be examined in detail in Chapter 2.

2

Urban Concentration and Individual Preferences: The Case of Paris

The
Growth of Paris

"**B**lame for the dominance of Paris in France has been variously ascribed to Louis XIV for assembling the court in Versailles, to the departmental system of Napoleon I, and to the beautification of the city by Louis Napoleon and Haussmann." [1] In any event, it is certain that the transfer of the political capital from Paris to Versailles in the seventeenth century did not halt the growth of Paris. Indeed, Paris profited from the proximity of Versailles not only by assuring its own supremacy in the arts but by increasing its dominance over the provinces. The royal highways were built to radiate from Notre Dame, which to this day remains the basic reference point in measuring distances. It is interesting that as early as 1724 a royal decree found that Paris had become so big that one could not imagine it getting larger "without exposing it to its ruin"; in consequence, a new boundary was staked out with a prohibition against construction in the suburbs, and the streets of the city were numbered in order to enforce this proscription.[2]

Under Napoleon I the dominance of Paris was permanently assured through the system of prefects, who exercised undisputed power in the newly created departments on the basis of instructions received from Paris. Thus at the beginning of the nineteenth century Paris was the center not only of political authority but of teaching, the arts, communications, and banking, owing to the creation of the Bank of France and the consequent development of the first great commercial banks. The financial predominance of Paris became overwhelming with the creation, between 1851 and 1864, of the Crédit Municipal, the Crédit Foncier, the Crédit Lyonnais, and the Société Générale.

After 1850 population growth in France fell off markedly. Whereas the annual growth rate was 0.5 per cent per year between 1831 and 1851, it fell to 0.045 per cent between 1851 and 1872, taking into account war losses in 1870–71. In the period from 1851 to 1872 both Germany and Great Britain had annual growth rates of 0.7 per cent. Moreover, the geographical distribution of France's population evolution during this interval strongly favored Paris. The three departments that recently constituted the Paris Region (Seine, Seine-et-Oise, Seine-et-Marne) increased by 40 per cent (2 per cent per year) while the rest of the country saw its population diminish by 1.7 per cent (0.07 per cent per year). The period from 1850 to 1880 was also one of rapid increase in railroad construction: the network during this time expanded from 3,000 to 24,000 kilometers. Moreover, the location of most lines tended to foster population movement toward Paris, since priority was given to lines radiating from the capital, often following the routes of the road network of Louis XIV.[3]

The rural exodus increased rapidly after 1875 owing to the importation of large quantities of cheap American wheat and to the devastating effects of phylloxera in the vineyards. In the single quinquennium 1876–81, 820,000 persons migrated from the farms, a number not equaled in any comparable period before or since. During the forty years between the Franco-Prussian War and World War I the Paris Region had an annual growth rate of 1.8 per cent, whereas that for the rest of the country remained virtually stationary. World War I fostered the growth of numerous industries in Paris, including the armaments, electrical construction, and metalworking sectors. The number of workers in the latter sector doubled from 165,000 to 330,000 in the fifteen-year interval from 1906 to 1921. The attraction of the Paris Region was particularly strong for the armaments industry since the state was the sole client. Moreover, a large influx of refugees from the North and East provided a considerable body of skilled laborers.[4]

Following the war, Paris accounted for nearly one half of national employment in banking, insurance, and exchanges, and 46 per cent of all university students. Armaments factories were converted and labor requirements constantly increased. The growth of the automobile industry was particularly marked; by 1931 it employed over 100,000 workers in the Paris Region. In general, industry in Paris expanded at a more rapid rate than in the rest of France, particularly in the aeronautical and radio-electrical construction sectors and other sectors whose primary market was the state. New industries dependent on technological progress were particularly attracted to Paris by the presence of numerous laboratory research facilities. Although the population of Paris proper remained stationary between 1906 and 1936, that of the suburbs of the Seine department doubled from 1.085 million to 2.142 million, a consequence of both the continuing rural exodus and foreign immigration.[5]

Although there was concern in some quarters regarding the high degree of concentration of population and economic activity before (primarily for military reasons) and during World War II, it did not become general until the late forties and early fifties. A widely-read study by J. -F. Gravier,[6] which dramatized numerous allegedly undesirable consequences of the concentration of French economic, administrative, and cultural life in the Paris Region, was in large measure responsible for arousing public opinion.

Demographic and Economic
Concentration in the Paris Region

The concentration of France's population in the Paris Region is indeed striking. As Table 2.1 clearly shows, the population of the region has not only increased substantially over time in absolute terms but also as a proportion of total French population. Today, the Paris Region contains nearly one fifth of France's total population on only 2 per

Table 2.1

Evolution of the population of Paris

and France, 1801–1965

(in millions)

Paris and France	Years							
	1801	1901	1921	1931	1946	1954	1962	1965
(1) Paris Region	1.403	4.816	5.769	6.797	6.691	7.424	8.597	9.117
(2) France	27.350	40.862	39.210	41.834	40.502	42.502	46.520	48.699
(1) as a per cent of (2)	5–1	11–8	14–7	16–2	16–5	17–5	18–5	18–7

Sources: Quelques chiffres sur la Région de Paris (Paris: District de la Région de Paris, 1964), p. 3; *Régionalisation du budget, 1966*, p. 165.

cent of the country's surface. Average population density in this area is about 700 persons per square kilometer, compared with an average of 85 for all of France. The population density of the central city itself is 32,000 persons per square kilometer and that of the suburbs immediately beyond the city limits, 6,000 per square kilometer.

Moreover, the rate of growth of the Paris Region is higher than that of any other French region. It is estimated that between January 1, 1963, and January 1, 1965, the population of the Paris Region grew by 4.3 per cent, whereas the corresponding figure for the whole of France was 2.4 per cent. Only two other regions had growth rates of over 3 per cent during this period: Rhone-Alps (3.2), and Provence-Riviera-Corsica (3.9).[7] At the present rate of growth the Paris Region will have a population of 11 million by 1975 and from 12 to 16 million by the year 2000.[8]

The degree of economic concentration in Paris is equally pronounced. For example, for all activities the Paris Region had 647,000 (or 28 per cent) of France's 2.299 million skilled workers in 1962. In terms of total salaries distributed in 1963 by place of residence, residents of the Paris Region received 34.745 billion francs (37 per cent) out of a total of 93.557 billion francs for all of France. Average annual salary in the same year in the Paris Region was 12,452 francs, against the French average of 9,466. No other region had an average above 10,000 francs, and only three, Upper Normandy, Rhone-Alps, and Provence-Riviera-Corsica, had averages greater than 9,000 francs. In 1964, the Paris Region accounted for 2.034 million (22 per cent) of France's 8.974 million personal and commercial automobiles, despite its highly developed system of public transportation. Telephone subscriptions in the Paris Region in 1964 numbered 106,071 (39 per cent) against a total of 273,118 for France as a whole. Total short- and long-term bank deposits in the Paris Region as of December 31, 1964, amounted to 39.843 billion francs (42 per cent) out of a total of 94.100 billion francs for all of France.[9] Total new industrial surface (excluding projects involving less than 500 square meters) added to the Paris Region from 1949 to 1963 was 89.060 million square meters (15 per cent), compared with a national total of 580.470 million square meters.[10]

The continuing growth of population and economic activity in Paris has been accompanied by high levels of public expenditure. For example, in the regional breakdown of the national budget for 1964, the Paris Region received 24.6 per cent of allocations for national education, 31.0 per cent for health and welfare, 38.9 per cent for specially supervised education, 55.5 per cent for cultural affairs, 13.6 per cent for postal service and telecommunications, and 16.9 per cent for urban equipment. Although these figures represent only a single year, and although the regionalized parts of the budget of each sector vary considerably (from 50.6 per cent in the case of national education to 83 per cent in cultural affairs and public works), it is clear that Paris benefits substantially from these expenditures.[11]

Paris also is in a relatively favorable position with regard to tax revenues available to local authorities. Receipts of this nature in 1962 amounted to 306 francs per inhabitant in the Paris Region, as against a corresponding value of 203 francs for the rest of France. Borrowings by the Paris Region from the Caisse des Dépôts et Consignations, a public credit institution whose main resources are derived from social security funds, pension funds, and redeposits of savings banks, have also been relatively large. For the four-year period from 1961 to 1964, the region borrowed 3.834 billion francs, whereas borrowings in the rest of France amounted to 13.231 billion francs. In per capita terms, using 1962 population figures, this amounted to 446 francs and 349 francs respectively. Moreover, the Paris figure excludes loans made to the subway system authorities. Despite these considerations, per capita investment expenditures of local authorities (departments, communes, and local public enterprises) in the Paris Region have not been particularly high. Although it ranked fourth among France's twenty-one planning regions in 1960 in this regard, it ranked only eighth in 1961 and only twentieth in 1962. Part of the reason certainly is the rela-· tively high operating expense burden of the Paris Region. Per capita outlays in this regard for the years 1960–62 were, respectively, 456, 503, and 552 francs. The next highest expenditures for these years were in Provence-Riviera-Corsica, whose respective corresponding values were 310, 353, and 362 francs.[12]

However, another difficulty has been the inability of local authorities to obtain necessary authorizations from the national government for increased borrowing. For example, although the Seine department borrowed a total of 66 million francs in 1959, 170 million in 1960, 200 million in 1961, 225 million in 1962, 250 million in 1963, and 260 million in 1964, these credits represented only half of what was borrowed during a comparable period before World War II. Michel Drancourt described this situation in an article in *Réalités:*

> Although the municipal council voted to borrow funds and to levy the taxes necessary to cover the annuities of relevant projects, the state, in its role as guardian, refused the authorizations. . . . the responsible state officials believed that the underequipment of Paris would limit its growth. In fact, its principal effect has been to make the taxes associated with the growth process more difficult; when nothing is replaced or constructed, in the end one is faced with the necessity of making constant costly repairs. . . . The debt of the city has only been a ridiculously low 5 per cent of its budget.[13]

In summary, public expenditures in Paris have been high relative to the rest of France as a result of continuing growth of population and of economic activity; but the primary emphasis has been on maintaining a given stock of public capital under increasing pressure rather than on supplying new capital. However, more recent policy decisions will produce a shift of emphasis in the future. Before considering these measures in detail, however, it is necessary to examine the effects of the highly concentrated living and working conditions which prevail in Paris.

The Consequences of Urban Congestion

Of the 3.2 million housing units in the Paris Region, half have two rooms at most and over half were built before World War I; only 16 per cent have been built since 1948. About 66 per cent have neither bathtub nor shower, 60 per cent are without central heating, 45 per cent are without inside toilets, and 15 per cent have no electricity. Average living space per inhabitant in the region is 0.95 room, whereas the corresponding averages for larger provincial cities and the remaining provincial areas are, respectively, 1.08 and 1.12. An extra 1.2 million rooms would be necessary to give residents of the region the same housing space as the rest of France.[14]

Congested conditions also prevail on the streets, where 2 million vehicles vie for insufficient parking space or stand "lined up bumper-to-bumper at the stop lights of Paris' wide avenues and major intersections and jammed together in the old narrow streets just as in crosstown Manhattan." [15] Half of the employed population of Paris work outside of their arrondissement of residence, necessitating more than 2 million trips a day. Moreover, since the war the number of trips to work has increased faster than the population, indicating that on the average places of work and residence have become increasingly separated. It is estimated that the average worker spends one hour and twenty minutes daily going to and from work.[16] It also has been estimated that the total marginal social cost associated with each extra vehicle in the Paris Region is 40,000 francs.[17] Whatever the difficulties involved in this type of calculation, it is certain that the increase in traffic congestion results in numerous external diseconomies. One of these is pollution of the atmosphere. Professor Truhaut recently announced that "for the first time in the history of medicine, we have succeeded in provoking cancers in laboratory animals simply by making them inhale toxic substances contained in the air which people in Paris breathe each day." [18]

Philippe Lamour finds that the traffic problem has resulted in serious psychological and physiological consequences for Paris citizens:

> It literally spoils the existence of many of them, bent over the steering wheel from morning on, exasperated by traffic jams, obsessed by the search for a parking place. The abnormal nervousness of most Parisians makes them lose not only all good humor but all courtesy, and the provincials are the afflicted witnesses of this deplorable evolution. The politeness of old has been replaced by egoism and invective.[19]

In view of these and similar aspects of the city's congestion, Lamour concludes that "Paris lives on a literary legend which nothing any longer justifies." [20]

The number of such subjective condemnations of congested conditions in Paris could be multiplied indefinitely. However, there also exist a number of estimates of the marginal social cost of establishing a new household in Paris versus that of establishing one in a provincial city. A study made by the Commissariat à la Reconstruction et à l'Urbanisme of the Paris Region in 1954 indicated that total public and private investment per marginal household in Paris was 4.25 million old francs as against 2.8 million in the provinces (excluding differences in land prices).[21] In 1959, it was estimated that each new household in the Paris agglomeration cost the nation over 5 million old francs; the establishment of a new household in the provinces, on the other hand, would cost 3 million. If the head of the household could find employment in close proximity to the family's present place of residence, it would cost practically nothing. At the then prevailing rate of immigration into the Paris Region it was estimated that the annual marginal cost of new households in Paris was 70 billion old francs.[22] In a more recent publication, Delmas "evaluates at 40,000 francs the cost of equipment for public services caused by the location of a new family in the suburbs (roads, schools, hospital equipment, fire and police protection, subsidies to mass transportation, etc.), as against 25,000 in a provincial city." [23] It should also be noted that numerous psychological and physiological costs of congestion would not be reflected in these calculations.

On the other hand, Wellisz maintains that there is no evidence in the French case which would justify tampering with the market mechanism. Specifically, he states that (1) possible external diseconomies of large urban agglomerations have not been demonstrated, and (2) even if diseconomies did exist in the public sector they might be outweighed by economies in the private sector. In support of the first point, he argues that the evidence showing that public per capita expenditures in Paris are substantially higher than elsewhere in France does not in itself indicate the presence of diseconomies, for per capita services may be correspondingly great, i.e. the values of the marginal product have not been compared with the marginal costs.[24]

Several factors do not accord with this evaluation. First, even if the short-run ratio of marginal product to marginal cost for investment in

Paris were equal to or greater than that in other regions, the long-run effect is likely to be undesirable because, as argued in Chapter 1, the increase in economies to private firms will tend to increase further the concentration of population and economic activity and result in concomitant increased social costs. Furthermore, there is considerable evidence in recent public opinion surveys to show that net external effects in the Paris Region are negative. These studies need to be considered in some detail.

The fact that population and economic activity are so concentrated in Paris does not imply a corresponding residential preference pattern. This is clearly indicated by a well-designed survey of 2,318 persons in 185 French localities which was conducted in 1959 and 1960.[25] The purpose of this survey was to establish the nature of public opinion regarding the nation's demographic evolution; proportionate sampling was employed with respect to age, sex, community size, region, and occupation of family head.

Seventy-five per cent of those interviewed believed that questions of population size and its geographic distribution and evolution are "important" or "very important," and 68 per cent indicated that they had discussed such matters with friends and relatives. Eighty per cent of the total sample were aware of the growing population of the Paris Region; 50 per cent advocated a diminution of the region's population, 34 per cent thought it should remain the same, and only 3 per cent preferred a larger population. The sample of Paris residents showed that 70 per cent wanted a decrease in the region's population, whereas the proportion of persons expressing a similar view did not vary by more than 5 percentage points from 50 per cent for any other population size class.

Similarly, respondents were asked the following question: If you were absolutely free to choose and could dispose of the same resources as you now have, would you prefer to live and work in the country, in a town of moderate importance, in a large provincial city, or in Paris? The responses, by actual place of residence class, are presented in Table 2.2. They show that most people would prefer to remain where they are or in a locality of more or less similar importance, except in the Paris agglomeration, where only 44 per cent would choose to remain where they are. It is also pertinent to note that in the subsamples for the other classes of actual residence, the proportion of persons who would choose to live in Paris ranges from a minimum of 3 per cent to a maximum of only 8 per cent. The proportion of the entire national sample who would prefer to live in Paris is only 9 per cent.

Respondents were also asked where they would prefer to live in terms of geographic regions of France, again assuming that they would be absolutely free to choose and could dispose of the same resources

Table 2.2

Preferred place of residence by actual
place of residence, France, 1959–60

	Actual residence (by population size class)					
Preferred residence	Less than 2,000 inhabitants (per cent)	2,000 to 5,000 inhabitants (per cent)	5,000 to 100,000 inhabitants (per cent)	More than 100,000 inhabitants (per cent)	Paris and suburbs (per cent)	Total (per cent)
Countryside	64	48	14	14	18	38
Small town	24	31	57	15	23	33
Large provincial city	8	14	20	60	14	18
Paris	3	5	7	8	44	9
No response	1	2	2	3	1	2
	100	100	100	100	100	100

Source: Alain Girard and Henri Bastide, "Les problèmes démographiques devant l'opinion," *Population,* XV (April–May, 1960), p. 271.

as they now have. The responses in this regard are grouped by region in Table 2.3. Again, those persons who would most willingly leave their present location are the Parisians. Furthermore, the results show that other regions of heavy urban concentration, such as Flanders, the Artois, and the Lyon Region, would also favor a diminution of their populations, presumably for reasons similar to the Parisians'. From the general results of their study, Girard and Bastide conclude, "If the expressed aspirations could be satisfied, the movement away from the countryside, however vigorously condemned, would continue, but a regroupment would be made to the profit of medium and large provincial cities, and Paris would cease to grow. Thus, one of the most important results of this study is that decentralization efforts conform to the wishes of the population." [26]

A comparably designed survey made in 1963 indicated that given present growth trends, public opinion favored government action to

Table 2.3

Regional residential preferences in France, 1959–60

| | Preference | | | Regional poplulation structure | |
| | Different region or undetermined (per cent) | Same region (per cent) | Total (per cent) | | |
Present residence				Preferred (per cent)	Actual (per cent)
Provence	17	83	100	31	6
Seine	80	20	100	9	12
Paris Region (without Seine)	78	22	100	4	7
Pays de la Loire	48	52	100	7	4
Brittany	43	57	100	6	6
Normandy	57	43	100	6	4
Coastal Aquitaine	44	56	100	5	5
Savoy, Dauphiné	51	49	100	4	4
Flanders, Artois	65	35	100	4	8
Languedoc	55	45	100	4	3
Western Lorraine	60	40	100	3	4
Auvergne, Velay	63	37	100	3	2
Interior Aquitaine	72	28	100	3	5
Lyon Region	79	21	100	2	4
Alsace-Lorraine	67	33	100	2	5
Other Regions	73	27	100	7	21
Total	64	36	100	100	100
No response	——*	——	——	17	——

*The dash is used throughout in the tables to indicate that no information is available.

Source: Girard and Bastide, p. 274.

Note: The Paris Region includes Seine-et-Oise, Seine-et-Marne, Loiret, and Eure-et-Loir.

curb the growth of the Paris Region. This attitude was expressed by two thirds of the respondents living in provincial regions and by a slightly higher proportion of those living in the Paris Region.[27]

Whether or not these phenomena should be of concern to economists depends on the nature of the issues and problems behind these responses. The 1963 survey included the following question: "According to you, what are the three most harmful or disagreeable things that one experiences in the city of Paris and the surrounding urban area?" [28] Over one third of the replies listed pollution of the atmosphere or similar health hazards (43 per cent), traffic problems (41 per cent), noise (34 per cent), and insufficient and uncomfortable public transportation (34 per cent). Each of the other problems mentioned (cost of living, tempo of life, etc.) were cited by one fifth or fewer of the replies. Thus, even though many social scientists have devoted considerable attention to the analysis of such "urban" phenomena as hyperintensity of individual and collective activity, absence of satisfactory social life, egocentrism, and the like, these factors were not frequently mentioned in the Paris responses. It is quite possible, of course, that problems of a sociological or psychological nature are considerably more important than the respondents themselves realized. Nevertheless, insofar as government preferences and actions are a response to individual preferences, these findings imply that policy should be oriented primarily toward the solution of problems in large measure economic, for the single common element in all of the major grievances expressed by Paris residents is that of space economy.

These survey results clearly demonstrate that the social costs of urban congestion are considerable and that they are significantly felt by the populations involved. Even so, it may be argued, as Wellisz has done, that it would be "capricious" to prohibit expansion of the Paris Region, because even if it were possible to prove that there are external diseconomies related to its expansion, "then enterprises in the Paris Region should be charged an amount equivalent to the estimated gap between private and social costs." [29] While this proposal may be theoretically sound it is not operationally feasible, for it is generally impossible to measure the social costs of adding a given firm or plant. How, for example, would one weigh the effects of smoke or fumes from a particular plant against those from homes, other plants, and automobiles? To what extent must public investment be increased to provide parks, police protection, and streets for population attracted by employment opportunities at a new plant, and to what extent must intensive investment (both public and private) be increased to compensate previous residents for the increase in congestion directly or indirectly attributable to a new plant? What is the present value of the operating costs that will be associated with this capital stock expansion? Even if it were possible to compute over-all regional averages for these various cost categories, how could they be applied to a given plant when space is not homogeneous, i.e., when the social costs attributable to a plant would vary according to its location within a region? To make policy decisions dependent on our ability to answer questions like these is in effect to preclude public action.

Paris, the Provinces, and Europe:
Regional Policy and the Politics of *Grandeur*

The general view of the French government concerning the Paris Region has been that since space is markedly limited in a fast growing urban area, it "becomes necessary for government to assume the initiative in land acquisition and space design in order to assure a functional and attractive public matrix into which private parts constructed by private enterprise will fit without congestion." [30]

However, while there may be very little quarrel over this general objective—even Wellisz admits that "there is a virtual absence of dissent to the policy of 'decongestion' which the French government has been pursuing with increasing vigor" [31]—the various concrete policy measures which have been proposed to achieve it often reflect a radically different emphasis. Although a whole spectrum of thought exists on the subject, and although parties at each extreme may frequently give lip-service to some of the general aims of the opposition (while attempting to withhold the means for their realization), it would not be amiss to speak of two principal approaches. The first is that of what may be termed the "decentralization" school, which has emphasized the need to check the expansion of Paris to the benefit of provincial regions. Partisans of this viewpoint frequently are accused of fostering hostility between Paris and the provinces and of being false Cassandras by those who favor emphasizing the development—or redevelopment —of Paris. The latter group includes those who believe that Paris is not too big and that its growth should in fact be stimulated, or at least not checked. For example, M. Michel Drancourt, editor-in-chief of the influential review *Entreprise,* writes that "it is not Paris which is overpopulated, but France which has too few people." [32] Similarly, M. Bertrand Akar writes, "if, indeed, the Paris agglomeration with its 8 million inhabitants were the capital of a nation with 80 million inhabitants, the situation would be normal, but it so happens that for reasons independent of our will, the French nation is a century behind in the evolution of its population." [33]

Those who maintain that not only is Paris not overconcentrated but should grow further base their position largely on two arguments, one economic and one political, with the latter usually taking precedence. Mme. J. Beaujeu-Garnier holds that "at this moment the concentration of Paris appears to be an incontestable opportunity for France, especially in the international sphere." [34] However, proponents of this view generally take the position that Paris' international role is not a detriment to the provinces but is, rather, a necessity for their well-being under the hypothesis of an opening of Europe's frontiers. According to this argument, the further development of Paris would at once give France an opportunity for increased political prestige and provide a bridge connecting the most active part of Europe to France's least developed regions.[35]

Yet to the extent that increasing investment in Paris means foregoing alternatives in other regions, it is not likely that provincial leaders will welcome the opportunity to achieve economic advance in their own territories by observing and learning from the experience of Paris. It is difficult to see, after all, how such a policy would be anything more than an extension of what has already been happening. Nevertheless, it would seem at present that Paris may be accorded a high place in the regional scale of priorities because of foreign-policy considerations, especially with the return of Michel Debré to the government.

It is essential here to understand the relationship of the conflict between the "Europeans" and "Nationalists" in terms of France's policy toward an integrated Europe, and the conflict between those who emphasize "decentralization" and those who emphasize developing Paris in terms of domestic policy. On the one hand, the Europeans, who form a significant part of DeGaulle's opposition, tend to favor decentralization within France and frequently are characterized by federalist tendencies, whether on the scale of France or of Europe. On the other hand, the Nationalists generally support a "Europe of the Fatherlands" wherein each nation retains a large measure of political independence, while on the domestic front they tend to favor strong centralization of authority and prestige in Paris. They would, of course, also like to see Paris become the center of Europe as well as of France.

The consequences of this division are well illustrated by the reactions to a study undertaken by a group of experts for the European Economic Community.[36] The study divided the Common Market into thirty-one "large regions," nine for France, eight for West Germany, ten for Italy, two for the Netherlands, and one each for Belgium and Luxemburg. Though the report had, of course, no binding practical consequences for the present, it did invoke an image of the form that a united Europe might eventually take. The response of the Nationalists was represented in M. Debré's contention that "To create large regions strongly independent of central power—is this not to prepare an 'integrated' Europe, where the idea of France would have only a folkloric character since the nation would be 'disintegrated'?" [37]

In view of this position, it is not surprising that the question should be raised as to whether Paris will receive certain priorities in investment localization primarily as a result of a deliberate intention to put the capital in a better position to compete with other metropolitan areas of Europe: "Will *aménagement du territoire* be linked to high considerations of foreign policy just as scientific research is now subordinated in its programing to the imperatives of national defense?" [38]

Public policy statements still are far from clarifying the degree of importance which will be attached to investment in Paris in the future. A recent report by the Delegate General of the District of the Region of Paris to the Prime Minister maintains that of all the regions of France, Paris is the only center with which other regions maintain important economic and "human" relations. Therefore, it is argued, any economic stagnation affecting Paris would relegate it to a secondary position relative to other major European centers, with harmful consequences for all of France.[39] Yet in the same context the report emphasizes that for Paris to compete adequately on an international level, equipment of the highest quality will be necessary for transportation, telecommunications, business and financial affairs, facilities for conventions, and "exceptional distractions." Thus, for Paris to conserve "its place in a world of rapid progress and continual change," its resources must be improved and expanded "each year." [40] But just how it will be possible to continue year after year to concentrate population, industry, and the most up-to-date infrastructure in Paris and at the same time develop poorer regions through industrial decentralization is not revealed. Until those who insist on continuing large-scale public and private investment in favor of Paris deal frankly with this issue, their recommendations to practical policy-makers will continue to say, in effect: Paris must receive top priority now, but eventually we also hope somehow to find something for the provinces.

It might be expected, of course, that the District of the Region of Paris would emphasize, if only by implication, investment in Paris. However, statements concerning public policy in this regard are equally ambiguous or conflicting even at the national level. For example, the

Report on the Principal Orientations for the Preparation of the Fifth Plan, while acknowledging the congestion of Paris and the need to develop other French urban areas as a counterweight to Paris, maintains that one of the main objectives of the Plan should be a "modernization of the Paris Region," not just to satisfy the needs of its inhabitants, but "to permit the capital to play a national and international role under conditions comparable to those of other large urban regions of Europe." [41] Further on the report states, "The Paris Region should be disengaged from activities which congest it to a greater extent than they serve it, but maintaining its vitality, radiance, and prestige is one of the opportunities of France in European competition." [42] Thus, "the *aménagement* of the Paris Region must be considered as one of the essential objectives of the policy of *aménagement du territoire.*" [43]

On the other hand, the Fifth Plan, while advocating the modernization of the Paris Region (primarily by implanting new towns around the fringe of the agglomeration and providing better means of intra-region transportation), is completely silent on the matter of the international role of Paris.[44] Similarly, the *First Report of the National Commission for Aménagement du Territoire* makes no mention of any political motive which should inspire greater efforts on behalf of Paris. It attempts to treat the problem of Paris as an integral part of the economic and social development of the country, while it deliberately plays down the notion that there might exist any essential conflict between the capital and provincial regions, whose interests are held to be "increasingly complementary." [45] Nevertheless, the commission's attitude regarding Paris is clearly one of concern over the consequences of its continuing growth:

> In overpopulated agglomerations the cost of public services per inhabitant is increasing considerably, whereas in areas which are losing population existing capital remains insufficiently utilized. However, the problem of excessive concentration is especially critical from the social and human point of view: urban inhabitants are crowded together and provincial initiatives are emaciated. Thus, *aménagement du territoire* appears in many respects as the quest for a better equilibrium between cities and rural areas, between Paris and the provinces.[46]

It is clear that the views of the commission reflect more the necessity of confronting an unavoidable problem than any enjoyment of the prospect that Paris may have certain potentials which, if sufficiently developed, might be politically advantageous for France. This also would seem to be the more reasonable point of view in terms of public preferences. The argument of the Nationalist school that the problem of the size of Paris is a difficulty only because Paris is large relative to the rest of France does not seem tenable. Although the imbalance between Paris and the provinces may aggravate certain problems, it is not reasonable to believe that the congested conditions of Paris would pose fewer difficulties if somehow the population of the remainder of the country could be increased by 50 or 100 per cent. New Delhi is no less crowded because India has an enormous population.

The fact that most French citizens, including most Parisians, find Paris so overconcentrated already that they would prefer to live in other areas should in itself preclude any effort to deliberately stimulate further growth of the agglomeration, at least insofar as public policy is responsive to social preferences. The only justification for the policies of the Nationalist school concerning Paris would be that those favoring such policies know themselves what is best for the people. But they would have to demonstrate that gains in satisfaction from increased political prestige, assuming that it were attained (by no means a certainty), would more than compensate for losses of social and economic satisfactions. These losses would also have to include the cost of foregone alternatives in the provinces. Granted that objective calculations of this sort are not operationally feasible, the problem still must be posed and considered in these terms, and the burden of proof concerning the advantages to be gained from stimulating the growth of Paris largely rests with the Nationalists and those of similar persuasion. The rhetoric characterizing most of these arguments has yet to be replaced by a careful weighing of alternative actions in terms of social preferences. Moreover, the results of the first round of France's 1965 presidential election, in which De Gaulle received only 43 per cent of the ballots cast in France, were generally interpreted in France as a reaction against too great an emphasis by the government on politically motivated policies to increase France's international standing (for example, De Gaulle's stand on the Common Market and his desire to build a strong atomic force), and too little emphasis on domestic social and economic problems.

Of course, the Nationalists argue that the growth of Paris is the key to the development of the provinces, especially the lagging regions of the West and Southwest. Again, however, the burden of proof is with them, and little evidence has been offered to support the case. If the relatively rapid development of Paris in the past has not particularly benefited such regions, why should it do so now or in the future? Certainly, the prospect of a European customs union will not substantially benefit the lagging regions. In this regard, the Political and Economic Planning group has pointed out that

> The less developed region differs in its economic position from the less developed country in that it has already reached some form of coexistence with more developed areas within the national market. An international common market is likely to affect the less developed region not so much directly but by its impact upon the more developed regions of the same country. The more intensive interchange of goods and services between industrialized areas is likely to accelerate their rate of growth. But in poorer regions the creation of a larger market offers little prospect to small-scale industry and does suggest some likelihood of encroachment on local markets. In these circumstances such areas may remain economically backward, falling further behind the rest of the country in their development.[47]

It also is maintained that, at least for the short run, the Common Market would promote capital deepening rather than extensive investment, so that employment opportunities might not substantially increase. Moreover, "integration, with the possibility of realizing greater economies of scale, may also make it more difficult to 'decentralize' firms. Many industries also, uncertain of their relative competitive strength at the outset of the Common Market, will be disinclined to take new risks, and will resist government pressure to move to new locations."[48]

Finally, on purely political grounds, it is doubtful that Paris would ever become the capital of a federal union of European states. Fears of letting a large industrial and commercial metropolis dominate a more or less federal union no doubt explain in part why New York, Montreal, and Zurich are not the capitals of their respective countries, and why Bonn and Brasilia are. With this in view, it becomes all the more astonishing to see "the barely concealed candidature of Paris become one of the new justifications put forth for the unlimited development of an agglomeration which is already largely saturated."[49]

It has been pointed out that as an object of concrete public-policy measures, the problem of the Paris agglomeration has a double aspect: the development of the region itself, and the effort which has been made to decentralize industry to the benefit of the provinces. The remainder of this chapter will consider measures that have been taken to develop the Paris Region. The problems and achievements associated with decentralization policy, which more directly concerns the nation as a whole, will be discussed in detail in subsequent chapters.

Public Policy and the
Development of the Paris Region

Although the Prefect of the Seine department established a commission in 1911 to study problems related to the growth of Paris, not until 1928 was a committee set up with the authority and means to prepare a development plan for the region. It required another seven years before a plan was actually drawn up, and it was not until 1939 that it gained final approval from the government. The plan of 1939 was based on two main principles: to promote a better distribution of the agglomeration's population by decongesting the center; and to organize and redevelop the whole of the region to provide better living conditions for the existing population. However, the plan had serious gaps and flaws. Since it was primarily concerned with controlling the growth of the agglomeration, it neglected the central city. As has frequently been the case, the power of Paris' attraction was underestimated, and as a consequence the boundaries fixed for the agglomeration were unrealistic and the provision for public services inadequate. Because of their complexity and rigidity, the building-code regulations laid down in the plan were difficult to apply. Moreover, the attempts to develop the agglomeration in terms of what was held to be the public welfare were often frustrated by the rights of private property owners.[50]

Following World War II a new project for the development of the Paris agglomeration was prepared. It was finally submitted to the Ministry of Reconstruction and Housing in January, 1956. The principal aims embodied in this program were to decongest the center of Paris, primarily by renovating run-down sections, to modernize and beautify the center, to expand the amount of green space available, primarily at the expense of industry, and to foster consolidation and increased cooperation among suburban communes. It was also suggested that rural regions be made more attractive to help check the flow of population of Paris.[51] These studies became the basis for a *Plan for the Equipment and General Organization of the Paris Region* which appeared first in December 1958; it was approved in definitive form by the government in August 1960.[52] This new plan, generally referred to as PADOG (*Le plan d'aménagement et d'organisation générale de la région parisienne*), laid down general development principles for a period of ten years. It envisaged the creation of four or five "urban nuclei" surrounding Paris at a distance of about twenty kilometers. A system of expressways linking these centers and Paris was also called for. PADOG, however, like most previous planning schemes, underestimated the future growth of the region. It very quickly became evident that its estimate of one million new inhabitants during the sixties would be too conservative. Thus, in September 1965, the Ministry of Construction announced that PADOG would be revised so as to be in harmony with the new *Strategic Plan for Town and Country Development for the District of Paris,*[53] a document prepared by the District of the Region of Paris.

The District was anticipated by an ordinance of February 1959, and finally established as a governmental agency in August 1961. The executive organ of the District is the Delegation General, headed by a Delegate General, at present M. Paul Delvourier, who is directly responsible to the Prime Minister. The Delegate General is assisted by an administrative council with twenty-eight local elected representatives. The principal functions of the District are the study of problems of redeveloping, equipping, and organizing the region, providing subsidies to various public bodies within the region, promoting cooperation among local governments for mutually beneficial projects (the region includes 1,315 communes), and eventually providing common administration of public services. The District is autonomous financially; a special tax on equipment produced revenues amounting to 200 million francs in 1966, and borrowed funds are also at its disposition. The Delegate General is assisted by numerous specialized organisms, such as the Institute for Equipment and Urbanism, the Land and Technical Agency, and a consultative Economic and Social Committee. With their cooperation, the District has published several major studies of the region in the past few years, most important of which has been the Strategic Plan.[54]

For the first four years of its existence, which coincided with the period of application of the Fourth Plan, the District voted to authorize 1.360 billion francs in programs, while at the same time voting 742 million francs in credits. Many of the programs, and especially many of the most expensive, were scheduled for completion under the Fifth Plan, which would provide for additional credits to cover the full costs of authorized programs. About two thirds of total authorizations were for improvements in the region's transportation network; public transportation alone received 530 million francs, or about 40 per cent of all authorizations.[55]

For the future, the Strategic Plan views the creation of new urban centers as the only remedy for the underequipment of the suburbs and the overcongestion of the center. To assure an adequate amount of land for construction and green space, it will be necessary to choose sites on the fringe of the present agglomeration. This will facilitate construction of transportation facilities and enable the inhabitants to live close to their places of work and still be near the countryside and facilities for leisure activities. Thus, the growth of population will be channeled along certain "preferential axes," chosen to fit the physical, economic, and human geography of the region. The principal axis will move downstream along the Seine, a direction in which growth is already relatively rapid, toward the Norman agglomerations of Rouen and Le Havre, which together comprise the second-ranking port of France. The activity of this port complex is for the most part directed toward Paris, and this interrelationship will be strengthened by an electrified railway link in 1968, an automobile expressway expected to be completed in 1970, and three oil pipelines. Secondary areas will be developed upstream from Paris along the Seine and along the Marne. The axis of the Marne Valley will be linked to that part of the principal axis which lies north of the Seine, and the secondary Seine axis above Paris will be linked to that part of the principal axis which lies south of the Seine downstream from Paris. The new scheme thus would break with the radial-concentric pattern which has heretofore contributed to the region's difficulties. Along these new axes a series of new towns will be built, and transportation facilities will be provided to link them with one another as well as with Paris. One of the main aims of the new towns will be to provide self-sufficient communities where people can live and work without having to make long trips. This implies, of course, that each new town must be able to provide a complete

range of commercial activities, services, and amusements. It is anticipated that each new town, by the end of the century, will be able to
provide for the needs of from 300,000 to 500,000 persons and will
serve the more specialized needs of from 1 million to 1.5 million persons. The present as well as the projected populations of these new
urban centers are shown in Table 2.4.

Table 2.4

Actual and projected populations
of new towns in the Paris Region

New towns	Years		
	1962	*1985*	*2000*
Noisy-le-Grand and			
Bry-sur-Marne	40,000	90,000	700,000 to 1,000,000
Beauchamp	12,000	60,000	300,000 to 500,000
Cergy-Pontoise	40,000	130,000	700,000 to 1,000,000
Tigery-Lieusaint	5,000	35,000	400,000 to 600,000
Evry-Courcouronnes	7,000	100,000	300,000 to 500,000
Southeast of Trappes	3,000	100,000	400,000 to 600,000
Northwest of Trappes	2,000	100,000	300,000 to 400,000
South of Mantes	1,000	5,000	300,000 to 400,000
Total	110,000	620,000	around 4,500,000

*Source: Schéma directeur d'Aménagement et d'urbanisme de la Région de Paris
(extraits),* p. 6.

The Strategic Plan certainly is the most realistic effort made to date
to deal effectively with the problems of the Paris Region. Instead of
proceeding on the pious hope that somehow the region's growth will
be checked, it assumes that by the year 2000 the region will have
14 million inhabitants, that is, a population two-thirds greater than at
present. It also assumes that industrial surface will double, that office
surface will triple, that housing surface will increase fourfold, and that
the number of automobiles will increase from 1.7 million to 4 or 5
million. It repeatedly makes plain that these projections do not represent the desires of the planners, but rather are the facts the planners
will most likely have to face. Given this viewpoint, the Plan's attempt
to create real cities instead of mere dormitory communities is indeed
admirable, yet the Plan also presents numerous difficulties.

In the first place, it presents no detailed estimates of the financial
requirements of the projects which it envisages; nor is there any sug-

gestion of the financial means which would be most appropriate, much less any weighing of possible alternatives. It is merely assumed that in the future the means will be found to the extent that citizens are willing to devote more resources to the public sector to make the Paris Region more liveable. Thus, even if it is assumed that implementation of the Plan would be desirable, it is questionable whether public pressures will be sufficient to bring about improvements until problems of increased congestion have arisen. As the planners themselves clearly realize, it is much more expensive to improvise hasty solutions in the face of delays than to act in anticipation of future problems. Yet the absence of financial considerations in the Plan definitely represents an opportunity lost to inform and clarify public opinion in this regard.

If there is little evidence from the past to suggest that public opinion will effectively anticipate the region's future needs, there is no more reason to expect that this will change in the future. In fact, the local authorities who would be most directly concerned with implementing the Strategic Plan have already expressed their hostility to it. The Administrative Council of the Union of Mayors of Seine-et-Oise adopted a resolution in September 1965 which opposed any attempt to allow the communes, especially those of a rural or "dormitory" character, to assume greater financial responsibility for providing public overhead capital. At the same time, the mayors emphasized that it appeared "illegitimate to charge the present generation with the burden of investments which will benefit the future more than the present." [56] Moreover, a large section of the Municipal Council of Paris has expressed outright hostility to the Plan, while most of its members have formulated numerous reservations. The principal fear is that application of the Plan would benefit the fringes of the agglomeration to the detriment of Paris proper; the council would prefer to see the Plan emphasize the development of the central city and its immediate suburbs. [57]

It is increasingly evident that the development of new urban centers will have to depend on some administrative authority superior to that of the communes. In the relevant French literature there is considerable interest in the "development corporations" which have been given the responsibility for the creation of Great Britain's new towns. [58] The principal attraction of this form of administration is its combination of public responsibility (directors are appointed by the government) with the flexibility of an industrial and commercial enterprise. However, this alternative would also seem to have little chance of success. First, it is most improbable that the communes involved would cooperate in a scheme which would put them out of existence. Moreover, even if they could be persuaded or forced to give up their authority to a higher administrative body, it is still questionable whether or not the new towns would provide any real solution to the problems of Paris.

Certainly the new towns around London have not succeeded in decongesting London. During the period from 1950 to 1963 the greater London area increased by 900,000 persons, whereas the population of the new towns increased by only 250,000 persons during the same interval. After twenty years of considerable effort and expense, the new towns near London contain some 380,000 inhabitants. The problems posed by the growth of the Paris agglomeration clearly surpass these dimensions. Given present conditions, their solution would require the construction of sixty towns (assuming the type of new town found in Great Britain) over the next twenty years.[59] Moreover, the space surrounding the Paris agglomeration is less favorable with respect to building new towns than the "outer ring" of London. The latter "constitutes an already heavily urban area with eighteen cities of more than 50,000 population. No city of this size exists in the vacant space surrounding the densely-populated Paris agglomeration. Thus, for each new city it would be necessary to begin from scratch to build a completely new infrastructure at an immeasurably higher cost per project." [60]

Even with this relative advantage, British planners have had to seek new solutions for the problem of the growth of greater London. Without abandoning the system of new towns and development corporations, the planners have undertaken negotiations with such other large cities of southeastern England as Portsmouth and Southhampton with a view toward having them double the populations of their jurisdictions in order to take pressure off greater London. In other words, emphasis is shifting toward guiding urban growth in terms of existing urban centers.[61] Similarly, proposals have also been made in France to check the growth of Paris by developing existing cities at a distance of from 100 to 200 kilometers from the central city.[62] These cities would include Orléans, Rouen, Amiens, Reims, Troyes, Chateaudun, and Chartres. However, no concrete plans for such development exist.

In summary, then, the Strategic Plan for the development of the Paris Region presents four principal difficulties. First, it does not make adequate provision for financing projects which it proposes to undertake; second, it lacks necessary support from both Parisian local authorities and those in the surrounding communes; third, it fails to provide administrative machinery for the creation of new urban centers; and fourth, the evidence from relevant British experience, which has been characterized by relatively favorable conditions for the creation of new towns and more modest goals with respect to their size, indicates that any ultimate solution for checking the growth of a congested region such as Paris will have to involve the growth of existing urban centers at a fairly considerable distance from the congested agglomeration.

Finally, it is necessary to put the Strategic Plan in the context of an integrated policy for regional development in France as a whole. In this regard, considerable reservations concerning the Plan have been expressed by interested parties in the provinces and, more generally, by most persons who would give high priority to checking the growth of the Paris agglomeration. These views are given complete expression in the Economic and Social Council's *Opinions and Reports Concerning the Project of the Fifth Plan*.[63]

The council maintains that the very existence of a Strategic Plan for the Paris Region serves to create a situation of "disequilibrium" to the detriment of other regions, which have not been given ample opportunity or means to prepare similar documents for themselves. Thus the fear is expressed that because the Strategic Plan specifies precisely what projects need to be undertaken in the Paris Region, "it could have as a harmful counterpart the abandonment of operations anticipated, but less well defined, in other regions in cases where such a choice becomes necessary." In particular, the council expresses concern over the assumption that the Paris Region will eventually have 14 million inhabitants. Since it is admitted that neither the Plan nor the Paris District consider such a population desirable, the main objection seems to be psychological, i.e., that once the principle of growth is admitted the Plan may come to be viewed as a more or less adopted program of development. In contrast, the council would favor improving the existing public overhead capital of Paris to ameliorate living conditions for present residents, but on the condition that a more vigorous effort be made, throughout the period of application of the

Fifth Plan, to stop the agglomeration's growth.[64] In addition, the council proposed that "projects for re-equipping the Paris Region should be financed in increasing proportion by the region's own financial means, both to avoid a curtailment of the limited means for developing other regions and to pave the way for a policy of prices which reflect true costs, which constitutes, in the long run, one of the basic solutions to the problem in question." [65]

The Fifth Plan also takes up the theme of having Paris pay its own way to a greater extent. If Paris requires modernization, then "it would be unjust and antieconomic for the strongest region not to support directly an important part of the effort undertaken to equip it." The principal measures foreseen in this regard include raising prices for the use of public transportation, payment for parking, and raising prices for water. Moreover, the Plan makes clear that this is a matter not just of raising funds, but of creating a price structure to facilitate rational decision-making in terms of regional policies. "In order to clarify the ends and means of *aménagement du territoire* it is appropriate to introduce progressively pricing and fiscal measures which tend to make enterprises and households pay the true costs associated with their localization at any given point in the country." [66]

While the aim of French policy-makers to charge rational prices in the public sector certainly is desirable, there has been relatively little attention paid to the exact meaning of a rational price. For a dozen years now, the nationalized Electricité de France has successfully applied one of the most advanced systems of marginal cost pricing attempted anywhere,[67] but aside from this, efforts at rational pricing have been quite rare.

The general impression given by official documents is that prices should be high enough to cover average costs, and one reason is that government subsidies could then be withdrawn from numerous undertakings. This in turn would facilitate the achievement of a balanced budget and reduce inflationary pressures, which have been among the recent major preoccupations of Gaullist policy. But in view of the rising average costs which characterize the provision of most services in the Paris Region, charging a firm or household a price that covers the average cost associated with its locating in Paris would not require payment of an amount equivalent to the true cost of implantation, i.e. the marginal cost. Thus average cost pricing, though it may improve on the present situation, would still not provide correct signals in terms of either economic rationality or the stated aims of the Fifth Plan. As has already been pointed out, marginal cost pricing may frequently prove operationally unfeasible, but this should not cloud the basic issue or leave one satisfied with incorrect choices.

Of course, a rational price is not always necessarily that which covers the marginal cost of a given activity. If, for example, the French authorities were to raise prices for the subway system, buses, and the suburban railway system in such a manner as to guarantee marginal cost pricing, this would probably have undesirable side effects. Unless analogous measures were taken with respect to motorists, the consequent substitution of private for public transportation would only aggravate congestion. The general aim of price policy should be to encourage more economical use of scarce resources. Where excess demand results in congestion or other undesirable consequences prices should be raised. On the other hand, underutilized resources do not justify price increases. Where feasible, prices should be varied to reflect differing intensities of use during different time periods. Moreover, price policy concerning any given activity should take account of its effects on other activities, i.e., mutually interacting activities should be regarded as parts of a general system and not as isolated cases. Public policy relating to Paris as well as to France as a whole (as is the case in most other countries) is far from realizing these objectives, and often it is doubtful if they are really understood. But official concern regarding the principle of rational prices is at least a step in the right direction.

Summary
and Conclusions

There is little doubt that the Paris agglomeration is characterized by overconcentration of population and economic activity. The undesirable consequences of congested conditions in the region are clearly reflected in revealed public preferences: most Parisians and non-Parisians would prefer to live in other regions and a substantial majority favor public measures to stem the growth of Paris. Yet it continues to grow, largely because of the presence of considerable external economies which attract private enterprise, and because external diseconomies are not sufficiently incorporated into the costs of firms.

In addition, pricing policies relating to public services have further contributed to the problems of the region.

Pressures arising from both past neglect and continuing growth have created an obvious need to modernize existing public overhead capital and to provide additional facilities for new population and new activities. Past efforts in this regard have failed largely because possibilities for stemming the region's growth have been overestimated and future needs underestimated. The recent creation of the District of the Region of Paris and the preparation under its auspices of a Strategic Plan for guiding the growth and modernization of the agglomeration represent the first realistic attempt to present solutions on a dimension compatible with the problems posed. Nevertheless, difficulties remain.

To consider only the problems of its application to the region itself, the Strategic Plan (1) fails to make provision for financing proposed projects; (2) has little support from local authorities; (3) fails to provide the administrative instruments appropriate to the creation of the proposed urban centers; and (4) probably overestimates the extent to which new towns will solve the region's difficulties, especially in view of the disparity between the available means and the magnitude of projected aims.

In an interregional context, fears have been expressed that the very existence of the Strategic Plan, along with its assumption of (though not desire for) continued rapid growth of the Paris Region, will only serve to accentuate present regional disparities. This proposition deserves careful consideration, especially in terms of the opportunity costs associated with alternative public investment policies; it requires detailed examination of the nature and consequences of past decentralization efforts as well as the prospects of and difficulties involved in present efforts.

3

French Decentralization Policy

Early Decentralization Efforts

The first decentralization measures in France were adopted during the 1930's. These were largely inspired by considerations of military strategy and involved the transfer of numerous armament firms, principally in the aircraft industry, to the South and Southwest. Following World War II, the effort of rebuilding cities, industries, and ports that had been destroyed or damaged helped to direct attention to problems of urban and regional planning. However, it was not until 1950 that M. Claudius-Petit, the Minister of Reconstruction and Urbanism, published the first document which called for rational spatial organization on a national scale.[1] In general, as Professor Lajugie has aptly pointed out, the experience of the years from 1944 to 1953 was characterized by initiatives which were too often dispersed or incomplete. Responsible agencies generally lacked the means for action on a significant scale, and in most instances the will to act was deficient as well. On the other hand, "the years 1954 and 1955 marked a decisive turning point in French regional economic development policy. At this time an endeavor was made to replace empirical and fragmentary efforts with a systematic and coherent policy involving much more considerable technical and financial means." [2]

A Decree of September 14, 1954, marked the initial effort to grant to firms which would locate in lagging regions forms of aid analogous to that given for reconversion,[3] but the means created for this purpose were largely replaced by others provided in legislation enacted in the following year. Legislation enacted in 1955 provided—even though many original stipulations have been modified since—the basis for a large part of subsequent French regional policy. It is therefore necessary to consider in detail the positive and negative aspects of the principal measures which have evolved from this period. This involves examination, on the one hand, of the measures taken to limit over-concentration in the Paris Region and, on the other, those taken to encourage location in other regions.

Restricting the Growth of Paris: The Negative Aspect

The Decree of January 5, 1955, represented the first major effort to control the implantation or extension of private industry in the Paris Region. In an *exposé des motifs,* the document points out the "waste" associated with "expenditures caused by excessive concentration of population" in certain zones, namely, the departments of the Seine, Seine-et-Oise, and Seine-et-Marne, and five cantons of the Oise. As a consequence, it was stipulated that industrial buildings intended for manufacturing or storage could not be created, or older buildings enlarged beyond 10 per cent of the surface existing at the time of the decree, without the prior approval of the Ministry of Housing and Reconstruction (in consultation with certain other government agencies). This restriction did not apply to enterprises employing fewer than fifty persons or occupying less than 500 square meters of building space. Enterprises with a "social character," for example hospitals, were also excluded.[4]

However, the Decree of January 5, 1955, did not prevent the industrial potential of Paris from increasing because entrepreneurs could still intensively reutilize vacant buildings. This defect was corrected by the Decree of December 31, 1958, which stipulated that "the substitution of an industrial activity for a nonindustrial activity in an existing building is equivalent to the creation of an industrial installation." Moreover, the decree went still further in defining the types of activities requiring official approval, including establishments of a scientific and technical nature which were not under state control and all construction of private buildings whose principal use was for commercial or professional offices and whose floor surface exceeded 100 square meters.[5]

A more recent measure aimed at encouraging necessary modernization in certain parts of the Paris Region while continuing to check the extension of factories and offices in others was the Law of August 2, 1960, which simultaneously provided for levies on some construction activities and for grants to persons who would demolish or transform business premises for conversion to public purposes such as housing and schools. Levies and grants alike are based on the floor space constructed or eliminated, as the case may be, as well as on the particular zone of the Paris Region where the operation takes place. Thus, in a zone including the Seine department, much of Seine-et-Oise, and six communes of Seine-et-Marne, the levies or grants are fixed uniformly at 200 francs per square meter of office surface involved; in another zone the corresponding figure is 100 francs. In a third zone there is neither a payment nor a charge. A similar zoning system exists with regard to industrial premises, though in this instance the respective rates per square meter are 100 francs, 50 francs, and, as before, no grant or levy.[6]

The results of these efforts to limit further congestion in the Paris Region are open to varying interpretations. One study, for example, shows that between 1955 and the end of 1961, only 23 per cent of the 3,100 decisions taken with regard to construction approval resulted in outright refusal. The number of requests for approval and the number of accords granted each grew at an annual rate of 14 per cent during this period. Half of the requests involved extensions of existing facilities, and 80 per cent of the cases where an enterprise was transferred involved a movement of less than 15 kilometers. These transfers were nearly always made from the center of the agglomeration toward the periphery. In general, entrepreneurs sought to move only a minimum distance from the center, and few were interested in locating in rural zones of Seine-et-Oise or Seine-et-Marne.[7]

On the other hand, the data in Table 3.1 show that the proportion of approved industrial construction permits accounted for by the Paris Region has definitely tended to decline since 1955. The same situation exists with respect to the proportion of total surface and, to a somewhat lesser extent, the proportion of employees accounted for by the Paris Region. In contrast to this relative shift in favor of the provinces, the corresponding absolute values for the Paris Region show considerable variability and no definite downward trend. Although the 1963 absolute values are below those for 1955, it should be noted that those for the latter year were unusually high even in relation to previous years; 1955, therefore, is not a very representative base period (for absolute values). Thus, even though the relative position of the Paris Region with respect to these variables has declined, there has been little progress in checking the annual rate of flow of activity into the region and the increased congestion which this implies.

Table 3.1

Construction permits issued in the Paris Region as a percentage
of the French total for projects involving over 500 square meters, 1955–63

| | *Years* | | | | | | | | | |
| | *1955* | | *1956* | | *1957* | | *1958* | | *1959* | |
Permits	*Paris*	*Per cent of French total*	*Paris*	*Per cent of French total*	*Paris*	*Per cent of French total*	*Paris*	*Per cent of French total*	*Paris*	*Per cent of French total*
umber issued	193	25	222	20	175	15	264	20	210	17
urface involved (in thousands of square meters)	623	37	651	27	452	20	595	21	437	18
mployees involved	9140	34	6100	16	3390	11	7880	17	5720	12

| | *1960* | | *1961* | | *1962* | | *1963* | |
Permits	*Paris*	*Per cent of French total*	*Paris*	*Per cent of French total*	*Paris*	*Per cent of French total*	*Paris*	*Per cent of French total*
umber issued	284	17	276	15	224	12	173	9
urface involved (in thousands of square meters)	672	19	522	13	472	11	422	10
mployees involved	5550	10	4480	6	6110	8	7740	10

Source: B.S., Nos. 7-8 (July-August, 1964), pp. 100-101.

Of course, a more complete picture of the effectiveness of the legislation in question would have to take account of the space which has been liberated in the Paris Region, as well as of new implantations. Cumulative results (through 1963) of the application of the Law of August 2, 1960, indicate that grants were given for the abandonment of 1,836,000 square meters of industrial premises, whereas levies were applied to the construction of 568,000 square meters, making a net difference of 1,268,000 square meters of abandoned space. However, net additions to industrial space in the rest of the region bring this value down to 576,000 for the region as a whole. Office space, on the other hand, showed a net increase in both the Seine department and the remainder of the region. For the region as a whole, combined office and industrial space increased by 143,000 square meters. In the light of this evidence, the National Assembly's Commission on Production and Exchange concludes that "the decentralization of industrial and tertiary activities in the Paris Region has scarcely been begun, and such transfers as have taken place have simply been toward the periphery of the region, complicating still more the difficult problem of the suburbs"; thus, "the balance shows nothing positive. On the contrary, the movement is aggravating the concentration in the ring around Paris and thwarting all the efforts at liberation which have been undertaken." [8]

In general, it is clear that purely negative measures to limit the growth of the Paris Region have not been adequate in view of the magnitude of the problems created by the presence of considerable external economies to private firms. This is not to say that these efforts have been without value, since congestion would no doubt have increased even more rapidly in their absence. On the other hand, it is even more obvious that attempts to limit the region's growth will not necessarily benefit the provinces. Thus, positive steps have also been taken to provide incentives for enterprises to locate in relatively less well-developed regions.

Directing Growth Away From Paris:
The Regional Development Societies

The creation of Regional Development Societies (Sociétés de Développement Régional, or SDR) by a series of decrees in June 1955, represents one of the major innovations in French regional development policy. Under the terms of a Decree of June 30, 1955, the SDR were defined as stock companies "having for their sole aim to cooperate in financing industrial enterprises, by means of participating in their capital, in regions suffering from unemployment or from insufficient economic development." [9] Constituted with the participation of Paris' commercial banks and public financial institutions, the SDR have been formed in virtually all regions with the exception of Paris, and their means have been put at the disposition of firms for the purpose of developing or modernizing installations.

The SDR were given certain legal advantages under the conditions that their own capital should amount to at least 2.5 million francs (since raised to 5 million francs), that their participation could not exceed 35 per cent of the capital of any enterprise or 25 per cent of their own subscribed capital (to avoid any excessive confusion of interests), and that the societies agree to submit to certain controls by a government commission. The advantages they were accorded consisted of exoneration from the corporation tax and the tax on distributed profits, and the guarantee of a minimum dividend of 5 per cent of their capital stock.[10]

Soon after the creation of the SDR it became apparent that commercial and industrial firms preferred to borrow rather than to increase their capital by introducing outside stockholders. In response to this preference, the Law of December 25, 1956, authorized the SDR to grant loans for five years or more to firms in which they held stock. In addition, it was provided that "the SDR will be able to organize the floating of collective bond-issues for the accounts of enterprises having their operations in the region conforming to the program of action of the SDR. Their form, their appropriation, and their destination should be agreed to by the government commissioner." Moreover, it was provided that collective issues of debentures would be supported by the guarantee of the government. This law was later modified by the Law of August 14, 1960, which authorized the SDR "to grant loans of five years or more to enterprises in which they have a vocation to hold capital stock. They can, in addition, give their guarantee to loans of five years or more contracted by the said enterprises." The insertion of the words "have a vocation" in effect removed the obligation of the SDR to subscribe to the capital of firms which borrowed from them, a necessity which heretofore had been an inconvenience and which was often carried out only in token form.[11]

The fifteen existing SDR were all formed before or during 1960.

By the end of 1962 their combined operations had amounted to a total of 755 million francs. Of this amount, 679 million (or about 90 per cent) involved grouped loans, 43 million involved loans made from the societies' own capital, and 33 million consisted of capital stock participations. The last represented about one third of their own total capital (98.8 million). It will be noted that although taking shares in private firms originally was the only object of the SDR, this form of activity has in fact been of only minor importance.[12]

The overwhelming preference given to the use of grouped loans by the SDR "has spread to all regions, even to those which are little industrialized or thinly populated. Although the aid given in these latter areas sometimes appears small in absolute value, it is, in reality, important in relative value." [13] The cumulative amounts of loan funds raised through this means by the various SDR, as of the end of 1964, are shown in Table 3.2. It has been estimated that the activities of the SDR have permitted the realization of about 20 per cent of the private investment realized within the framework of regional economic policy,

Table 3.2

Group loan issues
by Regional Development Societies, 1957–64

Society	Headquarters	Number of loans	Number of enterprises benefited	Amount of loans (thousands of francs)
Bretagne	Rennes	5	66	47,130
Centrest	Dijon	5	81	79,255
Champex	Reims	3	52	44,905
Expanso	Bordeaux	5	88	70,030
Lordex	Nancy	4	73	64,240
Méditerranée	Marseille	4	75	73,670
Normandie	Rouen	5	85	81,130
Nord et Pas-de-Calais	Lille	6	158	133,275
Picardie	Amiens	3	43	45,250
SADE	Strasbourg	5	119	93,280
Sodecco	Limoges	5	122	79,930
Sodero	Nantes	7	160	149,350
Sodler	Montpellier	2	23	25,425
Sud-Est	Lyon	5	119	91,675
Tofinso	Toulouse	6	116	89,830
Total		71	1,380	1,168,375

Source: "Dixième rapport du Conseil de Direction du Fonds de développement économique et social," *S.E.F.*, No. 198 (June, 1965), p. 970.

and that they account for about 40 per cent of aid specifically intended for regional expansion.[14] Nevertheless, they have not generally lived up to many of the enthusiastic expectations originally held for them.

One of the major difficulties of the SDR has been lack of success in raising capital. Although private banks (mostly Parisian) subscribed to half of their original capital, these banks, with the exception of a few regional banks such as those in Alsace, have been reluctant to increase their capital participation. Much of this reticence may be explained by their unwillingness to facilitate the activities of decentralized competitors. In general, the large banks are represented in the administrative councils of the SDR, which gives them "a privileged position to limit the activity of the society as soon as it threatens to infringe on their interest." [15] Moreover, insurance companies, savings banks, and individual investors, as well as commercial banks, have generally preferred alternative investments which are more liquid and present a greater possibility for capital gains.[16]

It also is pertinent to note that on the one hand the SDR have been accused of an unwillingness "to take important risks by engaging their funds in operations whose profitability would not be assured at the outset," [17] while on the other hand it is held that their insufficiency of resources "is aggravated in numerous cases by the low rate of return on investments. Often their participation in small and medium-sized enterprises has been repaid only with great difficulty." [18]

In order to compensate at least partially for their lack of resources, it has been proposed that the SDR provide technical assistance to firms in which they have an interest, thus indirectly promoting these firms' profitability.[19] It also has been suggested that the SDR could be deliberately oriented toward the creation of societies which would in turn construct industrial facilities that could be leased to private firms, a formula which has worked with some success in Alsace.[20] In general, however, the practical means at the disposition of the SDR have not permitted such undertakings.

A final problem concerning the SDR is that relating to their integration into the general regional development framework of France. As early as 1957, Maurice Byé [21] pointed out the necessity for confronting the programs of the SDR with those to be prepared by the twenty-one newly-created program regions. Unfortunately, no real effort has as yet been made in this direction.

Another aspect of this problem concerns a certain divergence be-

tween the field of application specified for the SDR at the time of their
creation and their present activities. It will be recalled that their operations were originally limited to regions suffering from unemployment
or insufficient economic development. In fact, however, they have extended their actions to all regions except Paris. Their activity may be
examined by a breakdown according to program region of loans received through 1962 by firms from the various SDR. Although exact
figures are not given for each region, and although the ordering for
each group is alphabetical rather than ranked, the results show that
the group which benefited the most included the regions of Alsace,
Aquitaine, Midi-Pyrenees, Nord–Pas-de-Calais, Pays de la Loire,
Provence-Riviera-Corsica, and Rhone-Alps. The group which benefited the least, on the other hand, included Auvergne, Brittany,
Limousin, Lower Normandy, Upper Normandy, Picardy, and Poitou-
Charentes. The greater proportion of the regions in the first group are
among the more industrialized and wealthy regions of France, whereas
the greater proportion of the last group are among the poorest regions.[22]
Thus, in terms of the discussion in Chapter 1, the SDR have tended
to be of greater benefit to intermediate than to lagging regions. Although this situation has been a source of concern in many quarters,
and although it obviously runs counter to the official objectives prescribed for the societies, it is by no means necessarily out of harmony
with economically rational resource allocation.

The Economic
and Social Development Fund

The Economic and Social Development Fund (Fonds de développement économique et social, or FDES) is a special account of the
Treasury; in the words of M. Byé, "it practically holds the key for
putting regional policy into operation." [23] Created in June 1955 and
presided over since by M. Bloch-Lainé, the FDES' domain of action
was set out in the following terms in the Decree which still constitutes
its basic charter:

> In order to assure the financing of projects anticipated by the plan
> of modernization and equipment and programs of regional ex-
> pansion, as well as operations for increasing productivity, for in-
> dustrial and agricultural conversion, for worker retraining, and
> for industrial decentralization, there is instituted a single fund en-

titled the "Economic and Social Development Fund."

This fund replaces the funds which have performed the same functions until now, and, under the conditions stated in the following articles, disposes of the same resources.[24]

The field of activity of the FDES as here defined is clearly quite vast.

The FDES is managed by the Minister of Finance, assisted by an administrative council including seven other ministers whose functions are particularly relevant to the economy, the Director of the Treasury, the Director of the Budget, the directors of several large financial institutions (Bank of France, Crédit national, Crédit foncier, Caisse des dépôts et consignations), the General Commissioner of the Plan, the Delegate General of the Region of the District of Paris, the head of the Délégation à l'Aménagement du Territoire et à l'Action Régionale, and several other heads of public agencies. Ministers who are not members of the council participate in deliberations involving their area of activity.[25]

The functions of the administrative council, as defined in a Decree of October 18, 1955, include examination of programs of investment which are to be executed by public administrations and by public enterprises, as well as all investment programs financed with the direct or indirect aid of the government. The council must also give its opinion regarding the order of priority and rhythm of execution of the projects which it examines, as well as the modes of finance applicable to these projects. This task is performed in reference to the dispositions of the national Plan, the state of public finances, resource availabilities, and monetary stability. Before the end of September of each year the council is informed about programs under its competence which are intended for execution during the following year. Subsequent revisions of these programs also are examined. The council is informed periodically as to the state of execution of projects on which it has been consulted.[26]

The work of the administrative council is prepared by a number of committees which have been altered, divided, and regrouped several times since 1955. Although nominally there are twelve such groups, only eight are still active, and these vary considerably in importance. The administrative council decided as early as October 1955 that any unanimous opinion concerning any particular project expressed by a specialized committee would be equivalent to the council's own opinion.[27]

The principal responsibility for regional policy has been delegated to a subcommittee, Committee No. 1b, of Committee No. 1. The president of Committee No. 1b is the Director General of the Caisse des dépôts et consignations, which also serves as the committee's secretariat. Its composition includes representatives of the Ministry of Industry, the Ministry of Construction, the Direction générale of Work and of the Labor Force, the Secretary of State for Domestic Commerce, the Ministry of the Interior, the General Planning Commission, the Prime Minister, the Treasury, the Bank of France, the Crédit national, the Caisse des dépôts, and the secretariat of the administrative council of the FDES. In addition, representatives of other administrations participate with the committee in the examination of matters that come under their competence.[28]

The principal object of Committee No. 1b is to allocate the various financial advantages which may be accorded by the government in favor of regional development, productivity, and collective tourist equipment. In this capacity it examines requests for special equipment grants, loans, rebates of interest, and guarantees intended to facilitate the realization of operations of conversion, specialization, or industrial decentralization; for allowances for transfers of domicile and subsidies for professional retraining; for loans to increase productivity; and for collective tourist facilities.[29]

The Decree of July 15, 1960, created a special account called "Loans from the Economic and Social Development Fund" to record payments and repayments of loans made within the general framework of the Plan or resulting from "specific actions, especially regarding productivity, regional action, congestion, and decentralization." The decree further provided that decisions to allocate funds are the responsibility of the Minister of Finance, who should take account of the division of credits proposed by the administrative council of the FDES. The sums to be lent are put at the disposition of beneficiaries either directly by the Treasury or through specialized financial institutions.[30]

Conditions governing the allocation of special equipment grants were subject to frequent change after they were first instituted by a Decree of June 30, 1955. The Decree of April 2, 1959, however, is probably the most representative in terms of the aims and methods which have been associated with this type of aid.[31] This document stated that an equipment grant could be allocated in localities or regions where technical and economic conditions permit the implantation of viable enterprises and which present at least one of the following characteristics: (1) exceptionally important partial or total unemployment or a very high number of unsatisfied requests for employment; (2) a risk of unemployment, either as a consequence of decided or anticipated closing of firms or of an important reduction in their activity, or because of the existence of an especially high number of young persons finishing school in relation to present and anticipated employment opportunities; (3) a permanent and significant excess of labor of rural origin, taking into account the foreseeable evolution of agricultural production and the improvement of methods of cultivation.[32]

Furthermore, to be eligible for a grant a firm should create a new establishment or put an abandoned one into operation, or extend or convert existing establishments so as to substantially increase productive capacity. Moreover, the investment program should involve the creation of a minimum of twenty jobs. Grants are limited to 20 per cent of the amount of investment expenditures borne by the enterprise. It was also provided that "in certain zones where the demographic and economic situation justify exceptional aid, and which, account taken of their collective equipment possibilities, ought to constitute centers of development for underdeveloped regions," a system of higher rates for grants could be established.[33]

Table 3.3 shows the number of requests for grants or loans which were accepted or rejected by Committee No. 1b from 1957 to 1964.

Table 3.3

Number of requests for grants or loans
from the FDES rejected or satisfied by Committee No. 1b, 1957–64

	1957	*1958*	*1959*	*1960*	*1961*	*1962*	*1963*	*1964*	*Total*
Requests received	300	183	269	297	356	264	230	234	2133
Requests rejected	153	75	83	79	97	55	45	24	611
Requests satisfied	127	107	152	229	259	202	174	210	1460

Source: "Dixième rapport du Conseil de direction du Fonds de développement économique et sociale," p. 968.

The relatively high proportion of rejections in the early years probably resulted indirectly from an ambiguity in the test of the relevant Decree of June 30, 1955. It was undoubtedly never intended that aid should be given to any firm which wanted to decentralize its operations. The area receiving the new establishment should be in need of help, and the form of activity should be economically feasible. However, this was not originally specified. In consequence, by their desire to avoid creating precedents of freely dispensing loans and grants, the authorities overstressed the security aspects of requests they received. Once the conditions were stated formally, however, there was no longer any need to adopt such a conservative stance. It may seem curious to promote liberalization by restrictions, but such paradoxes are by no means unknown to observers of economic behavior.

Table 3.4 shows the amounts of aid which were accorded in the form of loans and grants from 1955 to 1964 by Committee No. 1b. The amount of loans in 1964 diminished substantially in relation to the previous year, falling back to a level approximately equivalent to that of 1962. However, 1963 was an unusual year in this regard because of an exceptional effort made on behalf of the naval construction

Table 3.4

Loans and grants accorded by Committee
No. 1b, 1955-64
(in thousands of francs)

	1955	1956	1957	1958	1959	*Years* 1960	1961	1962	1963	1964	*Total*
Loans	16,000	34,000	46,100	37,770	20,605	49,042	21,045	15,375	67,683	16,362	323,98
Grants	——	8,000	5,400	5,719	45,856	88,394	53,005	58,377	61,595	75,936	402,71

Source: "Dixième rapport du Conseil de direction du Fonds de développement économique ∢ social," p. 968.

sector. Whereas 44 million francs were lent to finance reconversion in that industry in 1963, none were allocated in 1964. As to grants, the average rose from 225,000 francs in 1961 to 287,000 in 1962, then 354,000 in 1963, and finally 362,000 in 1964. The average amount of grants in relation to total investment costs was 10.2 per cent in 1961, 13.7 per cent in 1962, 10.8 per cent in 1963, and 10.2 per cent again in 1964. These values were of course well below the legal maximum of 20 per cent. It also is relevant to note that of the total demands for aid satisfied in 1962, 23.5 per cent involved the creation of new facilities, as opposed to transfers, extensions of existing facilities, conversions, or regroupments. This proportion rose to 32.8 per cent in 1963 and to 36.7 per cent in 1964. Transfers, meanwhile, fell from 24.7 per cent of total programs in 1962 to 19.6 per cent in 1964. The other major type of program, extension of existing facilities, accounted for about 42 per cent of the totals for 1962 and 1964. Thus, recent trends in programs involving FDES aid show a relative increase in the importance of new creations, largely at the expense of transfers.[34]

Table 3.5 shows the amounts of FDES subsidies accorded for professional retraining and relocation for the years 1959 to 1964, as well as the number of workers benefited. In each case there is a definite upward trend in terms of persons benefited, despite a temporary drop in 1963. Nevertheless, the results are quite modest in terms of overall needs.

Table 3.5

FDES subsidies benefiting the labor force, 1959–64

	Years					
Subsidies for	*1959*	*1960*	*1961*	*1962*	*1963*	*1964*
Retraining:						
Requests received	62	99	185	209	186	241
Requests not satisfied	3	5	8	——	3	6
Requests in process, Dec. 31	56	103	146	226	269	583
Number of aids accorded	52	47	134	128	134	184
Amount of aid (000 francs)	2,314	2,649	6,688	14,037	7,425	13,468
Number of workers readapted	3,918	3,499	9,861	12,809	9,765	16,909
Average cost per worker (francs)	590	757	677	1,095	760	796
Allowances for transfer of domicile:						
Requests received	361	345	768	1,192	1,015	1,414
Requests not satisfied	21	42	17	109	111	48
Requests granted	418	303	751	1,083	904	1,366
Amount of aid (000 francs)	593	452	1,226	1,797	1,621	1,466
Average value of allowances (francs)	1,564	1,503	1,632	1,659	1,793	1,073

Source: "Dixième rapport du Conseil de direction du Fonds de développement économique et social," pp. 972-973.

Firms locating in regions benefiting from FDES loans and grants may also receive certain fiscal exonerations from the Ministry of Finance, acting on advice from a specialized subcommittee of Committee No. 1b. Of 825 requests for reduction of the transfer tax in 1964, 581 were granted. These concerned total acquisitions amounting to about 150 million francs. Reductions or exemptions relating to the *patente* tax were accorded to 296 firms, out of a total of 489 requests. Accelerated depreciation benefits (25 per cent) were the object of 144 requests, of which 91 were approved. The value of constructions benefiting in this regard amounted to about 78 million francs, of which about 45.5 million concerned the relatively underdeveloped regions of Brittany and Pays de la Loire.[35]

In addition to these activities, the FDES is also linked to the work of the SDR, since the guarantee of a minimum dividend which the SDR receive from the Ministry of Finance is made only after they have consulted with the FDES. The FDES also cooperates with Regional Expansion Committees in certain cases involving grants. The creation of these organizations was authorized by a Decree of December 11, 1954, which specified that their field of action should correspond as closely as possible with program regions, and that they should include qualified representatives from all economic sectors—banking, professional associations, and so forth. Although the SDR, as well as the FDES, are obliged to consult with these committees, their role and their powers have never been very precise.[36]

The data in Table 3.6 show the amounts of investment made in connection with various types of aid extended directly or indirectly by the FDES or in close collaboration with other organizations.

Since the FDES is France's "most powerful instrument of financing regional expansion," [37] it is necessary to consider to what extent its operations have in fact corresponded to the tasks prescribed for it; moreover, it is equally necessary to examine carefully to what extent the objectives it had tried to achieve have in fact been realized.

The first problem, then, is to consider the effectiveness of investment outlays aided by the FDES in terms of regional needs. In the following discussion, this effectiveness is measured by new jobs per 100,000 population created by FDES aided investment. As indicators of differences in regional living standards we have three variables: television sets per 1000 population; per capita income; and per capita kilowatt-hour low-tension electricity consumption. The latter variable is made up primarily of lighting, public service, and domestic uses. (High-tension consumption, on the other hand, would primarily reflect industrial, and in the French case, railroad power demands.) The number

Table 3.6

Investments realized with the aid
of the FDES and cooperating organizations, 1963–64
(in thousands of francs)

Type of aid	Years 1964	1963
(1) Grants or loans of the FDES after consultation with Committee No. 1b	742,460	638,794
(2) Grants accorded after consultation with Regional Expansion Committees	31,962	61,909
(3) Special temporary FDES loans and grants for naval construction	——	167,532
(4) FDES loans for collective tourist equipment	34,776	16,463
(5) Grouped loans of the SDR	1,010,070	817,366
(6) Productivity loans	10,432	5,403
Total	1,829,700	1,707,467

Source: "Dixième rapport du Conseil de direction du Fonds de développement économique et social," p. 971.

of television sets would, of course, also tend to reflect level of communication with the outside world and level of information. Observations for these variables taken for the twenty-one program regions give the following regression equation:

$$\log_e Y = 30.498 - .7059 \log_e X_1 - .1431 \log_e X_2 - 3.766 \log_e X_3,$$
$$\quad\quad\quad\quad (.5739) \quad\quad\quad (.3420) \quad\quad\quad (.9036)$$

where Y = new jobs per 100,000 population created with FDES help through 1963, X_1 = television sets per capita in 1962, X_2 = per capita income (dollars) in 1962, and X_3 = low-tension kilowatt-hour consumption per capita in 1962.[38] The values in parentheses are the standard errors for the corresponding regression coefficients, all of which are negative. The relevant beta coefficients are $\beta_1 = -.1947$, $\beta_2 = -.0568$, and $\beta_3 = -.6628$. Thus X_3 clearly is the most influential independent variable. For the equation as a whole, $R = .814$ ($R^2 = .663$), and the F ratio is 10.51, highly significant at the 99 per cent level ($F_{.01} = 5.18$). It may be concluded, therefore, that investment aided by the FDES has been most effective in regions where it is most needed. It should be emphasized, too, that this is not just a matter of helping poor as opposed to more wealthy regions, but of a fairly close relationship between degree of effectiveness and degree of need over the whole range of twenty-one regions.

Of course, it might be objected that these results would be biased by the inclusion of the Paris Region, since FDES aid there is nil, and since the values of the observations for the independent variables are quite high. However, with the omission of the Paris Region, the following regression equation is obtained:

$$\log_e Y = 25.53 - .2891 \log_e X_1 - 1.439 \log_e X_2 - 1.577 \log_e X_3$$
$$(.2940) \qquad\qquad (.9406) \qquad\qquad (.5899)$$

Here the relevant beta coefficients are $\beta_1 = -.1515$, $\beta_2 = -.3213$, and $\beta_3 = -.4826$. Although the relative importance of X_2 is greater in this case, the most influential independent variable is still X_3. Moreover, the significance of this equation is even greater than that of the first, since now $R = .857$ ($R^2 = .734$), and the F ratio is 13.80 ($F_{.01} = 5.29$). It is clear, then, that inclusion of the extreme values associated with the Paris Region distorts the results obtained by the FDES unfavorably.

There is still further evidence to support the case that investment financed with the help of the FDES has been distributed in accordance with the aims of regional policy. In the twenty-region case considered alone, for example, variable Y is significantly correlated at the 98 per cent level of significance with, respectively, per capita sales in 1960 of commercial and industrial firms ($r = -.519$) and percentage population change from 1954 to 1962 resulting from migration ($r = -.557$). In other words, aided investment has tended significantly to favor regions lacking commercial and industrial importance and characterized by out-migration.[39]

We must now consider to what extent investment aided by the FDES, as well as the multiplier effects associated with it, have in fact promoted increased decentralization of economic activity as a whole. To provide an indication of this, existing commercial and industrial importance is compared with the location of new economic activity. More specifically, in the following regression equation relating to the twenty regions discussed above $Y =$ per capita value of newly authorized commercial and industrial construction (1961 through 1963) and $X =$ per capita sales of commercial and industrial firms in 1960:[40]

$$\log_e Y = 3.111 + 1.104 \log_e X$$
$$(.2661)$$

Here $R = .680$ ($R^2 = .463$), and the F ratio is 14.63, highly significant at the .99 per cent level ($F_{.01} = 8.28$).

In other words, it is clear that despite government efforts to make location of commerce and industry in less developed regions more attractive, firms continue to locate primarily in regions already prosperous and industrialized. The external economies provided by government grants, loans, and tax advantages simply are not sufficient to offset the advantages of external economies available in more advanced regions.

Decentralization of Government Activities

In addition to fostering industrial and commercial decentralization, the government has tried to encourage decentralization of its own agencies and activities. Here again, the first step was taken in a Decree of June 30, 1955. This document, with certain subsequent modifications, provided that all civil and military establishments and services of an administrative, industrial, scientific, technical, cultural, or social character which belong to the state or are subject to its control should prepare an inventory of their operations in the Paris Region. On the basis of this inventory, it was required that a list be drawn up of services and establishments whose presence, in whole or in part, in the Paris Region would not be a necessity. It was further stipulated that measures be proposed to the government to assure the progressive transfer of such activities outside of the Paris Region, according to a plan whose realization would be staggered in relation to "material and financial possibilities." [41]

As the Hacketts have pointed out, "The central government and nationalized industries together undertake directly each year over one-third of total fixed capital formation. As the choice of the location of these investments is by no means predetermined by technical, administrative or other considerations, a considerable margin of latitude remains which can be put to good effect in promoting regional growth." [42] Although this rather overstates the degree of flexibility open to the government and state enterprises (technically optimal operations of the Electricité de France, to choose an obvious example, certainly are limited by locational considerations such as availability of coal or water power), the extent of these activities is considerable, not only because of their share in total investment, but also because of their content and their strategic position. This influence extends to transport and communications (railways, Air France, the most important shipping companies, postal and telegraph services), fuel and power (gas, electricity, coal, atomic energy, basic oil prospecting and research, an important share of refining), general manufacturing (Renault, Sud-Aviation, Nord-Aviation, Frigeavia, tobacco and match industries), the most important insurance companies, information (radio and television monopoly, press services, parts of the motion picture industry), machine tool and supply industries, various laboratories and research facilities, and public health and social security activities.[43]

By the time the Fourth Plan was prepared, some dozen transfer operations from the Paris Region to the provinces were prepared for execution during the period from 1962 to 1965. These included a partial transfer of the Sud-Aviation plant from Courneuve to a site near Marseille, and the movement of several *grandes écoles*, for example the Public Health School to Rennes, the Aeronautical School to Toulouse, and the Marine Engineering School to Brest.[44]

However, transfer of its own activities is only one aspect of the state's effort to decongest the Paris Region. Many public services have tended to keep reserves of land in the Paris Region far beyond those they may be realistically expected to utilize. The administrations involved often have no real intention to utilize these lands; however, ignoring the issue of alternative uses, they argue that holding the land is not detrimental to anyone since it has no cost.[45] Although this continues to be a problem, important breakthroughs have been made, especially with regard to military properties.

Any over-all evaluation of the effects of the transfer or conversion of government controlled or related activities is extremely difficult to make, since the motives and conditions which determine such actions are seldom fully known. This problem is especially troublesome with regard to nationalized firms, since this sector has not been constituted in any systematic manner.[46] In any event, even with the addition of direct state relocations and conversions to the decentralization measures created in 1954–55, the expected, or at least hoped-for, results have not materialized. Although transfers of government controlled or related activities continue to take place, it is clear that any substantial reduction in the relative importance of Paris will have to come about primarily through the creation of new activities in the provinces.

Summary
and Conclusions

Postwar regional policy in France was begun for the most part as an effort to check the growth of congested conditions in Paris to the benefit of relatively underdeveloped provincial regions. Purely negative measures to restrict location of economic activity in Paris have not prevented increased concentration, although the situation no doubt would have been worse in their absence. Moreover, prohibitions concerning location in Paris have had only negligible effect in stimulating growth in more distant regions, since "decentralization" generally has involved movements to the periphery of the Paris agglomeration (often resulting in an extension of congested surface) or to favorable localities within a 200-kilometer radius of the capital. Positive measures—grants, loans, fiscal incentives, attempts to decentralize state or state-controlled establishments, and incentives to channel regional savings into local investment projects—to promote economic growth in less developed or stagnating regions have failed to provide sufficient external economies to overcome the attractiveness of advanced regions.

In view of this, it has become necessary to formulate a more comprehensive regional policy. Efforts are now being made to give the various regions the means and the incentives for the greatest degree of development consistent with the nation's over-all needs. This object of national policy was first expressed in the Fourth Plan:

> The regional economic development policy which the government intends to promote is oriented toward directives fixed at the national level. . . . Thus, it is a policy which is not limited to insufficiently developed regions but which extends to the whole of the country, at the same time pursuing in each region activities of a nature which assure its economic expansion.[47]

The following chapter critically examines the framework that has been created in an attempt to assure a coherent national policy of regional development. The specific policy measures which have been or will be put into effect within this framework are discussed in subsequent chapters.

4

The Institutional Framework for Regional Planning

The
Program Regions

In its initial phase, the regionalization of French planning appeared as an attempt to reform and harmonize the diverse administrative structures of the various government agencies. Prior to 1955, each ministry typically established its regional operations according to criteria of its own choosing, without reference to the regional structure of the operations of other ministries. In consequence, some larger provincial cities were centers for twenty or thirty different circumscriptions grouping varying numbers of departments. On the other hand, some principal cities were dependent on as many as four or five other centers, which obliged local authorities to go from one to another depending on the problem at hand.[1] Bordeaux, for example, served as

74

a center for twenty-three different regional circumscriptions, of which seventeen had an economically relevant character. As a result, it was practically impossible to carry out studies or implement measures which required comprehensive statistical documentation.[2]

Since regional policy would require the collaboration of diverse government administrations, a basic change in traditional administrative structures was obviously required. In 1955, at the suggestion of the General Planning Commission, a decree (June 30) was promulgated which called for the establishment of "programs of regional action" to promote regional economic expansion, particularly in regions suffering from unemployment or "insufficient" economic development. It was specified that "these programs will coordinate the action of diverse administrations with projects undertaken by local authorities or with private undertakings benefiting from either government financial aid or the cooperation of a public agency." It was further provided that the programs should be prepared within the framework of one or another specified form of traditional administrative structure, or "in a different framework when geographic or economic factors lead to a divergence from administrative circumscriptions."[3] This new framework was defined by an Order of November 28, 1956,[4] which divided the country into twenty-two regions, each containing a number of departments. The delimitation of regions was slightly modified in 1960, so that now there are twenty-one "program regions."[5] A list of the departments within the respective regions is given in Appendix I (see also the map on page 76).

There certainly has been no lack of criticism concerning the delimitation of these regions, although the necessity for some reform of this nature was never denied by anyone seriously interested in problems of regional policy. At the one extreme, of course, it is not feasible to create too many regions, since the entities involved would be too small to have any meaningful claim to independence. It would be equally undesirable to create too few circumscriptions, since the whole notion of specifically regional policy would tend to disappear as the number of regions approaches one, i.e., the region which is the nation as a whole. Although they may differ on details, the critics are generally agreed that the creation of twenty-one regions errs in the direction of the first extreme.

FRANCE
The Program Regions and the *Métropoles d'Equilibre*

Gravier, for example, expresses the fear that too fine a regional division may result in a "balkanization" of the provinces which would only favor the continued dominance of the Paris Region. As a result, he has recommended the combination of a number of regions; under his scheme the region with the lowest population would be Poitou-Charentes, with 1,415,000 inhabitants (1962). At present, ten of the program regions have fewer than a million and a half inhabitants.[6]

Similarly, Boudeville has argued that from an economic point of view the minimum feasible size for a region would be on a scale such as that of Denmark or Switzerland. Belgium and Holland, on the other hand, would each constitute two regions. "It would appear that a region of 30,000 to 40,000 square kilometers, a population of 4 to 5 million inhabitants and disposing of a regional income of $4 to $5 million can aspire to an integrated regional life, if not to a national existence. . . . It is only on this scale that social accounting and regional programs are necessarily called for." [7] Given the present division, only Rhone-Alps and Nord, with the exception of Paris, approach this dimension.

Others emphasize the need to harmonize the delimitation of France's program regions with those which would be most feasible within the framework of the Common Market. The position of many European-minded persons in France is that the French government should delimit regions in line with an international perspective so that the present administrative reorganization will not be upset in the future "by another geographical division of a supranational origin." [8] This issue is the source of sharp political differences within France.

In spite of these diverse objections (all of which have a great deal of merit) to present regional divisions, major revisions do not seem to be feasible at the present. The pragmatic approach set forth in a report prepared by the Economic and Social Council in 1963 is no doubt correct in maintaining that whatever the conceptual difficulties, "it seems premature to modify the present number of program regions during the elaboration of the Fifth Plan, since regional planning experience has scarcely begun. However, the present organization must be considered primarily as an experiment whose framework can be modified according to the results it gives." [9] Meanwhile, of course, maximum cooperation should be encouraged where two or more regions have an obvious affinity, so that any eventual regroupment may be carried out with a minimum of friction. A certain amount of spontaneous cooperation has in fact already been initiated. For example, officials from Rennes (Brittany) and Nantes (Loire-Atlantique) have initiated steps to define a common program "to counterbalance the considerable weight which the Paris Region represents in our region." Toward this end, historical links between the two regions have been emphasized, and initiatives have been taken to make two complementary regions around the Rennes-Nantes axis.[10]

Early
Regional Plans

On the basis of the 1955 decree calling for "programs of regional action," plans were prepared and approved for Brittany, Poitou-Charentes, Corsica (which was later merged with Provence-Côte d' Azur), and Lorraine. A Law of August 7, 1957, gave the central government the task of defining the conditions for establishing regional development plans "intended to favor a harmonious geographic division of the population and of its activities and, especially, to orient the location of public and private investment." [11] The government was also required to consult with local authorities and "interested regional organisms." Three plans were prepared and approved on the basis of this text: Midi-Pyrenees, Alsace, and Languedoc. A Decree of December 31, 1958, however, combined the principles set forth in the two documents. This decree called for the preparation, for each region, of a "regional plan for social and economic development and *aménagement du territoire*." [12]

At the time of this writing, regional plans based on the Decree of December 31, 1958, have been prepared, approved, and published for all regions; the last, that for Upper Normandy, was published in 1966. These documents have been prepared in a more or less similar manner. A first part gives a description of historical, geographic, infrastructure, and resource characteristics of the region. Another section is devoted to demographic factors, including projections of future trends. Then, the general strengths and weaknesses of the region are set forth. Finally, orientations are proposed for ameliorating the weaknesses and building on existing strong points. Many plans also contain a substantial statistical annex.

Unfortunately, these regional plans have tended to be plans in name only, since for the most part they constitute inventories of what existed in a given region at a given time. Moreover, their appearance at different times over a period of ten years means that even this aspect of the various plans is not really comparable. As to future projections, orders of priority generally are not specified and modes of finance are at best only vaguely hinted.

Already in 1960 the Economic and Social Council regretted that the elaboration of regional plans was being hindered by a lack of adequate information among officials who should have been actively involved in this. It was pointed out that they had not been given firm directions on how to proceed, and that printed maps of the program regions had not even been prepared. Regional plans which had been prepared very early by some regions were not made available as guides to other regions, and rulings concerning regional coordination were all but ignored. The council further pointed out the prevalence of "indifference, incomprehension, refusal to cooperate, and even ill will" which characterized "the resistance of structures to economic growth." It was strongly inferred that much of the difficulty resulted from the continued habit of each government administration to think of its mission only in the vertical terms of its own particular hierarchy. Each high official received instructions directly from his Paris ministry, and provisions to coordinate the disparate efforts of varying administrations were wholly inadequate. In the face of these obstacles, the council proposed the creation of an authority capable of coordinating administrative activities at the regional level.[13]

Yet another obstacle to the elaboration of the plans has been a tendency for hostilities to develop between subregions of given program regions. For example, during preliminary discussions for the preparation of the plan for Rhone-Alps, local authorities and collaborators were more disposed to think in terms of two regions, one a "Rhone" region centering about Lyon, and the other an "Alps" region grouping together departments whose economies are conditioned by the mountains. A report by a representative from the latter area held that the whole notion of discussing a plan for Rhone-Alps was wrong because it was by no means a unified region, since "the problems of the alpine economy are distinct and call for their own separate solutions." [14]

Human misunderstanding and obstinacy would be present in the face of plans prepared and put into operation under the best of practical circumstances. In this instance, however, much of the difficulty lies in the nature of the plans themselves. As Lanversin has pointed out, for any administrative act to have value as a juridical command it must be unequivocal and it must go beyond a simple sketch concerning orientations which can be variously interpreted; it must specify conditions (form, time, place) for its realization, on the one hand, and the person to whom its injunctions are addressed, on the other. Otherwise the responsibility for its execution or the lack of it cannot be exactly determined. This has been the case for the regional plans, whose juridical scope has been purely indicative.[15] Thus, even though the approval of a regional plan requires that all public administrations cooperate in its execution, and that each conform to it concerning its operations in the region, "the plans are badly provided with practical means of execution," and consequently they have "in fact only a rather limited influence on the conduct of the regional policy of the state." [16] Since this was generally known, it was not surprising that public opinion, as well as the activities of officials who were, or should have been, directly engaged in formulating and executing the plans were characterized by considerable indifference.

Despite the many shortcomings involved in the creation of the various program regions and their respective plans, the experience has not been without value. The very existence of program regions has represented an important step in directing attention toward problems of economically rational spatial resource distribution. At the national level, the General Planning Commission has been confronted with the need for horizontal consultation, coordination, and planning in regional terms as a complement to already well-elaborated vertical planning by economic sectors. At the regional level, many persons (though by no means a sufficient number) have acquired the habit of interdepartmental consultation, and of thinking in regional terms. Limited though they may be, these gains still represent important acquisitions at the outset of the present effort to regionalize the budget of the government.

Administrative Reform

By this time the reader may have inferred that one of the principal obstacles to meaningful regional planning in France has been the nature of its traditional system of administration. The structure of this system is essentially vertical and hierarchic; each ministry has its central administration in Paris and exterior services in the provinces. Until quite recently, organic links among the exterior services of the various ministries had been practically nonexistent at the local level. The principal representative of the central government in each of the ninety-five departments is the *préfet,* who is appointed by the Council of Ministers. The *préfet* is charged with, among other things, representing all public administrations and controlling their services, controlling subordinate district *préfets* and mayors at the local level, keeping the central government informed, and watching over the execution of laws and regulations. Although in principle the *préfet* represents the whole government, in practice his coordinating role has consistently declined, and he has more and more tended to become primarily the representative of the Ministry of the Interior. It has become increasingly evident that greater decentralization and a higher degree of horizontal coordination at the regional, departmental, and local levels are essential prerequisites for local initiative and more rational planning. Thus, a number of reforms, some frankly experimental, have been introduced in recent years. As M. Bloch-Lainé has pointed out, these measures are "inspired by a triple preoccupation: (a) to render the administration more capable of making choices as to the order of priority and the localization of investments; (b) to make the administration more operational; (c) to deconcentrate the administration more, and thus prepare the way for a closer association of local forces in decision-making." [17]

A step in this direction was taken by a Decree of January 7, 1959, which called for a harmonization of administrative circumscriptions with a view to putting programs of regional action into operation. Toward this end, it authorized departments to group themselves into circumscriptions which would be finally defined at a later date (these were in fact the twenty-one program regions, which were definitively fixed by a Decree of June 2, 1960). It further stipulated that a *préfet* would be appointed for each of these new regions, who should organize and preside over interdepartmental conferences. The aims of the conferences should be to study and coordinate the application of measures concerning programs of regional action, *aménagement du territoire,* and, more generally, the economic policy of the government. Finally, the decree stipulated that within one year, the district boundaries of administrations and of state and state-controlled services which were relevant to regional programs should be harmonized with the boundaries of the program regions.[18]

In fact, the services and administrations concerned were generally opposed to this decree on the ground that it constituted a threat to the relations between the central administrations in Paris and the external services.[19] Moreover, the designation of the *préfet* of one department as *préfet coordinateur* for a program region was widely interpreted as a promotion for the individual concerned and as a subordination for his colleagues. In addition, the training and experience of the *préfet* as a government official did not necessarily give him adequate competence in the coordination of economic matters.[20] Thus, the interval provided for adjustment of administrative circumscriptions passed without the realization of the intended reforms.

In response, a Decree of June 2, 1960, called for the immediate harmonization of relevant administrative circumscriptions with those of the twenty-one program regions, which this decree designated in final form.[21] The administrations affected were those with an economic or social character; in all, they numbered some thirty agencies. Their boundaries now correspond with those of the regions, if not exactly, by grouping several regions or by subdividing regions. "Thus an end has been put to the old quarrel which for a number of years paralyzed regional policy, and a homogeneous framework has at last been traced for it. One may contest the validity of the framework, but it does have the merit of having clarified the situation." [22]

More recently, a series of Decrees of March 14, 1964, helped complete the reform of the administrative structure by defining more carefully the powers of the regional *préfet* as well as the aims which should guide his actions, and by strengthening the institutional bases for consultation and coordination of policy at the regional level. It was stipulated that the mission of the *préfet* is to put into operation in his circumscription government policy concerning economic development and *aménagement du territoire*. Moreover, he is to "animate and control" the activity of *préfets* of departments in his region, as well as that of certain other services with a regional character.[23] An instruction for the application of these decrees also specified to the *préfet* that "the government intends to affirm your pre-eminence over regional chiefs of services." In addition, it stated that "the general power of coordination which is conferred on you . . . permits you to give the necessary directives to interested chiefs of services when a matter goes beyond the limits of a single service in its objective or by virtue of its repercussions." [24] The importance of these measures is that they clarified the issue of whether the regional *préfet* would have real authority or simply remain a kind of "first among equals." They thus marked a clear defeat for parties hostile to administrative decentralization.

At the same time that the powers of the regional *préfet* were being enlarged, Regional Administrative Conferences were created to replace the interdepartmental conferences established by the Decree of January 7, 1959. The principal function assigned to each conference is to consider "problems posed by public investments and their effects on the economic and social life of the region." Because of the vagueness of this stipulation it is not yet certain what role the conferences will be called on to play, though this will undoubtedly vary according to the knowledge, needs, and personalities of the various regional *préfets*, who will serve as their presidents.[25] Unfortunately, the decree makes no provision for consulting with competent persons outside of the administration, although it states that "it may be useful to call in experts in order to throw light on debates on an individual problem." [26] Consultation of experts will, of course, vary from region to region, though it may be hoped that competent opinion will be sought whenever possible.

Yet another organism created by a Decree of March 14, 1964, is the Regional Economic Development Commission. One commission is designated for each program region. Each commission may have a minimum of twenty members and a maximum of fifty, and a quarter of its members must be chosen from among local authorities, i.e. mayors and municipal councilmen. The mayor of the principal city of the program region is automatically a member of the commission. Half the members are designated in part by associations representing local commerce, industry, agriculture, and crafts, or by the organism which represents all of these groups at the regional level; and in part by professional organizations and syndicates of employers, industrial workers, agriculture, and commerce. However, the president of the Regional Expansion Committee (see Chapter 3) is also automatically a member. The remainder of the commission's members are designated by the Prime Minister and are chosen on the basis of competence in economic, social, familial, scientific, or cultural areas. A commission is designated for five years, and a president and two vice-presidents are chosen by its members. Although their authority is purely consultative, consultation with the commissions is obligatory during the elaboration of regional plans, and, more specifically, during the preparation of the regional sections of the national Plan.[27]

The planning effort at the regional and local level is by no means limited to the organisms just described. Numerous private groups are also more or less actively engaged in this effort; these include, among others, the regional expansion committees, Chambers of Commerce, university institutes and study centers, and various political and professional groups. However, because of their highly varied nature and importance and the lack of any systematic integration of their activities with those of the public organisms, it is impossible to evaluate their over-all significance. The relevance of their activities must be considered in a regional context.

The *Délégation à l'aménagement du territoire et à l'action régionale*

Until recently the efficacy of French regional planning was sharply limited because the responsibility for executing regional policy was badly defined. Although the Ministry of Construction had a bureau devoted to problems of *aménagement du territoire,* the bureau could not coordinate the efforts of the various ministries and services of the government, whereas the need for such coordination was becoming increasingly apparent. Moreover, such reforms as the creation of the District of the Region of Paris and an interministerial committee for regional problems were also far from answering the need for more comprehensive and integrated formulation and execution of regional policy.

In response to these deficiencies, the government held that it had become necessary to assure a unified conception of planning, and to reinforce the means for implementing regional policy objectives. The first of these tasks faced a certain divergence of approach which had come to exist between the General Planning Commission and plans for *aménagement du territoire* conceived by the Ministry of Construction; the former operated within the perspective of the four-year national Plans, whereas the latter took a long-term view. The government held that it was essential to end this duality by assuring, at conception, greater coherence regarding the perspectives for the future.[28]

To deal with these issues a Decree of February 14, 1963, created a new organism, the *Délégation à l'aménagement du territoire et à l'action régionale* (DATAR). To avoid possible conflicts or jealousies it was provided that the creation of the DATAR would not greatly modify the structure of government or constitute in any strict sense a new administration. Rather, the DATAR was confided the tasks of coordination and impulsion. Its role was defined to include (1) operating on the basis of the general directives established in the national Plan; (2) preparing and coordinating the elements necessary for government decisions concerning *aménagement du territoire* and regional planning; (3) ascertaining that technical administrations adjust their respective activities in these domains; and (4) fostering the convergence of actions toward regional policy objectives on the part of these administrations when the objectives involved surpass the competence of any one of them. The last task, since it involves problems at the interministerial level, would be carried out with the possibility of recourse to the arbitrage and authority of the Prime Minister.[29]

The head of the DATAR, the Delegate (*Délégué*), is attached directly to the Prime Minister, which gives him direct access to the Interministerial Committee for problems regarding regional activities and *aménagement du territoire*. Moreover, the Delegate is expected to prepare the deliberations of the Interministerial Committee in liaison with the ministers concerned and the General Planning Commission. The committee is then given the function of synthesis, arbitrage, and impulsion, though supervision of the application of its decisions is a function of the Delegate. The Committee, the General Planning Commission, and the Delegate are also responsible for preparing the regional sections of the national Plan and reporting on their execution.[30]

To assure unity of conception concerning the national Plan and regional policy, the General Planning Commissioner is required to prepare studies on the guiding conceptions of *aménagement du territoire* policy and to integrate their conclusions into the national Plans. The studies, however, are based on a longer-term perspective than the national Plans. In carrying out this task, the General Planning Commission is assisted by a National Commission for *Aménagement du Territoire* (CNAT), which replaces the comparable section of the Ministry of Construction. The Delegate of the DATAR is closely associated in this work, since he participates in the formulation of the national Plan as a vice-president of the Committee for Regional Plans, and participates in the management of the National Fund for Land and Urban Planning. The latter is attached to the Ministry of

Construction and is used to facilitate certain land acquisitions relating to operations of urbanism, industrial implantations, and reserves for future utilization. In addition, the Delegate is a member of the Executive Council of the Economic and Social Development Fund, and his participation in certain specialized committees permits him to maintain permanent contact with operations concerning industrial decentralization and investments of local authorities. The work of the Delegate extends to the regional level through the newly instituted regional *préfets,* Regional Administrative Conferences, and Regional Economic Development Commissions, with whom he maintains continuing contacts. In addition, he keeps in contact with the private Regional Expansion Committees to assure that they are associated in the realization of local objectives; he must also propose to the Prime Minister the amounts of subsidies to be made available to the Regional Expansion Committees to assure their necessary functions. Finally, the Delegate has at his disposition a Fund for Intervention for *Aménagement du Territoire* (FIAT) which is intended for the financing of certain activities considered necessary for the realization of regional policy.[31] In general, then, it may truly be said that the DATAR is located at "the hinge linking thought and action" with respect to regional policy.[32]

Despite these elaborate measures concerning the institution of the DATAR, doubts have been expressed concerning their efficacy. For example, Lajugie maintains,

> One may fear that the desired unity of conception in this matter is not yet completely assured. In place of the dualism General Planning Commission–Ministry of Construction will there not be substituted a dualism General Planning Commission–DATAR which will present the same drawbacks so long as the two organisms are simply juxtaposed under the Prime Minister, without one having any hierarchic authority over the other? Doubtless it will be necessary in the near future to clear up this matter by completing the reforms instituted at the national level, just as had to be done on a regional scale with regard to the *préfets coordonnateurs,* whose authority was also too imprecise at the outset.[33]

It would seem that the creation of the DATAR did result in a certain apprehensiveness on the part of the General Planning Commission, primarily because the commission felt that to superimpose a new administration on the previously existing structure would only complicate the decision-making process. In fact, the role of the DATAR as an initiator of regional policy has been ambiguous. The regional objectives of the Fifth Plan, which will be considered in detail in later chapters, have been determined more by the First Report of the National Commission for *Aménagement du Territoire* than by the DATAR, but the latter has given every evidence of close cooperation to facilitate their realization.[34] Of course, this does not mean that the potential difficulties raised by Lajugie may not eventually materialize; however, the evidence certainly would not indicate that this will necessarily be the case. Thus, the principal problems at the present time relate not so much to conflicts in the formulation of objectives but to their appropriateness and the means available for their application. The first of these issues will be examined in the discussion of concrete policy measures; the second, however, requires consideration of a major innovation in the structure of French planning, namely, the regional sections.

The
Regional Sections

The principal mechanism for the regionalization of the national Plan is the "regional sections." In the French literature these are generally referred to as *tranches opératoires,* or occasionally *tranches régionales.* The limited relevant references in English have employed the term *tranche opératoire,* which literally means "operative slice" and sounds as bizarre in French as in English. As two French authorities have pointed out, "reform experiences often produce awful nomenclatures; curiously, here have been combined terms with culinary and surgical resonances, two domains which it is hardly fitting to bring together." [35] The choice of the term "regional section" has been made in concordance with this judgment and because it is a fairly accurate reflection of the phenomenon it designates.

As we have seen, the regional plans formulated on the basis of 1955 legislation constituted little more than inventories of regional resources and suggestions for future projects, without any real schedule of executions or provision for financing. To remedy this situation, it was decided in 1962, on the initiative of the General Planning Commission, to introduce regional sections in the elaboration of the Fourth Plan. The sections are, in theory, parts of the respective regional plans; but in their totality they also represent the regional breakdown of the national Plan, since they are intended to project to the regional level the objectives specified in the national Plan. Like the national Plan, the regional sections include a schedule of realizations, an order of priorities, and indications of the corresponding modes of finance, that is, precisely what the previous regional plans lacked. Of course, the regional sections are also, as is the case with national Plan, indicative.

The Fourth Plan provided that regional sections should be prepared by collaboration among regional organisms, interested administrations, and the General Planning Commission, with final decisions the responsibility of the Interministerial Committee for regional action and *aménagement du territoire*. In addition, it was stipulated that the regional sections would not be limited to public investments, but would also include forecasts of the creation of new employment and private investment. "Regional planning is thus tending to become what it should be in order fully to play its role, that is to say, the indispensable complement to national planning." [36] Of course, since its inception in 1963, the DATAR has also been closely associated in this process, both in the preparation of the regional sections and by verifying that the regional objectives of the Plan are being respected in practice.

For the period corresponding to the application of the Fourth Plan, the preparation of the regional sections was directed primarily toward a four-year perspective on the economic development of the respective regions, and toward the public investments to be realized from 1961 to 1965.[37] In each case, the work demanded of regional organisms consisted of making projections over the entire four-year period and not of specifying annual values.

The preparation of perspectives on regional development was to be based on demographic studies, the evolution of regional production, and employment problems. As to the first, emphasis was put on population change, its urban-rural composition, migration, the age structure, and evaluation of the work force. Projections to 1965 were to be made for number of students, available labor force, and housing needs. Concerning production, regional activities were to be compared to the average trends for the nation as a whole. Employment studies were given particular emphasis, especially with regard to comparisons of supply and demand for labor, and estimations of new jobs which would have to be created by 1965.[38]

With regard to public investments, the procedure for preparing the regional sections cannot really be dissociated from the regionalization of the budget of the state. These investments have been, insofar as possible, regrouped by program region; they concern, on the one hand, direct operations of the state (highway construction, water supply, school construction, etc.), and, on the other hand, subsidies to organisms engaged in activities of a public nature (cheap housing, regrouping of rural land, etc.)

The preparation of the regional sections involves three categories of investments: those which can be individualized at the national level; those which can be individualized at the regional level; and those fixed in general aggregates at the regional level. For investments in the first category, all the projects were known individually and were already mentioned in the Fourth Plan. The interdepartmental conferences were notified of their nature and of the expenditures involved in each case and were asked to comment on them and to present their opinions concerning the order of priority for their realization. Investments in the second category were anticipated by the Fourth Plan but had not yet been individualized. Investments in the third category included projects which it would not be feasible to individualize in detail at the regional level before they were established by the departments, subject to the annual determinations of the allocation of the state's budget or of the budgets of interested local authorities. This category included such projects as elementary schools, housing, rural and departmental roads, water supply, and reparceling of land. In other words, it was not generally possible for the planners at the national level to specify the financial limits of projects in the second and third categories at the outset of the Fourth Plan, though methods were suggested for their estimation. The interdepartmental conferences were also instructed to indicate what consequences would follow from an increase or a decrease of 20 per cent of the expected expenditures. This was intended to provide the basis for a certain flexibility in the financial framework of the Plan, as well as to encourage regional participants to consider carefully the issue of priorities.[39]

In general, the theoretical procedure for the elaboration of the regional sections consisted of six phases. In the first phase, documentation was to be prepared at the national level containing the principal information needed for the work of the interdepartmental conferences. In the second phase, these documents were to be examined at the regional level by the conferences, in collaboration with regional and departmental agencies. After the necessary studies, a program for the regional sections was to be prepared and submitted to the national level, where, in phase three, the relevant ministers and General Planning Commission were to adjust the projects to harmonize with national objectives. In the fourth phase, these revisions were to be submitted to the interdepartmental conferences for further suggestions or recommendations. Here the Committees for Regional Expansion were also to be brought into consultation. In the fifth phase, the revised regional sections were to be examined at the national level by the Committee for Regional Plans and by the ministries involved and then submitted to the Interministerial Committee for regional policy for definitive elaboration of their final form.[40]

In fact, the preparation of the regional sections for the Fourth Plan did not proceed in textbook fashion, owing both to the pattern of informal relations which inevitably arises in the operation of any complex administrative process and to the frankly experimental nature of this initial effort. Moreover, by the time the regional sections were worked out in 1963, the Fourth Plan had already been approved, its first year of application was already passed, and the annual budget for 1963 had already been prepared. The regional sections thus were of relevance only to investments of a rather residual nature. Moreover, it will also be recalled that even the basic institutional pattern for regional planning was changed during the course of the Fourth Plan, i.e., the DATAR was created only in 1963 and in the following year the interdepartmental conferences were abandoned in favor of the Regional Administrative Conferences and the Regional Economic Development Commissions.

Thus, the elaboration of the sections did not take place as had been intended, largely as a result of institutional changes and the haste caused by the relative lateness of their preparation. The first three phases generally went according to the prescribed order, but the second phase was the only one where direct regional participation in fact occurred. After a synthesis of the regional sections by the relevant ministries and the General Planning Commission in phase three, the sections were submitted directly to the Committee for Regional Plans for discussion in phase four. The fifth phase comprised the preparation of a report on the regionalization of the state budget for 1964 by the DATAR. The final phase involved discussion and approval of this report as an annex to the annual budget bill by the parliament.[41]

In addition, numerous difficulties not related solely to lateness of planning and the administrative reform were evident. In the first place, there was a lack of agreement between the methods of preparation proposed by the General Planning Commission and those proposed by certain ministries, for example, that for agriculture. Moreover, many of the exterior services of the Paris ministries were hostile to the whole enterprise, for numerous reasons including repercussions from uncertainties in the central offices, the increase in work required of them, the presence of conflicting directives from the General Planning Commission and the ministries, and, not least, "an endemic resistance of administrative structures which it is necessary to take into account when attempting any act of reform or progress." [42]

A particular disappointment to advocates of greater local initiative was the lack of real power accorded the interdepartmental conferences. It was often difficult to elaborate the regional sections at the regional level because of the rigid and narrow directives and advice communicated by the ministries in Paris. In general, the ministries seemed to show little respect for either the spirit or the letter of the experiment to promote decentralized initiative. Although the coordinating *préfet* and his colleagues were theoretically supposed to work out a synthesis of the various programs communicated to them, they generally had little choice in the matter; representatives of the central authorities tended to impose their own views and often "considered with humor that anyone could seriously contest their programs." Sometimes, of course, changes were impossible because of technical constraints, and the last-minute nature of this initial effort also meant that many changes were not feasible, especially where they involved altering a project which would in turn affect an entire set of interdependent projects.[43]

There was also considerable lack of coordination at the local level. The consultation of the Committees for Regional Expansion seemed to be particularly disappointing, both because of a lack of enthusiasm on

the part of administrations to consult with them, and because of the
frequent failure of the committees to furnish adequate information and
studies where these were requested of them. The latter problem was
aggravated by insufficient statistics, lack of time, and confusion resulting from the many texts concerning the process of working out the
regional sections. A further difficulty was the tendency of the committees to pretend to be the representatives of the entire private sector
of the economy, to the exclusion of groups such as the industrial and
commercial Chambers of Commerce, the agricultural chambers, and
other private associations. Moreover, in their attempt to rally support
from the entire private sector, the committees often attracted those
elements which were the least favored by competitive circumstances,
creating the danger that these groups would unduly influence the participation of the committees.[44]

One of the principal advantages of the regional sections over the
previous regional plans was to be, and remain, the effort which they
represent at quantification of means and ends. Unfortunately, the degree of availability of economic, demographic, and social statistics was
not sufficient to permit the precision desirable in evaluating regional
needs and the position of individual regions with respect to other regions and the nation as a whole.[45]

Before we consider the changes which have been made to improve
the procedures for preparing the regional sections for the Fifth Plan,
it must be pointed out that even if the difficulties just discussed were
greatly ameliorated, certain inherent limitations to the regionalization
of the national budget would still remain.

Regionalization
of the Government Budget

The extent to which the budget may be regionalized and the interpretation which may be attached to the results vary according to the
type of activity in question. Many types of investment credits cannot
always be localized. Such would be the case for many funds allocated
to studies and research. For example, a credit allocated to a university
in northern France for technological research on a project whose results could only be exploited in southern France could not properly be
assigned to any one section of the country. Similarly, it would be impossible to give a meaningful breakdown by regions of expenditures

for projects such as interregional express highways, international cables, and high-tension electricity lines. General provisions for adding flexibility to or adjusting future operations whose time and place of application cannot be known in advance provide another category of credits which cannot be localized.

For those credits which are amenable to regionalization, problems of interpretation pose numerous hazards. Comparisons of percentages of public investments among regions can be particularly misleading, especially when it is a question of narrow categories rather than broad aggregates, or when the data relate to a single year rather than a longer period of time. In addition, the danger always exists that their inclusion in tables showing the regional distribution of expenditures will provoke alarm on the part of less-favored regions, even though the latter may be substantially benefiting from a project (for example a maritime port) whose stimulating effects on economic activity spread to a number of regions. As the DATAR has correctly pointed out, "it is not possible to seek equity at any cost: the needs of a region naturally differ according to the climate (Brittany does not need snow plows as much as the Auvergne), the nature of the land surface, the population, the activities, the degree of industrial development, etc. Taking account of the present state of our measuring instruments, criteria permitting the measurement of the degree of 'justice' involved in the distribution of investments are nonexistent." [46]

Another difficulty in the interpretation of regional investment allocation relates to the type of policy being pursued in any particular case. Here it is fitting to introduce the distinction which the French literature makes between a policy of *entraînement* on the one hand and of *accompagnement* on the other. The former refers to the choice of investments designed primarily to have a stimulating or inducing effect on the rest of the economy; thus, after World War II the early national Plans made a special effort to restore the transportation network and the energy base of the country, since these in turn would encourage the growth of other sectors. In contrast, the latter type of policy is designed to accompany the expansion of other sectors. In an area where economic activity and population are growing there is an increasing need for dwellings, so aid to housing construction would constitute an operation of *accompagnement*. For the sake of convenience these concepts will hereinafter be referred to by their closest English equivalents, i.e. "inducing activities" and "induced activities," especially since these are the terms employed in the theoretical discussion in Chapter 1. The Fourth and Fifth Plans have both distinguished between regions where public policy should play an inducing role and those where it should be characterized by an induced nature. However, it is risky to attempt to evaluate the magnitude of these respective effects by singling out certain regionalized categories of investment as induced and others as inducing, since in reality they rarely exist in pure form. "Depending on its location, the same category of operations will have either an induced or an inducing effect. A technical college constructed in an industrial region is induced by development; established in a weakly industrialized region it will have an inducing effect. Moreover, when certain induced operations undertaken at a given place are combined and harmonized the resultant totality may lead to the creation of an inducing effect." [47]

In view of these considerations, the regionalization of the budget of the government does not pretend to show the degree of equity in the geographical division of public funds; rather, it attempts to establish "in what measure and under what limits the investments of the state, which contribute an important part to the growth of the economy, are capable of being localized." Furthermore, it presents the operations of the government as governed both by technical criteria and by criteria of deliberate choice. Investments subject to technical criteria are closely related to induced investment, since they include actions of the government without which certain public or private undertakings would be rendered ineffective. The construction of an office building, for example, would require the provision of a telephone system. The regionalization of the budget also reflects the emphases of government policy at any given time. Thus, the 1964 budget reflected relatively high outlays for such priority items as regroupment of agricultural land, irrigation, and equipment for national education, whereas previous budgets had emphasized items such as rural habitations and equipment for energy and steel production.[48]

In the 1964 budget, eight major branches of activity were regionalized, with the proportion of each budget category regionalized varying from 50 to nearly 83 per cent. These sectors, with their corresponding rates of regionalization, were national education (51 per cent), health (81 per cent), specially supervised education (68 per cent), cultural affairs (83 per cent), public works (83 per cent), post and telecommunications (68 per cent), urban equipment (68 per cent), and agriculture (80 per cent). By the time the 1966 budget was prepared, the civil aviation, youth and sports, scientific and technical research, tourism, water, and radio and television sectors were also added to this list. All sectors for which rates were available had at least 60 per cent of their respective budgets regionalized in 1966, with the exception of scientific and technical research (30 per cent), which presents special difficulties.[49]

Regionalization of the Fifth Plan

The preparation of the Fifth Plan marks the first time that decentralized planning measures have been undertaken with the full cooperation of each region. Although it is impossible at this early date to evaluate adequately the work that has been done, it already is obvious that substantial improvements have been made over the experience which characterized the Fourth Plan. This should not be surprising, since the current effort is the first in which the nature and mode of preparation of the regional aspects of the Plan have been an integral part of its basic constitution from the outset. Moreover, the new institutional framework for regional planning (see Figures 4.1 and 4.2) marks a definite improvement over the rather ill-defined and frankly experimental relationships characteristic of previous experience.

During the preparation of the Fifth Plan the only real modification made in the new institutions which have been described concerned the Committee for Regional Plans. A Decree of July 17, 1965, provided a badly needed clarification of the committee's nature and aims, which are essentially to aid in coordination. The committee is composed of the General Planning Commissioner; the Delegate of the DATAR; the Delegate General of the District of the Region of Paris; the tourism commissioner and representatives from other interested ministries and government agencies; and two representatives from the administrative council of the FDES. The committee has responsibility for harmonizing the directives transmitted to the regional *préfets* concerning regionalization of the Plan. In addition, it examines the reports prepared by the respective regional *préfets* with regard to the orientation of their activities and the preparation of regional sections, as well as the opinions expressed by the Regional Economic Development Commissions concerning these reports. The committee also organizes the information required by the Interministerial Committee for regional planning problems for its deliberations regarding the regional sections. Finally, the committee must consider annual reports on the execution of the regional sections.[50]

Regional participation in the preparation of the Fifth Plan began in the spring of 1965. Following parliamentary approval of the principal orientations of the Plan, the appropriate regional authorities were requested in April and May to make known their viewpoints concerning the orientations most appropriate for regional policy during the period from 1966 to 1970. This consultation was carried out in accordance with the stipulations laid down in the texts of March 14, 1964, on regional organization. Each regional *préfet,* in collaboration with his staff, prepared a report on the general orientation of regional policy concerning his circumscription and submitted it to the Regional Economic Development Commission. This consultation contributed to defining the main lines which would be followed later in the regionalization of the Plan. The generally well-documented reports which the *préfets* and regional commissions prepared were examined at the national level by the central administrations concerned, the modernization commissions of the Plan, and the Committee for Regional Plans. After Parliament approved the Fifth Plan in November 1965 there followed several months of exchanges of views between the national and regional levels in order to clarify various divergencies, especially concerning projections to 1970.

The general results of consultation with regional authorities prior to the preparation of the regional sections varied according to the three principal areas of study, which in general corresponded to the three separate parts of the reports of the regional *préfets.* The first concerned the long-run perspectives for *aménagement du territoire* and followed the same spirit as the national studies undertaken to clarify general lines of social and economic development until 1985. All of the regions were asked to study the long-run evaluation of their relations with the external world, their prospects for internal planning and development in view of both their actual state of development and potentialities for future growth, the principal paths which should be followed with respect to urban and rural development policy, and the

The Organizational Structure of Regional Planning

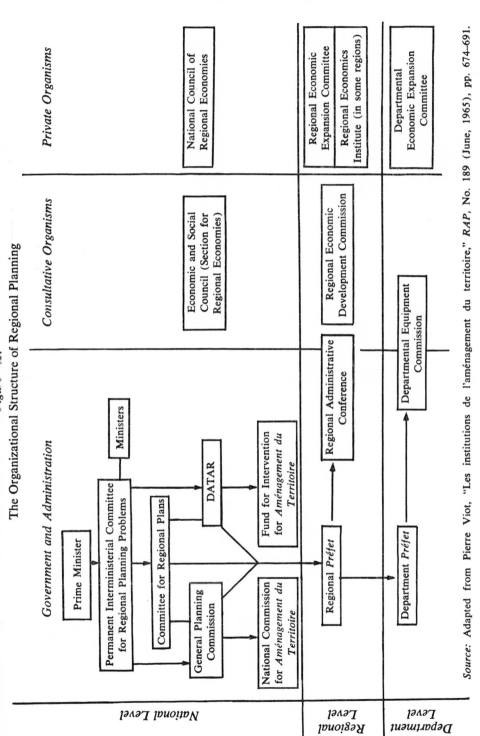

Source: Adapted from Pierre Viot, "Les institutions de l'aménagement du territoire," *RAP*, No. 189 (June, 1965), pp. 674–691.

Figure 4.2.
Preparation of the Fifth Plan

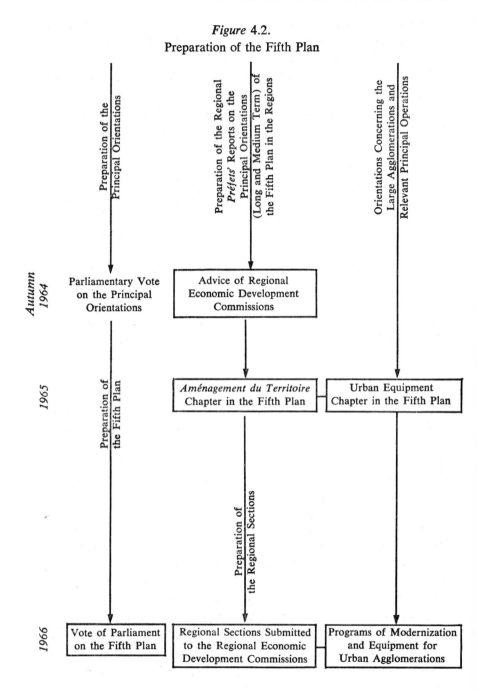

Source: Pierre Viot, "Les institutions de l'aménagement du territoire," *RAP*, No. 189 (June, 1965), p. 691.

long-term orientation which would be appropriate for programs of public investment within their boundaries. The regions carried out their research within a reference framework established by the National Commission for *Aménagement du Territoire* at the time of the elaboration of the principal orientations of the Fifth Plan. The commission attempted to forecast the breakdown of population and economic activity by region for 1985. In this regard three large zones were considered: the East, the West, and the Paris region. For the East, two different hypotheses of development were formulated according to assumptions of the maximum and minimum population which would be concentrated in the urban-industrial centers along the North Sea–Mediterranean axis. For the West, several development hypotheses and their respective effects on out-migration were formulated. An objective of obtaining a 35 to 40 per cent of the increase in national industrial employment was fixed for this region, which in turn would imply a reduction of one third in the present rate of out-migration. The long-run perspective for the Paris Region was established in conformity with the Strategic Plan discussed in Chapter 2. To supplement these hypotheses, the National Institute for Statistics and Economic Studies established three alternative perspectives on population change by region. These were based on past trends and took account of natural evolution from 1962 with assumptions concerning, respectively, no migration, interregional migration, and interregional and international migration. The reports submitted by the various regions indicated, however, that it was difficult for them to relate their probable rates of expansion to these hypotheses, since the former will depend in large measure on investment programs outside the control of local or regional authorities. Thus, most reports were based on the highest hypotheses.[51]

In addition to demographic studies, the long-term perspectives on relations of the respective regions with the external world also took account of evolutionary tendencies concerning agriculture, industry, and tourism, and the consequences which would follow the opening of national frontiers and the development of exterior exchanges. As to agriculture, most of the reports gave estimates of employment in 1985 based on results of national studies on the number of workers technically necessary in this sector. The preparation of industrial projections permitted considerable participation by professional groups, but it was not possible to deal very effectively with problems posed by the evolution of industrial structures because of the insufficiency of regional data on production or investment by branch of activity. These studies were limited, therefore, primarily to employment.[52]

Medium-run regional employment forecasts were prepared at the regional level during the first five months of 1965. These studies were based on data regarding manpower availability projected to 1970 by the National Institute for Statistics and Economic Studies from national figures which had been rectified in consultation with the modernization commissions. Manpower needs were also projected to 1970; these were based on trends since 1954, and were scrutinized at the regional level with regard to both the industrial and agricultural sectors. Forecasts concerning the tertiary sector were attempted but have only very limited value because of a general lack of sufficient data. The evolution of employment in agriculture was based on an average annual diminution of 116,000 persons up to 1970 (the average annual rate from 1954 to 1962 was 160,000), with allowances being made for particular regional conditions.[53]

As to industrial employment, the forecasts transmitted by the National Institute for Statistics and Economic Studies to the regions at the beginning of 1965 were based on several general tendencies, which were derived from both past trends and policy assumptions. These included an annual rate of growth of 5 per cent for the economy as a whole, an increase in international competition, and the application of measures to attain the objective of locating 35 to 40 per cent of all new employment during the Fifth Plan in the West. In nine of the twenty-one regions, the estimates presented by the regional reports corresponded closely to those formulated by the National Institute for Statistics and Economic Studies. The largest deviations with regard to higher estimates by regional authorities were those for Auvergne (11.0 per cent) and Languedoc (9.8 per cent), while on the lower side the largest deviations were those for Lorraine (−4.8 per cent) and Alsace (−4.5 per cent.)[54]

These results relate to regional consultations held prior to the final formulation and approval of the Fifth Plan. However, decentralized work on the Plan was carried on, following its approval, in the areas of regional studies on development perspectives, determination of criteria for regionalization of the Plan, and coordination of investment programs by various sectors. These efforts will be discussed after an examination of the body of thought which has been instrumental in shaping the means and ends of French regional policy.

5

Regional Economic Theory: The French Approach

Chapters 3 and 4 have traced the evolution of the institutional framework for regional planning in France. The specific economic policy measures which have been developed and applied within this framework are in large part the result of a body of thought which has similarly evolved since World War II, and especially in the past decade. Among the outstanding contributors to this movement have been Professors Jacques Boudeville, François Perroux, and Joseph Lajugie. Mention also must be made of the contributions of such Belgian economists as Jean Paelinck and Louis Davin, particularly in view of the close collaboration among French and Belgian scholars through the vehicle of the *Association de Science Régionale de Langue Française*. Finally, it is essential to note the importance of the Economic and Social Council's function as a liaison between the realms of economic scholarship and political action. The presence on the council of eminent scholars such as Maurice Byé and Jules Milhau has been particularly fruitful, since they have consistently provided constructive criticism of national and regional planning measures from the viewpoint of economic analysis. This is not to say, of course, that all misunderstandings and suspicions between "practical" officials and "abstract" scholars have been harmoniously resolved (nor would this necessarily always be desirable), but the degree of *rapprochement* is considerably greater on their account.

The French Approach
and Traditional Theory

Regional economic analysis in France, insofar as it has influenced regional policy, has been to a considerable extent a response, or better, a reaction to the purely deductive models of classical location theory,[1] as well as to highly simplified and abstract models of economic growth.

Dissatisfaction with traditional spatial theory certainly has not been limited to France, but the general orientation of French regional thought seems to have made a clearer break with the classical approach than has been the case, for example, in the United States. The extremely influential position held by Professor Isard is, despite the variety and richness of his contributions, itself cogent testimony to the continuing strength of the tradition of von Thünen, Weber, and Lösch. Unfortunately, most contemporary problems of spatial resource allocation necessarily involve urbanization patterns not amenable to treatment in terms of analyses which assume an undifferentiated transportation surface and which abstract from external effects. The following passage from a recent article by Lloyd Rodwin on the choice of regions for development deserves quotation because it succinctly and accurately focuses on a principal aspect of this difficulty:

> Turning to the spatial theorists is a disappointing experience since the assistance furnished by them on this topic is relatively meager whereas one might have expected them to be the most helpful. To begin with, the traditional approach of location theory, with few exceptions, has been largely from the point of view of equilibrium theory with extensions to take account of transportation and trade variables. This aspect of location theory is, therefore, subject to all the strictures of the growth economists about equilibrium theory and comparative advantage. . . .[2]

Similarly, Tiebout suggests that while classical location theory is "not unrealistic" with regard to agriculture in a country such as the

United States, its restrictive assumptions are not tenable when applied to urban location problems.[3]

Pierre Bauchet reflects the French consensus in rejecting classical location theory and Isard's models on the ground that they are too abstract and complex to give feasible solutions to concrete regional problems.[4] This is not to say, of course, that French economists have not kept up with foreign developments in this area, or that French theorists have not constructed highly complex and "impractical" models for regional analysis. Indeed the familiarity of French economists with the Anglo-Saxon literature is remarkable, whereas the opposite flow of communication seems to be at best very limited, largely because of inadequate language abilities on the part of most American economists. Moreover, the work being done in France in the area of pure theory is of high quality. Boudeville's studies have been especially noteworthy in this regard, and fortunately a number of them are now available in English.[5]

In general, while French thought has not denied the importance of some aspects of more traditional theories of location, it has been oriented toward concepts more relevant to immediate policy problems. As Bauchet has remarked, the traditional approach "has remained liberal: it has not proposed guides for action." [6] Since it explains and evaluates localization from the sole perspective of the private firm, it is not a very useful tool for dealing with the social costs of agglomeration; thus it fails to come to grips adequately with one of the central concerns of French thought and policy, i.e., the decongestion of Paris. Moreover, the classical theorists, by emphasizing the minimization of transportation costs, centered analysis on an area which has become less and less important in a nation such as France.[7]

Economic growth theory has been another common source of dissatisfaction. The classical theory of balanced growth and the steady-growth theories of Hicks, Harrod, and Domar differ primarily in that the latter group show that the dynamic equilibria of modern economies may be unstable. Both approaches, however, have been generally unsatisfactory in explaining French regional or national experience.[8] Here again, the dominant French approach has been directed more toward concepts which have greater prospective relevance as policy guides. Principal among these concepts has been that of "development poles" (pôles de croissance).

The Concepts of Development Poles
and Development Axes

The theory of development poles was first propounded by François Perroux,[9] but it is prominent in the writings of most French regional economists. Unlike the balanced and steady growth theories, Perroux's approach holds that analysis of sustained growth of total production should concentrate on the process by which various activities appear, grow in importance, and in some cases disappear, and it emphasizes that growth rates vary considerably from sector to sector. Like Schumpeter, Perroux maintains that entrepreneurial innovation is a dominant factor in explaining the growth process, which takes the form of a succession of dynamic sectors, or poles, through time. A particularly regional flavor has been given to the pole concept by emphasizing that growth is concentrated in various spatial loci as well as in certain leading industrial branches.[10]

Another version of this theme, based largely on historic French experience, emphasizes that economic expansion generally follows a linear spatial path because of the influence of transportation routes which link important industrial centers. Pottier's findings indicate that in the last century the paths of these axes were influenced primarily by geographical considerations.[11] Growth of traffic along the original routes resulted in economies of scale and lower unit costs; new techniques could be more readily incorporated into the existing infrastructure because the volume of traffic guaranteed their "profitability." However, by lowering transport costs the resultant increase in traffic volume created added demand for still newer improvements. This cumulative process tended to concentrate and juxtapose various modes of transportation along the original major routes. Population, industry, and commerce clustered along these axes, which constituted extended, easily accessible markets attractive to new economic activity. Even agriculture in close proximity to development axes benefited relative to that in other areas because of its greater involvement in the dynamics of modernization and technological progress. These developments contributed to the economic expansion of the North, the East, and Paris, whereas the rest of the country remained relatively stagnant.[12] However, Pottier reflects prevalent French opinion when he states that "unlike the last century, it is now possible to create the bases for equilibrium growth throughout the country . . . by means of public intervention. Through its control or influence over public overhead capital the modern State holds a decisive development control lever." [13]

Of course, these formulations of the development pole and development axis doctrines do not in themselves provide adequate policy guidelines. Although Perroux's voluminous writings have originated numerous thought-provoking concepts, they are frequently couched in terms which are scarcely operational. Thus, in the case of regional analysis, more precise analytic formulation of the development pole notion has been almost entirely the work of other economists. Similarly, in the lines which were just quoted from Pottier, one may well ask precisely what is meant by "equilibrium growth throughout the country." Does this mean that equality of per capita public overhead capital, income, or economic activity (however that may be defined) should be a proper goal of regional policy? Should the growth of less developed regions be promoted solely by moving resources to these regions or creating new resources within their boundaries, or should population movements also be encouraged to reduce interregional inequalities? Precisely what public and private activities should be located in varying types of regions? What effects will the location of various types of activities in a given region have on other regions as a result of induced activities (on both the supply and demand sides) of an interregional nature? What conflicts might arise between maximizing regional and national welfare and how should they be resolved? Admittedly, answers to many questions of this nature involve explicit or implicit value judgments which the economist must take as given. However, whether or not this is the case it is obvious that consideration of these problems requires considerable refinement of the rather general notions discussed above. Some of the attempts which have been made within the context of French experience in this regard are therefore briefly examined in the sections which follow.

Development Poles
and Economic Space

Although the subject has been dealt with in numerous articles and books, there exists no definitive theory of development poles. Thus, the following material represents a synthesis of what, in my opinion, are the most important contributions made to date. This means, of course, that the approach of any given scholar may not correspond to the presentation here.

It is necessary to emphasize at the outset that although the theory of development poles may be useful in analyzing and comparing the differing consequences of alternative choices of location, it is not in itself strictly speaking a theory of location. In Perroux's original article on the subject, he insisted that "growth does not appear everywhere at the same time; it shows itself in points or *pôles de croissance,* with variable intensities; it spreads by different channels and with variable final effects for the economy as a whole." [14] This should not be construed to mean, however, that a development pole is equivalent to a key industry, an economic base, an industrial zone, or even some geographically concentrated phenomenon. Rather, Perroux's concept should be interpreted in its essentially economic and functional sense.[15] To appreciate fully this perspective it is necessary to place Perroux's article on development poles in the context of his somewhat earlier work on economic space.

Perroux's concept of economic space definitely is not to be confused with simple location as defined by geographical or political divisions. "A banal sense of space location creates the illusion of the coincidence of political space with economic and human space." [16] However, in reality there exist "as many spaces as there are structures of abstract relations which define an object. These *abstract spaces,* some of which are known to be extremely complicated, are sets of relations which respond to questions without involving directly the location of a point or a shape by two or three coordinates." [17] Thus, by distinguishing between Euclidean and abstract space "we may distinguish in our discipline as many economic spaces as there are constituent structures of abstract relations which define each object of economic science." [18] For Perroux, there are three types of economic space: economic space as defined by a plan, economic space as a field of forces, and economic space as a homogeneous aggregate. The first of these spaces is defined by "the set of relations which exist between the firm and, on the one hand, the suppliers of input (raw materials, labor, power, capital) and, on the other hand, the buyers of the output (both intermediate and final)." Second, as "a field of forces, economic space consists of centres (or poles or foci) from which centrifugal forces emanate and to which centripetal forces are attracted. Each centre being a centre of attraction and repulsion, has its proper field, which is set in the fields of other centres." Finally, the "firm has, or has not, a structure more or less homogeneous with those of other firms which are its neighbors topographically or economically—it belongs to a space where, roughly speaking, one price reigns." [19] It is quite clear, therefore, that Perroux's concept of economic spaces, and in particular the second type, which is most relevant to the present discussion, is centered on complex economic relations rather than on specifically geographical considerations.

In contrast to Perroux's approach, that of Boudeville emphasizes the regional character of economic space. Following Perroux, Boudeville maintains that from an economic point of view there are three types of space: homogeneous, polarized, and program, or planning, space. Thus, in the first place,

> The region can be characterized by its more or less pronounced uniformity: it is more or less homogeneous. In the second place, the region can be studied from the point of view of its more or less pronounced degree of coherence, that is to say, according to the interdependence of its diverse parts; it is more or less polarized. Finally, the region can be envisaged from the point of view of the goal that it pursues, of the program that it establishes; this is the program region or planning region.[20]

In Boudeville's thought, a homogeneous region corresponds to a continuous space wherein each of the constituent parts or zones has relevant characteristics as close as possible to those of the others. Thus, "from an economic viewpoint, Clermont, Lyon, Saint-Etienne, and Grenoble are equivalent to the North, that is to say, to the rich part of France." [21]

The notion of polarized space, on the other hand, is closely related to that of a hierarchy of urban centers ranked according to the functions they perform; a polarized region is a heterogeneous space whose different parts complement and support one another, and where these parts have more exchanges of goods and services with a dominant intraregional urban center, or pole, than with neighboring regions. In this sense, Lille would be the dominant pole for the Nord,* and Lyon would have a similar role in the upper Rhone Valley. However, following Alexandersson, Boudeville defines three types of polarization: national, regional, and local. This hierarchy corresponds to the hierarchy of specialized goods and services which are produced or

---

* The Nord Region refers to the program region which combines the departments of Nord and Pas-de-Calais.

furnished at these levels. Thus, national goods circulate throughout
a given country, regional goods are characterized by a distribution
network for the most part limited to the boundaries of a given region,
and local goods are generally provided for only a small local market.
A national center would therefore also be a regional and local center;
it would perform the whole range of polarized functions. It is thus
possible, given adequate data on the movement of goods, to classify
the polarized regions of any given country.[22] Despite pronounced data
inadequacies, Boudeville has made several studies which attempt to
analyze regional polarization both within France as a whole and
within certain of its broad subdivisions.[23]

Finally, the planning, or program, region "is a space whose various
parts depend on the same decision"; in addition, it is "an instrument
placed in the hands of an authority, whether or not localized in the
region, to attain a given economic goal." [24] The fact that the twenty-
one geographic units which have been created for regional planning
purposes are generally termed "program regions" is no mere coincidence, since a deliberate effort has been made to identify the
government's relevant institutional and policy measures with the corresponding theoretical concept. Boudeville himself has been quite
explicit in this regard.[25] Moreover, he has even linked to the purely
theoretical construct a time dimension which corresponds rather closely
to the five- and twenty-year perspectives adopted for the concrete
work involved in the preparation of the Fifth Plan:

> In a general and abstract fashion, the planning space is the analysis
> of the choice of available geographic means to realize a given end
> after a given time lapse: *five* or *fifteen* years, for example. These
> means can be the localization of a type of propulsive industry,
> the selection of propulsive sectors in a given regional space, the
> opening of new railway, highway, or river transportation sys-
> tems, the creation of new energy sources, the determination of a
> local salary level, or any other localized means favoring the ac-
> tivities which one seeks to maximize.[26]

Boudeville also acknowledges that there exist as many program regions as there are distinct problems, but that the interdependence of
diverse activities requires a program region chosen with the intention
of coordinating various problems.[27]

To briefly summarize, it has been argued that a proper understanding of the development pole concept requires its consideration in the context of the related theory of economic spaces. The latter was originated by Perroux with an explicitly nongeographical orientation. However, Boudeville (and others), even though he borrows Perroux's terminology *in toto,* maintains that the theory of economic space "is the application of a mathematical space on or in a geographic space." [28] From this he develops, among other ideas, the theoretical notion of a program region which corresponds quite closely to the program region of French regional planning. The question which must be posed, therefore, is whether or not it is possible to have a consistent theory of development poles without a correspondingly consistent theory of economic space. However, before taking up this problem it is necessary to consider another aspect of the development pole theory, that relating to the concept of dominance.

Economic Dominance and the Process of Polarization

The concept of dominance is yet another ubiquitous notion in French economic literature which owes its inception to Perroux, and along with the concept of development poles, it marks a key element in his general effort to provide a dynamic interpretation of economic activity. For Perroux, the effect of domination "consists of an irreversible or partially reversible influence exercised by one unit on another. An economic unit exercises this effect by reason of its dimension, its negotiating strength, the nature of its activity, or because it belongs to a zone of dominant activity." [29] The effect of domination has both a purely economic dimension, abstracted from any consideration of geographic space, and a spatial dimension. In addition, "as soon as any inequality among firms appears, the breach is opened by which the cumulative effect of domination insinuates itself." [30] Given these notions, it follows that the dominant, or propulsive, firm will generally be oligopolistic and large and will exert an important influence on the activities of suppliers and clients. Moreover, in terms of geographic space, dominant and propulsive industries make the cities where they are located the poles of their regions.[31]

This briefly outlined approach seems to have considerable validity when applied in abstraction from spatial considerations, but its significance in the latter regard is more ambiguous.

As to the first of these propositions, it is instructive to consider an input-output model proposed by H. Aujac, since it provides significant evidence that the concept of dominance does in fact have a corresponding empirical counterpart.[32] Aujac's model succeeds in ordering sectors in input-output form, in such a manner that relatively large intermediate demands are situated below the principal diagonal, whereas those which are relatively weak are situated above it. This triangularization of the matrix is carried out on the basis of the "best customer." If Aij represents sales from industry i to industry j and Aji the converse, then j is said to dominate i if $(Aij \ Pi) > (Aji/Pj)$, where Pi and Pj are, respectively, the total sales of i and j. On the basis of such calculations a hierarchy is established in which each sector dominates the one which follows. Thus, changes in output in a given industry will affect industries coming after it in the hierarchy, but will have only negligible effects on preceding industries, i.e., indirect effects do not travel up the triangular matrix and distort the hierarchy. The order of the hierarchy established by Aujac for France is as follows: construction and public works; diverse services; food and agricultural industries; agriculture; mechanical and electrical industries; textiles and leathers; wood, paper, and furniture; diverse industries; chemicals; steel; nonferrous metals; transportation and communications; energy; rubber; tenant farming.

It might be supposed that Aujac's model would provide a convenient tool of regional analysis even though it is not formally constructed in regional terms. If, for example, one wished to examine the direct and indirect effects of the transfer from Paris to the provinces of firms in various industries, it might be possible to calculate the importance and number of suppliers who would tend to follow one or another migrating industry. Similarly, the comparative effects of establishing different industries in a given region could be examined. To analyze the effects of introducing a steel complex, for example, it would only be necessary to calculate modifications in industries following steel in the matrix hierarchy. However, the difficulties involved in any straightforward application of the national pattern of flows on a regional level would be formidable. Depending on the number and magnitude of interregional linkages, which are certain to be very great for areas on the scale of the French program regions, many interindustry effects will pass to the rest of the world. Thus, links between local production and local consumption, as well as the effects of investment on employment, would require a great deal of special attention. Moreover, the prospects for utilizing operationally feasible interregional matrices are not bright. As Rodwin has aptly remarked, ". . . the neglect of price effects, the difficulty of getting data for these models, the vastly increased computational problems which regional breakdowns entail coupled with the egregious simplifications of industry categories and the unrealistic linearity assumptions make one skeptical of the immediate, not to mention the long-term usefulness of this instrument." [33]

It should be pointed out that numerous attempts have been made in France to construct regional input-output tables similar to that employed for national accounting purposes.[34] However, their usefulness for solving concrete regional problems remains for the most part to be seen. Even on a national level, "the precision of the input-output table in a medium sized economy like France, more and more open to foreign markets, actually seems questionable." [35] Moreover, the particular difficulties which have characterized French efforts at the regional level can only add to doubts concerning their feasibility as policy aids. Industrial statistics at the regional level have been generally insufficient. It is extremely difficult to identify the respective shares of the differing activities of multiproduct firms. Declarations concerning salaries and business receipts are not available in uniform fashion, and they are sometimes reported according to plant location and at other times according to location of home office. Moreover, interregional monetary, financial, and merchandise movements are often impossible to evaluate, and the "final demand" category, including government, firm, and individual purchases, is difficult to specify because the planning system is only indicative.[36]

In general, then, while the notion of dominance has been given empirical verification for the structure of industry in the nation as a whole, it is not now operationally feasible to regionalize or otherwise give spatial content to the relevant national model. Nor is there any likely prospect that this end will be realized in the foreseeable future. However, the problem of analyzing the role of dominant sectors as localized development poles need not be limited to input-output techniques. As Paelinck has stated, it is not sufficient for the economist working on regional development problems to limit analysis to "the classical interdependencies (of either the Walras or Leontief type) of economic flux, whether in quantity or value terms. He must be able, in addition, to recognize the *technical origin* of this interdependence, which explains its ever increasing complexity.[37]

It has already been pointed out that the notion of economic dominance is closely related to that of development poles, and that both are employed in the relevant French literature as tools to explain the dynamics of economic change. Here, however, it is necessary to raise again the problem which was posed at the end of the first section of this chapter. It will be recalled that the concepts of economic space and development poles have been defined both in terms of abstraction from spatial location and in terms of concrete geographical areas. It also should follow, then, that the dominance of a propulsive industry could be treated both in abstraction from spatial considerations and in terms of specific regions. This in fact has been the case.

Perroux's treatment of the growth process is consistent with his theory of economic space in that the industry remains his point of departure and the essential element in subsequent development. Philippe Aydalot has correctly maintained that while Perroux sometimes "seems to study the localization of the growth process, in fact, this localization seems secondary to him," since "the primary phenomenon is 'the appearance and disappearance of industries,' 'the diffusion of the growth of an industry.' "[38]

The effects generated by a propulsive industry which qualify it as a development pole have been thoroughly explored by numerous writers. Some of these effects are internal to the industry itself; that is, its own growth generates increased investment, employment, and distribution of factor payments, including profits which may be retained and reinvested. The internal growth of an industry also generates numerous external effects. Vertically and horizontally induced effects may of course be analyzed within the framework of input-output matrices. The effects of polarization may be further examined, at least in theory, by the application of appropriate matrices or vectors to the initial Leontief-type matrix. Here several possibilities are available. For example, dynamic effects which alter the structure of industry as given by the original matrix may be introduced. Structural change involving lateral, or horizontal, production increases is termed a Perroux effect in the literature on development poles. There is also the so-called Keynes effect, which involves the classic multiplier based on marginal propensities to consume applied to income increases. Yet another effect is that relating to the interplay of prices among related sectors and enterprises; this is generally called the Scitovsky effect.[39] Nor does this list by any means exhaust the possible effects which a dominant industry may have. There is, in addition, a feedback phenomenon which generally is termed the Aftalion effect. This involves increased investment resulting from the operation of the accelerator principle in connection with increases in final demand, which of course is related to the effects just mentioned. There is also psychological polarization, which refers to the impacts on investment decisions of small and medium-sized firms resulting from the creative activities of dominant propulsive sectors. Here the degree of availability of technical information is important. The latter has a special designation, namely, the publication effect.[40]

Although still other polarization classifications can be found in the literature, it is apparent that a propulsive industry (or firm) must have at least three basic characteristics. First, it must be relatively large in order to assure that it will generate sufficient direct and potentially indirect effects to have a significant impact on the economy; second, it must be a relatively fast-growing sector; and third, the quantity and intensity of its interrelations with other sectors should be important so that a large number of induced effects will in fact be transmitted.

The importance of bigness, first emphasized by Perroux, has been equally stressed in subsequent writings of other scholars. Bauchet, for example, writes that the growth of an underdeveloped region depends on the actions of large economic units. "Their mass alone is capable of starting the region on the path of economic growth." [41] Similarly, Davin maintains that "the principal poles are found in heavy, highly capitalized, industry, and are the domain of large firms." [42] Thus, "the multiplicity of firms of small dimension, working in dispersed fashion, without relying on a few large firms, is not of a nature to set in motion a truly dynamic regional economy." [43] Nevertheless, as will be discussed shortly, the notion of industrial bigness as an initiator of economic growth is not without its difficulties. That a propulsive firm or industry should be rapidly growing is unquestionable. However, when it comes to the third criterion, that of interrelations with other sectors, several problems may be raised.

Aydalot has argued that all things considered, the simplest definition which may be given of a propulsive industry is that it is a pro-
ducer of external economies.[44] Here again, though, the question must
be posed as to what kind of economic space is involved. Aydalot is
quite correct in pointing out that a priori the concept of polarization
does not imply geographic concentration. Polarization "is the process
by which the growth of an economic activity termed propulsive sets
in motion that of other economic activities by the channel of external
economies." [45] But this process takes place in abstract economic space.
Thus, although a propulsive industry must certainly have a location
in geographic space, the *process* of polarization is not amenable to
unambiguous geographic location.

Taking this definition of the polarization process, it is possible to
say that the automobile industry is an example of a propulsive industry, and that the Régie Renault would be an example of a propulsive firm. It may then be said that "the activity of the Régie Renault
makes its effects felt as far as Saint-Michel-de-Maurienne and
Hayange, and indeed, as far as New York, by means of its affiliated
branches (SAFE, the Temple steel mills, Renault Incorporated)." But
if "Renault is a pole whose center is Paris and whose periphery
embraces most of the world, this would be to deny to the pole an
autonomous spatial existence." In other words, if the above discussion permits an understanding of why Renault is a pole, "one still
cannot understand why Paris is a pole." [46]

Moreover, if a propulsive industry is to initiate regional expansion,
as the usual discussion would have it, it is essential to inquire into the
criteria which govern the choice of location by a propulsive industry.
In this regard,

> it is insufficient to bring in the effects of agglomeration once a
> propulsive industry is established. In other words, to say that
> Paris is a pole owing to the agglomerating power of its propul-
> sive industries does not resolve the problem; it remains to explain
> why these propulsive industries are themselves agglomerated in
> Paris.
>
>   One is necessarily led to the conclusion that the poles (spatial)
> possess characteristics which have a causal role in the implanta-
> tion of propulsive industries.
>
>   This is to say, and here is the essential point, that contrary

> to the conclusions of certain contemporary economists, the pro-
> pulsive industry is not the primary phenomenon in the process of
> polarization.[47]

Thus, even if the propulsive industry does induce other activities, it is itself induced, and thereby constitutes only one link in the process of polarized growth; the propulsive industry as such "does not merit either the pedestal where it has been placed, or the prestige which has been given to it." [48] In conclusion, Aydalot finds that the propulsive industry does not represent the origin of the polarization; it is only an effect of it. Here he concentrates on the importance of agglomeration effects, and particularly those of a tertiary nature, in attracting industries, including those which in turn induce other activities.[49]

In sum, it is apparent that Aydalot's approach to the problem of the polarization process is consistent with that given in Chapter 1. Assuming no specific policy role on the part of the government, industrial growth will tend to occur for the most part in already industrialized centers, because of the external economies these centers generate. Furthermore, these are considerably more varied than the tertiary benefits to which Aydalot limits his analysis. Also, as in the case of the analysis given in Chapter 1, he argues that insofar as a central government has a regional policy, external economies provided by the state can be used as an effective instrument to modify economic activity along chosen lines.

A Critique
of Development Pole Theory

Although the foregoing outline of the theory of development poles does not pretend to give a complete picture of the richness of the many writings now available on the subject, it does provide a basis for criticism of some of the major problems and deficiencies present, in greater or lesser degree, in a representative portion of these works. In addition, it permits an appreciation of some of the theory's positive contributions to the formation and implementation of concrete planning measures within the institutional framework of French regional planning.

One of the basic common denominators in the development pole literature is the notion that the process of economic growth has its origin and continuing stimulus in big industrial undertakings, a notion which derives from the theory of dominance. Some of the more naively enthusiastic interpretations of the theory would maintain that to generate economic growth in a region it is merely necessary to implant a large firm, or several large firms, preferably in a relatively fast-growing industry. The fact that bigness alone is not sufficient in this regard is well illustrated by the case of the steel industry in Lorraine. The development of the steel industry in this region was not accompanied by a corresponding development in the region of industries consuming steel. As a result, Lorraine became highly dependent on exterior sources of supply for machinery and other equipment. Despite the existence of coal mines, energy sources, transportation facilities, and markets in close proximity to the steel complex, it would appear on the basis of input-output data that less than 10 per cent of steel production in the region was consumed by manufacturing industries in the region. Thus, there exists the paradox of relatively weakly developed industry existing side by side with conditions highly favorable to industrial location.[50] As Paelinck has emphasized, "the facts do not indicate that one can consider any isolated industrial implantation as a necessarily efficient development pole, by which effective polarization relations, technical or otherwise, are produced." [51]

In Chapter 1 it was argued that government efforts to induce economic growth will be most effective in the presence of external economies. Of course, as was also pointed out, exponents of unbalanced growth such as Hirschman would maintain that a glaring need for external economies, made evident by the introduction of a propulsive activity, is in fact just what is needed to generate their appearance.[52] The evidence thus far in this regard has not been impressive. Aydalot, in fact, states that "development theory has tried to integrate the theory of development poles, but without great success. Indeed, the great complexes of 'propulsive industries' which have been implanted in certain African countries have not in most cases fulfilled their role." [53] The experience of underdeveloped countries would also apply to regional situations in more developed countries, even though the latter have external economies to a degree far exceeding that in the former. The case of Lorraine has already been cited, and relevant French experience with respect to the implantation of a propulsive industry in the lagging region of Lacq will be discussed at greater length in Chapter 7.

If the stimulating effects on general economic growth of big industrial undertakings often have been overestimated, so have the importance of both bigness and industry. Boudeville, as was mentioned earlier, considers that on a European scale Denmark just fulfills the minimum requirements to qualify it as an "independent" region. However, the prosperity of this region was not initiated and has not been sustained by a big propulsive industry, but rather by scattered (though closely cooperating) and relatively small agricultural units.

Moreover, even if a propulsive industry is considered to be as much an effect of the polarization process as a cause of it, it is clear that development pole theory, as it has been elaborated, fails to give a satisfactory explanation of the agglomerating process. As Vernon has shown,[54] the industries most attracted by the external economies generated by large urban areas are not characterized by a highly oligopolistic structure, but are rather industries with numerous small and medium-sized firms, highly dependent on auxiliary business services, which need frequent direct personal contacts with buyers and sellers.

Another difficulty with development pole theory is that criteria for regional policy which have been proposed within its frame of reference have often not been explicitly related to the goals often sought in practice. For example, Davin poses the following question: From the point of view of political economy, what is the nature of the principal polarizing activities (active or potential), and how can the flux among these poles be created or increased? In reply, he maintains that the industries or industrial sectors most favorable to regional growth (defined as a significant increase in the flux of products and of revenues) are those where (1) the value added per worker is the highest or most likely to increase; (2) the foreseeable increase in production indicates an accelerated rate of expansion, and where technical progress is the most rapid and the most probable; (3) the process of automation or semiautomation can be most easily applied; (4) the flux of products and of services with the development poles is the most intense; and (5) the constitution of large production units is achieved most easily, since these units are capable of releasing a maximum of induced reactions (through the existence of interenterprise or intersectoral technical linkages, and the possibility of making general use of small, dependent suppliers), and of realizing a maximum of technical and commercial productivity.[55]

One problem raised by these criteria is that in themselves they do not really give insights into the objective, or objectives, of regional policy. Is the "increase in flux of products and of revenues" supposed to increase hourly earnings of workers, annual income per employed inhabitant, the number of persons employed, or some other possible regional variables? The emphasis put on automation and high worker productivity would conflict with what is perhaps the most generally sought-after goal of regional policies, namely, increased employment opportunities. Even if one adds, for example, the goal of increased earning power per employed inhabitant, it is not clear that these criteria would guarantee success. In this regard, the outcome would depend in large measure on the extent to which induced effects actually are localized in the region in question. If regional policy is to aim for increased flux in economic activity in lagging regions, the flux may be dissipated as a result of linkages with other regions. A particular difficulty in this respect would be income flows to owners of capital who reside outside of the region. Lagging regions generally would not be the type to furnish the savings which would be invested in the big, capital-intensive undertakings described by Davin. The reality of this difficulty will be illustrated when the case of Lacq is discussed in Chapter 7. In addition, there is the probability that increased commercial and industrial activity will be accompanied by higher per capita costs of public services. I have already described this phenomenon on the basis of highly standardized Belgian data.[56] In general, it is evident that development pole theory itself is not very helpful in providing goals for regional policy; in addition, it is equally evident that its criteria for the formation of specific regional policy measures are not very useful without some prior conception of regional economic goals. Fortunately, in the French case some determination of goals can be ascertained from public opinion surveys, as well as from the institutionalized interaction of interested regional and national groups working through the planning mechanism.

Finally, it cannot be emphasized too much that the theory of development poles is badly in need of a thorough semantic reworking; the concepts and language which characterize it need more precise definition and more consistent usage. Even the notion of a development pole itself suffers in this regard. For example, Davin states, "The idea of a development pole is made more precise by that of a propulsive industry and of a key industry. The first engenders activities in other industries, either suppliers or clients for merchandise or services; the second determines the increase of maximum activity." [57] Paelinck, on the other hand, states,

> The development-pole concept has often been misunderstood. It has been confused with the notions of key industry, basic industry, and industrial ensemble; from this follows the erroneous conception according to which the development pole would be an industrial monument raised to the glory of future regional industrialization, a guarantee of certain economic growth. Or again, to make this scarcely rigorous concept more precise some would have as a development pole any important implantation of firms, preferably industrial, which would exercise salutory effects on the geographic area where it is introduced.[58]

Then, too, there is the question of economic space. The same concepts are sometimes employed in the context of abstract, nongeographic space, at other times in the context of certain more or less well-defined geographic areas, and at yet other times in a fashion which indiscriminately mingles abstract and geographic space in the same context. Of course, a scholar should be free to define the terms of his own discourse, and there would be no objection to his doing so, provided that he then proceeds to employ them in a systematic and consistent manner. In the present instance, however, one finds all too often that once the writer has defined (no matter how vaguely) his essential concepts, he proceeds in the development of his thought to bring in references from other writers to nominally identical concepts which, unfortunately, have been defined or used differently by the other writers. Even this would not be objectionable if the various definitions or usages were critically contrasted or otherwise differentiated, but this is rarely the case.

A greater emphasis on conceptual clarity might also have the virtue of making the concepts of development pole theory more operational. It has been noted that in some respects development pole theory may be viewed as an effort to grasp the complex technical origins and dynamic interrelations of the growth process to a degree not possible with classical input-output techniques. Yet practical expositions of the theory (or better, individual versions of it) are generally presented in an input-output framework, usually in terms of a regionalization of the basic Leontief-type model, or by applying modifying vectors or matrices to the basic model, or both. In other words, although this approach is more complete from a theoretical viewpoint than the simple classical model, it necessarily limits the analysis of the polarization process to essentially static effects. In any event, it has been through an input-output format that the development pole approach has made its most important original contributions to operationally meaningful theory; otherwise, this literature has been extremely eclectic, borrowing such well-known analytic devices as location coefficients, simple graph theory, and Edgar Dunn's distinction between proportionality and differential employment shifts. However, on the level of operationally feasible models it is questionable that development pole theory has really contributed any fundamentally new method of analysis, since the theoretically useful modifications which it has made in classical input-output techniques suffer not only from the usual difficulties in this regard, but also from the frequent impossibility of actually quantifying the modifying variables which it employs.

On the positive side, it may be said that the difficulties involved in unifying the basic concepts of development pole theory within the context of operationally feasible models are a result of its effort to come to grips with the complexity of the growth process, a phenomenon which frequently tends to be oversimplified for the sake of "elegance." Perhaps the best approach to development pole theory as applied to regional problems is that given by Paelinck, who proposes that it be regarded as "a *conditional* theory of regional growth; it is valuable, above all, to the extent that it clearly indicates the conditions under which accelerated regional development can occur." [59] Of course, this conditional approach implies that the relevance of the theory to individual regional cases must be judged on the basis of the nature and prospects of the particular regions, or types of regions, in question; the value of the theory to regional policy problems is not independent of the actual context in which it is to be utilized. Thus, the relevance of the theory to French regional policy is best seen in terms of the specific policy measures carried out or proposed for the program regions.

Summary
and Conclusions

The theory of development poles has been elaborated by French (and Belgian) economists concomitantly with the evolution of the institutional framework for regional planning in France, although the connection between the two, as will be seen in greater detail later, has varied considerably according to the nature of various specific policies and regions. In many respects, development pole theory arose in response to the inadequacies of traditional location theory and over-simplified growth models. However, it has itself been characterized by a number of shortcomings and difficulties, including certain ambiguities and inconsistencies in the definition and usage of terminology; too exclusive an emphasis on the role of bigness and industry in the development process; too much emphasis on the function of propulsive firms and industries as generators of external effects and too little attention to the process of polarization as a consequence of the presence of existing external economies; and an inability to elaborate operationally feasible models capable of incorporating all of the principal concepts and relationships elaborated in the theory. The extent to which these problems are present varies, of course, from writer to writer, and even among the different works of any given scholar.

But the theory has proven valuable in some respects. Its emphasis on the disequilibria involved in the growth process, and on the various and complex ways in which growth may be transmitted (or inhibited), has provided numerous valuable insights for the preparation of regional policy measures, if not criteria for policy goals. Moreover, insofar as it has been applied to regional problems, the theory has been elaborated largely with reference to concrete problems or relationships, even if quantification has been limited by data inadequacies. Boudeville's contributions to the development and application of the theory deserve particular recognition in this regard. In general, the literature has provided a conditional theory of regional development, whose practical application requires specific consideration of the nature of the areas where policy measures are to be applied. These conditions will be examined with regard to the program regions of France in Chapter 6.

6

The Regional Structure
of the
French Economy

Demography

The data presented in Table 6.1 show that only four of the twenty-one program regions—Paris, Rhone-Alps, Nord, and Provence-Riviera-Corsica—have more than 3 million inhabitants, and only five have more than 2.5 million inhabitants. On the other hand, Limousin and Franche-Comté each have a population of less than 1 million persons. It also is pertinent to note that the three regions with the greatest recent population growth are among the four largest in absolute size. At the other extreme, the region with the smallest population, Limousin, is the only one which lost population from January 1, 1963, to January 1, 1965. Of the six regions with least population change, none ranked higher than thirteenth in terms of absolute population size. Thus, population growth tends generally to be greatest in the larger regions and least in the smaller regions.

Table 6.1

Demographic data by Program Region

Regions and France	(1) Population (thousands) Jan. 1965	(2) Rank	(3) Per cent population change Jan. 1963 to Jan. 1965	(4) Rank	(5) Median age Jan. 1963	(6) Rank
Paris Region	9,117	1	4.3	1	33.8	14
Champagne	1,248	18	2.0	10	30.6	7
Picardy	1,532	12	1.9	11	30.5	5[a]
Upper Normandy	1,452	15	2.2	7[a]	30.3	3[a]
Center	1,917	10	1.5	12	33.3	13
Nord	3,784	3	2.2	7[a]	30.3	3[a]
Lorraine	2,300	8	2.9	4	29.1	1
Alsace	1,373	16	2.4	6	31.9	9
Franche-Comté	973	20	2.5	5	30.8	8
Lower Normandy	1,226	19	0.7	18	29.7	2
Pays de la Loire	2,523	5	1.4	13[a]	30.5	5[a]
Brittany	2,416	6	0.3	20	32.4	10
Limousin	737	21	—0.4	21	38.7	21
Auvergne	1,302	17	0.9	17	35.3	17
Poitou-Charentes	1,480	13	0.6	19	32.8	12
Aquitaine	2,405	7	1.4	13[a]	35.1	16
Midi-Pyrenees	2,172	9	1.3	15	35.7	18
Burgundy	1,478	14	1.2	16	34.2	15
Rhone-Alps	4,281	2	3.2	3	32.7	11
Languedoc	1,666	11	2.1	9	36.5	20
Provence-Riviera-Corsica	3,318	4	3.9	2	36.1	19
France	48,699		2.4		32.9	

Source: *Régionalisation du budget, 1966*, pp. 165, 175.
Note: Values in columns (1) and (3) are estimates.
[a]Two regions have this value and thus the same rank.

The issue of population change is particularly important with respect to migration, since in the French case, as in numerous others, one of the principal aims of regional policy has been to limit emigration from regions characterized by relatively large out-migration "to a reasonable level." [1] In view of this, some knowledge of the determinants of population movements is desirable. In the case of France, regional migration rates may be explained largely by three variables: number of doctors in relation to population; the importance of agriculture to a region;

and per capita kilowatt-hour low-tension electricity consumption. Observations of these variables for the twenty-one program regions give the following regression equation:

$$Y = -11.553 + .6977\ X_1 - .1272\ X_2 + .0268\ X_3,$$
$$(.2208)\qquad (.0937)\qquad (.00867)$$

where Y = per cent of population change due to migration (1954–62), X_1 = number of doctors per 10,000 inhabitants in 1962,[2] X_2 = per cent of employed persons engaged in agriculture in 1962,[3] and X_3 = per capita kilowatt-hour low-tension electricity consumption in 1962.[4] The values in parentheses give the respective standard errors. The corresponding beta coefficients are $\beta_1 = .4136$, $\beta_2 = -.1424$, and $\beta_3 = .4798$. For the equation as a whole, $R = .932$ ($R^2 = .868$), and the F ratio is 37.26, very significant at the 99 per cent level ($F_{.01} = 5.18$). Since X_1 may be taken as an indication of the state of health facilities, X_2 of the degree of agricultural importance, and X_3 as a reflection of living standards (see Chapter 3), it may be concluded that migrants are leaving agricultural regions characterized by relatively low levels of health facilities and relatively low standards of living in favor of regions with opposite characteristics.

It might be objected, as in the cases involving regression analysis in Chapter 3, that inclusion of the extreme values associated with the Paris Region would tend to bias the degree of closeness of fit of this equation. In fact, however, if the Paris observations are omitted, the closeness of fit is improved. In this event the following regression equation is obtained:

$$Y = -13.825 + .979\ X_1 - .1726\ X_2 + .02794\ X_3.$$
$$(.1959)\qquad (.0769)\qquad (.0070)$$

Here the beta coefficients are $\beta_1 = .4896$, $\beta_2 = -.1967$, and $\beta_3 = .4508$. The multiple correlation coefficient, R, now becomes .947 ($R^2 = .8959$), and the F ratio increases to 45.95, again very significant at the 99 per cent level ($F_{.01} = 5.29$).

The usefulness of these independent variables in explaining migration patterns is noteworthy even when observations are taken at the department level. Again excluding Paris (as well as Corsica and the territory of Belfort, for which comparable data were not available), the following regression equation is obtained for the eighty-seven relevant departments:

$$Y = -8.3168 + .8420\, X_1 - .1445\, X_2 + .0223\, X_3.$$
$$(.1876) \qquad (.0358) \qquad (.0065)$$

In this instance, $\beta_1 = .3524$, $\beta_2 = -.3199$, and $\beta_3 = .3032$; $R = .797$ ($R^2 = .6355$), and $F = 48.2$ ($F_{.01} = 4.04$). Although the goodness of fit as indicated by the coefficient of determination is somewhat less than when regional observations are employed, the F ratio is even higher in this case. The significance of the regression coefficients also is greater because of the large number of observations. In addition, whereas X_1 and X_3 contributed most to explaining variations in Y when regional observations were used, the three independent variables are about equal in importance here.

Of course, these results should not be interpreted to mean that these independent variables per se explain migration patterns in such high degree, since they themselves are functions of other related phenomena. For example, in the twenty-regions case, the number of doctors per 10,000 inhabitants is significantly correlated with per capita purchasing power at the 99 per cent level of significance ($r = .595$). Similarly, agricultural importance is closely related to commercial and industrial importance as measured by per capita sales of commercial and industrial enterprises, the relationship, of course, being negative ($r = -.861$). Per capita low-tension electricity consumption, as might be expected, is also closely related to per capita purchasing power ($r = .810$).

Comparison of data in Tables 6.1 and 6.2 gives further evidence of the nature of regions with negative or low rates of population change. In Limousin, where natural population increase is not sufficient to offset out-migration, the median age (38.7 years) is the highest of all regions, as is the proportion of the total population engaged in agriculture (18.7 per cent). In terms of agricultural productivity, Limousin ranks twentieth in terms of both value added per worker and per hectare. Moreover, the conveniences of agricultural life, as measured by the proportion of agricultural population with running water, are low in Limousin, which also ranks twentieth in this regard.

Brittany, which ranks twentieth in terms of population increase, has a relatively young population but one which obviously is too large in

Table 6.2

Agricultural data by Program Region

(1962 and 1963)

Regions and France	(1) Per cent of population employed in agriculture, 1962	(2) Rank	(3) Average farm size (hectares) 1963	(4) Rank	(5) Value added per worker (100 francs), 1962	(6) Rank	(7) Value added per hectare (100 francs) 1962	(8) Rank	(9) Per cent of agricultural population with running water, 1962	(10) Rank
Paris Region	0.7	21	40.7	1	137	3	10.8	9	88.7	2
Champagne	8.4	13	35.9	3	120	5	7.8	14	73.1	8
Picardy	7.5	14	37.4	2	164	1	11.8	7	86.3	3
Upper Normandy	6.5	16	21.2	6	125	4	13.3	3	66.0	12
Center	11.7	9	25.1	4	83	11[a]	6.5	16	68.4	11
Nord	3.5	20	16.7	13	151	2	19.2	1	85.2	4
Lorraine	4.0	19	21.1	7	109	7	7.1	15	80.2	6
Alsace	5.6	17	7.4	21	84	10	13.8	2	95.0	1
Franche-Comté	8.5	12	18.8	8	71	14[a]	6.3	17	80.9	5
Lower Normandy	17.0	3	15.5	15	83	11[a]	11.7	8	53.5	18
Pays de la Loire	14.4	5	15.9	14	71	14[a]	9.6	10	52.8	19
Brittany	17.5	2	11.8	18	64	17[a]	13.1	4[a]	47.8	21
Limousin	18.7	1	16.8	12	51	20	5.8	20	51.3	20
Auvergne	13.7	7	18.4	10	60	19	6.0	19	63.3	15
Poitou-Charentes	13.8	6	18.5	9	87	9	8.7	12	61.4	16
Aquitaine	13.4	8	12.5	17	64	17[a]	13.1	4[a]	55.6	17
Midi-Pyrenees	15.4	4	18.1	11	50	21	5.3	21	63.6	14
Burgundy	10.8	10	24.0	5	72	13	6.1	18	65.5	13
Rhone-Alps	7.3	15	12.8	16	65	16	8.2	13	69.5	10
Languedoc	10.5	11	11.4	19	118	6	12.4	6	77.6	7
Provence-Riviera-Corsica	4.6	18	11.2	20	96	8	8.9	11	72.8	9
France	8.3		16.9		82		9.1		68.3	

Sources: Col. 1: *Annuaire Statistique*, 1963, p. XVIII. Cols. 3, 5, 7, and 9: *Régionalisation du budget, 1966*, pp. 186, 198, and 205.

[a]Two regions have this value and thus the same rank.

relation to existing resources. Brittany ranks second in proportion of population engaged in agriculture, and the prevalence of small farms is reflected in its ranking of eighteenth with regard to average farm size. Although value added per hectare is quite high, the large number of workers relative to available land makes value added per worker quite low. In addition, the proportion of the agricultural population provided with running water is the lowest of all regions. Lower Normandy, which is geographically close to Brittany, shares many of Brittany's characteristics.

Poitou-Charentes, the nineteenth-ranking region with respect to population change, does not have particularly low values concerning agricultural productivity and its median age is close to the national average. However, it ranks sixth with respect to proportion of population in agriculture and sixteenth with respect to proportion of agricultural population with running water.

Limousin is bordered on the east by Auvergne, whose characteristics are similar. Like Limousin, Auvergne is small in absolute population size, has a high median age, is low in terms of population growth, and has a relatively high proportion of its total population engaged in agriculture. Moreover, it ranks nineteenth, just ahead of Limousin, with respect to both value added per worker and per hectare. It ranks fifteenth with respect to agricultural population with running water.

In general, then, the five lowest-ranking regions in terms of recent population change are all relatively highly agricultural in nature and are all in western France, south of the Seine. Furthermore, of the next five lowest regions with respect to population change, four are relatively agricultural regions in this same geographical area. These four regions are Midi-Pyrenees, Pays de la Loire, Aquitaine, and Center.

It will be noted that Pays de la Loire is similar in most respects to two of the regions which it borders, namely, Brittany and Lower Normandy. Aquitaine and Midi-Pyrenees, on the other hand, are more similar in character to Limousin and Auvergne.

In contrast, the Center presents a much more mixed picture than other regions of the West and Southwest. This should not be surprising, however, since it constitutes a transitional region, bordering prosperous Upper Normandy and the Paris Region in the north, and Limousin and Auvergne in the south.

In summation, the regions of the West and Southwest rank low in terms of population increase, a consequence of large out-migration. They are relatively highly agricultural and the level of amenities of their agricultural populations, as reflected in the proportion provided with running water, is low. However, apart from these unifying characteristics, they may be differentiated into two fairly distinct groups. The more northern regions (Lower Normandy, Brittany, and Pays de la Loire) have relatively young populations and small, intensively worked farms. Thus, value added per hectare is considerably larger in this group than value added per worker. The regions in the Southwest (Limousin, Auvergne, Aquitaine, Midi-Pyrenees), on the other hand, have relatively old populations. Limousin, Auvergne, and Midi-Pyrenees have the lowest levels of both value added per hectare and per worker in all French agriculture; Aquitaine ranks only seventeenth in terms of value added per worker, but is exceptional in ranking fourth with respect to value added per hectare. However, the latter phenomenon may be partly explained by its relatively large total population and the relatively large proportion of total population engaged in agriculture. Poitou-Charentes represents a transitional area between the two major groups, and the Center represents a transitional area between the regions of the West and the more dynamic regions of the North.

In contrast to regions with low rates of population growth are the Paris Region, Provence-Riviera-Corsica, Rhone-Alps, and Lorraine, each of which has a recent two-year growth rate of over 2.5 per cent. These regions all have relatively high absolute population values, a low proportion of total population employed in agriculture, and a high proportion of the agricultural population supplied with running water. In general, the regions with the highest rates of population growth are found in the North or in the East.

Industry
and Commerce

The industrial and commercial data presented in Table 6.3 again show a clear difference between the West and Southwest and the remainder of France. The five lowest-ranked regions in terms of turnover tax on businesses are all in the former areas, whereas the seven highest regions are in the North and East. The high proportion of taxes paid in the Paris Region, however, gives a somewhat exaggerated picture of its importance. The tax payments of an enterprise are attributed to the region where the enterprise has its headquarters, even if a large part of its operations actually take place in other regions. In particular, the taxes of nationalized enterprises and automobile manufacturers are nearly all paid in the Seine department.

Industrial energy consumption is highest in regions characterized by the presence of significant natural energy sources, as well as in the Paris Region. Thus, the two highest-ranking regions, Lorraine and Nord, benefit from the coal of the North, while the next highest-ranking regions (excluding Paris), i.e. Rhone-Alps, Midi-Pyrenees, and Provence-Riviera-Corsica, benefit from relatively abundant hydro-electric power. With the exception of Midi-Pyrenees (which includes

Table 6.3
Industrial and commercial indicators
by Program Region
(1963 and 1964)

Regions and France	(1) Turnover tax on businesses (million francs), 1964	(2) Rank	(3) Industrial energy consumption (in equivalent thousand tons of coal), 1963	(4) Rank	(5) Number of important business headquarters, 1963	(6) Rank	(7) Net change in commercial enterprises, 1964	(8) Rank
Paris Region	15,046	1	7,376	4	2,681	1	1,022	2
Champagne	649	9	1,674	11	117	8	77	13
Picardy	412	15	2,453	9	85	12	95	10
Upper Normandy	1,252	7	2,842	7	119	7	176	8
Center	432	13	1,253	16	82	13	122	9
Nord	2,747	2	10,747	2	399	3	−308	21
Lorraine	1,596	4	16,615	1	178	6	305	6
Alsace	1,300	5	1,896	10	186	5	53	16
Franche-Comté	474	11[a]	1,463	12	51	17	82	12
Lower Normandy	234	20	1,319	13	44	19	36	17
Pays de la Loire	610	10	1,292	14	98	10	87	11
Brittany	355	17	638	20	90	11	−214	20
Limousin	172	21	337	21	23	21	−54	18
Auvergne	431	14	943	18	40	20	−59	19
Poitou-Charentes	352	18	860	19	50	18	67	14
Aquitaine	741	8	2,816	8	114	9	538	3
Midi-Pyrenees	474	11[a]	3,370	5	73	15	260	7
Burgundy	356	16	1,271	15	62	16	62	15
Rhone-Alps	2,740	3	8,680	3	410	2	374	5
Languedoc	346	19	1,120	17	74	14	389	4
Provence-Riviera-Corsica	1,342	6	3,332	6	209	4	1,568	1
France	32,062		72,297		5,188		4,678	

Source: *Régionalisation du budget, 1966*, pp. 219, 220, 230, 231.
[a]Two regions have this value and thus the same rank.

the gas resources of Lacq), it is clear that the North and East have benefited most from natural power advantages, and the West and Southwest least. The seven highest-ranking regions, excluding Midi-Pyrenees, are all in the North and East and the six lowest-ranking regions are all in the West and Southwest.

The geographical distribution of important business headquarters presents a picture similar to that for the variables just discussed. An "important" enterprise is one which, following the usage of the Ministry of Finance, has an annual turnover of over 14,950,000 francs. Here again, of course, a somewhat exaggerated importance is given to the Paris Region.

The figures in column 7 of Table 6.3 on changes in number of commercial enterprises present a more mixed picture, though the general tendency concerning geographic distribution tends to remain the same. In any event, these values must be interpreted with considerable prudence, since numerous omissions and extensions are not included. Moreover, a diminution of number of commercial establishments may not necessarily be unfavorable, since it may indicate a more efficient concentration of activities in a region in the process of significant modernization.

Finally, it will be recalled from the regression analyses presented in Chapter 3 that there is a pronounced tendency for new commercial and industrial activity to locate in regions already characterized by commercial and industrial activity, that is, in regions of the North and East.

Education

The variables listed in Table 6.4 require a brief explanation. The *baccalauréat* is awarded to graduates of the *lycées* (secondary schools), which include classical, modern, and technical sections. Students awarded the *baccalauréat* generally are about eighteen years old. The *Grandes Écoles* are institutions of higher learning which are for the most part under government administration but independent of the universities. The *Grandes Écoles* provide most of the future leaders in teaching, industry, public administration, the army, and other branches of national activity. Entering these schools is quite difficult, and often only one candidate out of ten is accepted. The values given in column 5 include students from eleven to fourteen years old in the initial stage of various types of secondary instruction—the *lycées, collèges, collèges d'enseignement technique, collèges d'enseignement général,* etc. Some of these students are prepared for clerical work or skilled labor on completion of secondary education, while others are prepared for more advanced study.

Table 6.4
Education data by Program Region
(1964)

	(1)	(2)	(3)	(4)	(5)	(6)
Regions and France	Baccalauréats delivered, 1964	Rank	Students preparing for Grandes Ecoles, 1964	Rank	Students in secondary education first cycle, 1964	Rank
Paris Region	18,264	1	10,046	1	332,063	1
Champagne	1,878	17	375	15	44,789	18
Picardy	1,976	15	202	19	52,852	12
Upper Normandy	1,662	20	301	16	49,554	15
Center	2,731	11	525	10	64,687	10
Nord	5,499	4	1,276	4	137,565	3
Lorraine	3,509	9	617	8	79,740	7
Alsace	1,934	16	410	13	43,547	19
Franche-Comté	1,700	19	292	17	42,030	20
Lower Normandy	1,809	18	155	20	44,947	17
Pays de la Loire	3,470	10	603	9	61,251	11
Brittany	4,302	7	793	7	72,592	8
Limousin	1,440	21	133	21	29,592	21
Auvergne	2,478	11	449	12	46,465	16
Poitou-Charentes	2,313	13	226	18	51,309	14
Aquitaine	4,458	6	927	6	88,979	6
Midi-Pyrenees	5,021	5	942	5	93,362	5
Burgundy	2,195	14	396	14	52,475	13
Rhone-Alps	8,297	2	1,826	2	149,173	2
Languedoc	4,243	8	466	11	71,455	9
Provence-Riviera-Corsica	7,550	3	1,738	3	131,592	4
France	86,729		22,698		1,739,948	

Source: Régionalisation du budget, 1966, pp. 238, 241, 242.

For the most part the rankings of the various regions correspond closely to their relative positions with respect to absolute population size. However, it is interesting to observe that noteworthy departures from this general tendency favor the West and Southwest. For example, education in the northern industrial regions of Upper Normandy,

Lorraine, and Picardy lags behind what might be expected. Upper Normandy ranks fifteenth in population but third in terms of youthfulness of the population (see Table 6.1), yet for the three variables shown in Table 6.4 it ranks, respectively, twentieth, sixteenth, and fifteenth. Lorraine ranks eighth in total population but has the youngest median age in France; it ranks ninth, eighth, and seventh for the respective variables in Table 6.4. Picardy ranks twelfth in population and fifth in terms of youthfulness, but occupies positions fifteen, nineteen, and twelve in the rankings of the respective education variables. Only one region of the West or Southwest—Pays de la Loire— presents similar characteristics.

On the other hand, Auvergne and Midi-Pyrenees rank higher than might be expected with regard to education. Auvergne ranks seventeenth in population and has a relatively old population, yet for the three education variables it ranks, respectively, eleventh, twelfth, and sixteenth. Midi-Pyrenees, which is ninth in population and also has a relatively old population, ranks fifth for each of the corresponding education values.

In general, the regions of the West and Southwest do not seem to be at any disadvantage with respect to education through the secondary level, unless there are significant regional differences in quality of education. However, they do seem to be at a disadvantage with respect to higher education. Of 10,588 *licences* awarded by French universities in 1962, 3,298 were delivered at the eight universities located in the ten regions of the West and Southwest (Caen, Nantes, Rennes, Clermond-Ferrand, Poitiers, Bordeaux, Toulouse, and Montpellier). In other words, although these regions contain 37 per cent of France's total population, they accounted for only 30 percent of the *licences* awarded. The situation with respect to doctoral degrees is even more striking. Of the 3,909 doctoral degrees conferred in all disciplines in France in 1962, only 963 were conferred by universities in the West and Southwest; this represents a proportion of only 25 per cent.[5] It would be useful, of course, to analyze the number of students enrolled in various universities according to their families' places of residence, but unfortunately such data are not available.

Tourism

Rising per capita income and increasing leisure have combined to make the tourist industry one of the fastest growing sectors in most

advanced economies. Although it is not the panacea for the ills of
lagging regions that many enthusiasts would claim, its importance does
merit special consideration, especially since it plays a significant part
in certain aspects of French regional policy.

Table 6.5

Tourism data by Program Region

	(1)	(2)	(3)	(4)	(5)	(6)
Regions and France	*Change in gasoline consumption in July and August 1955–64 (1955 = 100)*	*Rank*	*Capacity (rooms) of hotels for tourists, 1965*	*Rank*	*Campers (thousands), 1964*	*Rank*
Paris Region	160.5	18	62,079	1	240	11
Champagne	161.8	16	3,807	19	191	14
Picardy	155.5	21	3,056	21	198	12
Upper Normandy	171.6	14	5,610	17	100	20
Center	188.4	8	7,496	12	320	7
Nord	161.7	17	6,157	15	159	17
Lorraine	159.2	20	10,133	9	170	16
Alsace	183.0	10	6,726	14	115	19
Franche-Comté	160.3	19	4,970	18	117	18
Lower Normandy	167.3	15	9,537	10	242	10
Pays de la Loire	192.9	6	8,789	11	431	5
Brittany	201.7	3	17,121	7	731	3
Limousin	200.8	4	3,171	20	88	21
Auvergne	178.9	13	21,246	5	198	12
Poitou-Charentes	181.7	11	5,930	16	302	8
Aquitaine	191.5	7	17,941	6	427	6
Midi-Pyrenees	194.8	5	28,106	4	289	9
Burgundy	180.7	12	6,932	13	181	15
Rhone-Alps	188.1	9	48,836	3	658	4
Languedoc	224.8	1	11,428	8	795	2
Provence-Riviera-Corsica	205.4	2	53,764	2	1,255	1
France	181.1		342,835		7,207	

Source: Régionalisation du budget, 1966, pp. 246, 247, 252.

The values shown in column 1 of Table 6.5, which gives the change
in gasoline consumption during the months of July and August between
1955 and 1964 (1955 = 100), provides an index of the relative increase in tourism for the various program regions during this ten-year
period. Of the eight highest-ranked regions, seven are in the West and
Southwest, the only exception being Provence-Riviera-Corsica. The

extent to which tourism has grown in Rhone-Alps, ranked ninth, undoubtedly is underestimated because of winter sports activities, which have grown rapidly in popularity in recent years. With the exception of Franche-Comté, the six lowest-ranked regions are all in the North, where the loss of numerous historically and architecturally interesting buildings during World War I, industrialization that has resulted in a great deal of drabness, and unfavorable climate have combined to create a relatively unfavorable environment for tourism.

With the notable exception of Paris the growth of tourism has tended to be greatest in areas which already have relatively high absolute levels of touristic activity, as reflected in hotel capacities for tourists and the frequency of campers. The first of these variables includes only the capacity of hotels of sufficient quality to be classified as suitable for tourists by the government's Commission for Tourism. Despite the relatively large proportion of rooms accounted for by the Paris Region, six southern regions have over half of the nation's total capacity. These regions are Rhone-Alps, Auvergne, Provence-Riviera-Corsica, Languedoc, Midi-Pyrenees, and Aquitaine. However, among these six regions the relatively low position of Languedoc is especially noteworthy in view of the government's efforts to develop the touristic attractiveness of this region. The figures concerning number of campers include only the number of persons arriving at campsites and do not take into account the duration of their stays. Nevertheless, the popularity of Provence is clearly evident, since in itself it has over 17 per cent of the national total. However, of the next nine highest-ranked regions, all are in the West and Southwest with the sole exception of Rhone-Alps. Thus, in terms of absolute level and growth of touristic activity, the regions of the West and Southwest are in a relatively favorable position.

Income
and Consumption

With respect to income and consumption levels, the highly favorable position of the Paris Region and the low standing of the West and Southwest are clearly seen in the data presented in Table 6.6. With respect to average white-collar salaries, only two of the twelve top-ranked regions are in the West or Southwest. The high ranking of one of these regions, Auvergne, undoubtedly is attributable to the presence of Michelin, which dominates its industrial economy; the other, Center, benefits from its close proximity to the Paris Region. The situation with respect to average blue-collar wage is even more striking. Not one of the eleven top-ranked regions is found in the West or Southwest; in other words, the ten regions which comprise this area are also the ten lowest ranked. The same situation obtains with regard to the proportion of wage earners earning less than 5,000 francs per year.

Table 6.6

Income and consumption data by Program Region, 1963

Regions and France	(1) Average white-collar salary (francs)	(2) Rank	(3) Average blue-collar wage (francs)	(4) Rank	(5) Per cent of wage earners earning less than 5,000 francs per year	(6) Rank	(7) Per capita low-tension electricity consumption (KWH)	(8) Rank
Paris Region	11,477	1	10,780	1	8.64	1	420	1
Champagne	9,339	8	7,913	10	23.05	8	260	5
Picardy	9,277	9	8,173	9	23.94	10	213	14
Upper Normandy	9,439	7	8,859	2	22.22	6	227	11
Center	9,220	10	7,280	16	29.14	16	252	7
Nord	9,214	11	8,188	8	21.77	3	192	17
Lorraine	10,007	5	8,426	5	21.79	4	226	12
Alsace	8,621	15	8,211	7	22.07	5	170	21
Franche-Comté	9,942	6	8,265	6	21.35	2	266	4
Lower Normandy	8,171	19	7,340	12	28.47	14	192	17
Pays de la Loire	8,500	16	7,256	17	28.89	15	207	16
Brittany	8,298	18	6,991	20	28.15	13	177	20
Limousin	7,812	20	6,638	21	35.70	20	180	19
Auvergne	10,385	2	7,315	14	27.07	12	254	6
Poitou-Charentes	7,240	21	7,094	19	33.86	19	207	15
Aquitaine	8,458	17	7,323	13	38.30	21	239	9
Midi-Pyrenees	8,909	13	7,101	18	31.63	18	228	10
Burgundy	9,034	12	7,445	11	26.27	11	250	8
Rhone-Alps	10,242	4	8,734	3	22.29	7	346	3
Languedoc	8,820	14	7,309	15	31.04	17	219	13
Provence-Riviera-Corsica	10,307	3	8,555	4	23.92	9	384	2
France	——		——		20.71		279	

Source: *Régionalisation du budget, 1966*, pp. 263, 265, 267

Per capita low-tension electricity consumption is a good index of household consumption, particularly in relation to home appliances, radios, and television. Its significance has already been demonstrated in the regression analyses designed to explain variation in economic activity aided by the Economic and Social Development Fund and variation in migration patterns. The regional rankings for this variable present a more mixed picture than is the case for wage and salary data. Nevertheless, none of the five regions with the highest values are found in the West or Southwest, and the two regions from this area which are represented in the eight highest-ranked regions are also the two which stand relatively high in terms of average white-collar salary. Moreover, the West and Southwest account for four of the six lowest-ranked regions.

Transportation and Communications

Column 1 of Table 6.7 gives the total number of kilometers of roads over seven meters wide by region. Considerable care must be taken in comparing these values since they do not indicate intensity of use. Moreover, it would be expected that a spatially large region such as Rhone-Alps would rank higher than a small region such as Alsace or Limousin. Nevertheless, the induced nature of highway construction is reflected in the data. For example, the relatively small Paris Region ranks high, whereas the ten regions of the West and Southwest, which represent 56 per cent of France's total area, have a combined total of 9,971 kilometers, or only 44 per cent of the national total.

The relative positions of the various regions with regard to letters distributed are much the same as those for telephone traffic and new telephones installed. Moreover, as would be expected, there is a close correspondence between the respective rankings for these variables and for absolute population size.

Finance

The values of bank deposits shown by region in column 1 of Table 6.8 include data for all financial institutions legally permitted to receive deposits from the public. They also include all types of accounts, from checking accounts to long-term deposits. It should be noted, however, that the value for the Paris Region reflects the concentration of industrial and commercial headquarters in Paris, even though many of the operations of these firms may be carried on in other regions. Despite

Table 6.7

Transportation and communications data by Program Region, 1964

Regions and France	(1) Roads over seven meters wide (kilometers)	(2) Rank	(3) Letters distributed (millions)	(4) Rank	(5) Telephone traffic (millions)	(6) Rank	(7) Phones installed	(8) Rank
Paris Region	1,088	7	1,718	1	3,451	1	74,102	1
Champagne	926	10	114	17	159	16	4,189	15
Picardy	714	17	126	12[a]	186	15	3,685	18
Upper Normandy	683	19	128	14	218	11	4,321	14
Center	1,000	9	167	10	225	10	4,611	12
Nord	869	12	310	4	410	4	6,855	6
Lorraine	2,114	2	180	8[a]	263	7	6,957	4
Alsace	689	18	122	15[a]	209	12	5,106	9
Franche-Comté	772	14	89	20	108	20	2,489	20
Lower Normandy	620	20	101	19	143	18	3,051	19
Pays de la Loire	1,160	6	214	6	271	6	6,034	7
Brittany	1,512	5	180	8[a]	247	9	5,022	10
Limousin	590	21	63	21	82	21	2,043	21
Auvergne	731	16	105	18	141	19	3,992	17
Poitou-Charentes	759	15	122	15[a]	150	17	4,667	11
Aquitaine	1,052	8	246	5	380	5	6,901	5
Midi-Pyrenees	1,773	3	190	7	263	8	5,314	8
Burgundy	892	11	126	12[a]	189	14	3,994	16
Rhone-Alps	2,234	1	452	2	631	3	12,754	3
Languedoc	774	13	146	11	203	13	4,421	13
Provence-Riviera-Corsica	1,588	4	365	3	724	2	17,916	2
France	22,540		——		——		188,424	

Source: *Régionalisation du budget, 1966*, pp. 305, 313, 318, 319.
[a]Two regions have this value and thus the same rank.

this qualification, the concentration of bank deposits in a few regions is striking. Three regions alone—Paris, Provence-Riviera-Corsica, and Rhone-Alps—account for 59 per cent of the national total. The ten regions of the West and Southwest, on the other hand, account for only 18.276 billion francs, or 21 per cent of the total. A similar situation exists with respect to bank credit outstanding (column 3).

On the other hand, the regions of the West and Southwest come off relatively better with respect to savings account deposits. Their combined deposits amount to 16.167 billion francs, or about 31 per cent of the total. With the exception of the four highest regions, the regions in the West and Southwest compare very favorably with other areas in regard to savings deposits.

Table 6.8

Financial data by Program Region

Regions and France	(1) Bank deposits (millions of francs) Dec. 1964	(2) Rank	(3) Bank credit (millions of francs) March 1965	(4) Rank	(5) Saving bank deposits (millions of francs) Dec. 1964	(6) Rank
Paris Region	37,412	1	64,130	1	12,245	1
Champagne	1,590	15	2,158	12	1,196	18
Picardy	1,646	14	2,265	11	1,221	15
Upper Normandy	1,536	16	1,811	14	1,439	13
Center	2,395	9	2,633	7	2,082	6
Nord	3,802	4	5,516	3	2,648	4
Lorraine	2,399	8	3,049	5	2,032	7
Alsace	3,076	5	2,562	8	1,227	14
Franche Comté	973	20	967	20	967	19
Lower Normandy	982	19	973	19	881	20
Pays de la Loire	2,082	11	2,114	13	1,990	8
Brittany	2,031	12	1,588	15	1,938	9
Limousin	632	21	441	21	805	21
Auvergne	1,188	18	1,133	18	1,218	16
Poitou-Charentes	1,339	17	1,238	17	1,210	17
Aquitaine	2,897	6	2,719	6	2,289	5
Midi-Pyrenees	2,251	10	2,378	9	1,929	10
Burgundy	1,665	13	1,492	16	1,578	12
Rhone-Alps	6,182	3	7,543	2	5,457	2
Languedoc	2,479	7	2,311	10	1,825	11
Provence-Riviera-Corsica	6,853	2	4,795	4	5,284	3
France	85,410		113,796		51,461	

Source: *Régionalisation du budget, 1966*, pp. 321, 324, 325.

In summation, then, the regions of the West and Southwest fare much better with respect to savings than to bank deposits, largely because of their relative lack of commercial and industrial depositors, but also because many of their activities are dependent on headquarters in other areas, a phenomenon indicated by data presented earlier. It is clear, therefore, that the difficulties presented by less developed regions in a country such as France cannot really be compared with those encountered in underdeveloped nations. In the former case there exists a significant amount of local saving; the problem is to channel it into local investment projects. As pointed out in Chapter 3, it is unfortunate that the Regional Development Societies have not been able to exercise a more active part in this regard.

Local
Public Finance

Despite the highly centralized nature of France's administrative structure, recent studies have shown that in the past few years local authorities have been responsible for the execution of about two thirds of all public investment. Approximately 28 per cent of the cost of investment projects of local authorities has been subsidized by the central government. Thus, about one half of total public investment expenditures have been borne by local governments.[6]

Regional data on local public finance is presented in Table 6.9. The fiscal receipts of local authorities (column 1) include the diverse types of taxes levied by communes and departments. Per capita operating outlays (column 3) refer only to the budgets of communes and departments, and not to local public enterprises. The interest costs of loans are included in these values. The data on per capita investment expenditures (column 5) include outlays by local public enterprises as well as by the communes and departments themselves.

Column 7 shows the amount of loans made to local authorities during the four-year period 1961–64 by the Caisse des dépôts et consignations, the most important public credit institution in France. The funds of the Caisse come primarily from Social Security funds, pension funds, and the Caisses d'épargne (savings banks), which redeposit private savings with it. Loans extended by the Caisse are particularly important in the area of construction. Most infrastructure provided for industrial zones, a large part of urban renewal projects, and most large housing developments are financed by it or by its branches. In addition, the Caisse lends funds to local public authorities for numerous types of public projects.[7]

As pointed out in Chapter 2, the tax income of the Paris Region (column 1) is relatively greater than its population; the former accounts for about 26 per cent of the French total, whereas the latter amounts to only 19 per cent of the national population. The local tax receipts of the regions of the West and Southwest are approximately

Table 6.9

Local public finance data by Program Region

	(1)	(2)	(3)	(4)	(5)	(6)	(7)	(8)
Regions and France	Fiscal receipts, (millions of francs), 1962	Rank	Per capita operating outlays, 1962	Rank	Per capita investment outlays, 1960–62 (francs)	Rank	Caisse des Dépôts loans, (millions of francs) 1961–64	Rank
Paris Region	2,628	1	552	1	572	16	3,834	1
Champagne	227	19	277	19	666	8	357	19
Picardy	296	14	310	13	575	15	367	17
Upper Normandy	341	12	343	6	722	3	544	11
Center	406	9	328	8[a]	687	6	718	9
Nord	661	4	266	21	448	21	867	6
Lorraine	374	11	269	20	584	14	479	14
Alsace	245	17	355	4	680	7	218	21
Franche-Comté	153	20	321	11	618	11	359	18
Lower Normandy	301	13	328	8[a]	716	4	384	16
Pays de la Loire	485	5	378	2	654	10	887	4
Brittany	439	7	295	16	532	20	860	7
Limousin	140	21	290	17	608	12	239	20
Auvergne	244	18	287	18	589	13	407	15
Poitou-Charentes	271	16	296	15	555	18	492	13
Aquitaine	440	6	298	14	561	17	877	5
Midi-Pyrenees	421	8	325	10	547	19	765	8
Burgundy	289	15	315	12	655	9	522	12
Rhone-Alps	880	2	335	7	688	5	1,855	2
Languedoc	379	10	350	5	816	1	584	10
Provence-Riviera-Corsica	720	3	362	3	738	2	1,387	3
France	10,340		—		—		17,065	

Source: Régionalisation du budget, 1966, pp. 329, 330, 331, 334.

[a]Two regions have this value and thus the same rank.

the same as their share of total population; these two proportions are, respectively, 34 per cent and 37 per cent. Thus, local tax income in the rest of the country is also slightly less than its share of the national population; these respective values are 40 per cent and 44 per cent. For the most part, the ranking with regard to local tax receipts corresponds rather closely to the ranking according to population size.

Per capita operating outlays (column 3) show no particular broadly regional pattern. Two of the five lowest-ranking regions are in the West or Southwest, but so are two of the five highest-ranking.

Because of their considerable variability, per capita investment outlays (column 5) are cumulated over a three-year period. Here again,
however, no broadly regional pattern emerges. A similar situation
exists with respect to borrowing from the Caisse des dépôts. Nevertheless, it will be observed that the two large and rapidly growing regions
of Rhone-Alps and Provence-Riviera-Corsica rank relatively high for
all of the variables considered in Table 6.9.

Regional Disparities and
the Evolution of Regional Employment

The foregoing examination of the regional patterns associated with
demographic, economic, and other relevant variables has emphasized
primarily the differences between three broadly defined areas: the
regions of the West and Southwest, the Paris Region, and the regions
of the North and East. In general, the first of these areas tends to
compare unfavorably with the others in many fundamental respects,
while the Paris Region generally has an importance out of proportion
to its population (see Chapter 2). This distinction among three areas
has been employed not only because of its usefulness in providing
insights into the spatial structure of the French economy, but also
because it has been widely utilized in the preparation of the regional
aspects of the Fifth Plan. For example, in its First Report, the National
Commission for *Aménagement du Territoire* points out that large-scale
movements of population and economic activity toward the relatively
dense urban and industrial concentrations of the North and East imply,
as at least a first approximation, a picture of France outside the Paris
Region as consisting of two main areas, "a more-developed part in the
East, and a less-developed part in the West." [8] This same distinction
is maintained in the Fifth Plan itself.[9] Nevertheless, as the foregoing
sections have indicated, there often is considerable variation within
these broad groupings, a fact which also has not been ignored by the
planners.[10]

Thus, analysis of regional differences again is confronted with the
difficult problem of defining regional boundaries in terms of operational
policy considerations, a problem examined to some extent at the outset of Chapter 4 in connection with the establishment of the twenty-
one program regions. In any event, it is clear by now that the issue
is more complex than a simple distinction between Paris and a more

or less uniform *désert français* would indicate. It is equally clear that certain contiguous program regions may be conveniently grouped together for planning purposes. However, before considering how this might best be accomplished, it is necessary to examine more closely the structure and dynamics of the sectoral and regional composition of French industry. As recently as a decade ago many persons saw in the importance of the French population working in agriculture one of the signs of 'the equilibrium' of the French economy and of its traditional harmony; today the idea increasingly is admitted that agriculture should occupy only a secondary place in French employment and production. Thus, one of the essential problems posed by this reorientation is that of assuring a place in industrial society for those persons destined to leave agriculture and rural society.

Adequate study of the evolution of the technical and geographic structure of French industry must proceed on the basis of employment data, since this is the only relevant variable for which complete, comparable statistics are available in both sectoral and regional terms over time. A very instructive study of the regional and structural composition of the evolution of regional employment in France between 1954 and 1962 has recently been published by Michel Beaud.[11] His approach is similar to that recently utilized to analyze American regional economic growth in terms of "proportionality employment shifts" and "differential employment shifts." [12] Regions specializing in relatively slowly growing sectors have net downward proportionality shifts in total employment, whereas regions characterized by growth industries have net upward proportionality shifts. Net differential shifts, on the other hand, occur because given sectors expand more rapidly (or slowly) in some regions than in others.

Beaud defines three ratios of growth which may be applied to a given region α; these are the average rate of growth observed during the time period considered in the country as a whole (T), the rate of growth observed in region α (t_α), and the hypothetical rate of growth of region α (t'_α). The latter is the growth rate the region would have had if each sector studied had the same growth rate in α as in the nation as a whole. With these three rates, it is possible to calculate the total deviation (E_α) characteristic of the region, i.e. $E_\alpha = t_\alpha - T$, and to break down E_α into structural (S_α) and regional (R_α) components. Thus, $S_\alpha = t'_\alpha - T$, $R_\alpha = t_\alpha - t'_\alpha$, and $E_\alpha = S_\alpha + R_\alpha$. In other words, the total deviation is simply the difference between the relative growth observed in the region and that observed for the nation as a whole. The structural component is the difference between the relative growth which would have been brought about in the region as a consequence of its economic structure and that actually observed for the nation as a whole. The regional component, then, is the difference between the relative growth observed in the region considered and that which "normally" would have resulted from the economic structure of the region. Beaud computes values for E_α, S_α, and R_α for the twenty-one program regions by using weighted averages based on each region's degree of specialization in each sector and the rate of employment growth for each sector. Thirty-six sectors were utilized, including agriculture, construction, and all of the principal industrial and tertiary branches.[13]

Total employment in France increased by .44 per cent between 1954 and 1962; in other words, it was virtually unchanged. Employment changes thus took place within a constant national aggregate, and as a result of shifts of employment among sectors and migration among regions, which are of course related. Relative to the national pattern, total employment increased most in the Paris Region (10.8 per cent) and in Provence-Riviera-Corsica (9.6 per cent). A moderate increase took place in four other regions: Lorraine (3.3 per cent), Rhone-Alps (2.6 per cent), Upper Normandy (1.4 per cent), and Picardy (1.3 per cent). As to the remaining regions, Languedoc had almost no change, while the other fourteen had declines. Total employment in Brittany, Pays de la Loire, Poitou-Charentes, Aquitaine, Auvergne, and Limousin diminished by more than 5 per cent in each case; the last two regions were particularly affected—their respective rates were 10.0 per cent and 12.4 per cent.

All of the regions of the West and Southwest are thus characterized by stagnation or decline of total employment. Moreover, the structural component is particularly negative, a reflection of the importance of agricultural employment in these areas. On the national level, employment in this sector diminished by one quarter. As to the regional component, some regions in this area had positive values, whereas others were negative. Among the favored regions in this regard are Lower Normandy and Center. As pointed out earlier, efforts to decentralize economic activity have tended to benefit areas close to Paris. Therefore, Lower Normandy and Center benefited from a marked increase in industrial employment as well as a substantial increase in tertiary employment. In contrast, Limousin and Auvergne had stagnation in industrial employment, a greater than average decrease in agricultural employment, and the lowest increase in tertiary employment in France. It will be recalled that the particularly unfavorable position of these regions was clearly evident in terms of numerous variables examined in the preceding sections.

Among the regions of the East, Provence-Riviera benefited from notably positive values with respect to both structural and regional components of total employment. This region has profited, and undoubtedly will continue to profit, from the "movement which, as in the United States, brings not only large numbers of tourists to the sunniest regions, but a great number of modern economic activities." [14] Finally, the Paris Region, because of its importance in industry, construction, and tertiary activities and the relative weakness of its agricultural importance, has benefited from the structural composition of its employment. The regional component, on the other hand, has been slightly negative, which indicates that decentralization measures have been significantly effective.

With respect to industrial employment alone, only one region, Auvergne, suffered primarily from an unfavorable tendency in the regional component. All of the other regions characterized by stagnation or decline in relation to the average national increase of 4.9 per cent were characterized essentially by weakness in the structural component, i.e. by the dominance of declining industries. These regions included Nord, Languedoc, and Midi-Pyrenees, and to a lesser extent Aquitaine, Brittany, and Limousin. The five industries wherein employment declined between 1954 and 1962 (solid mineral combustibles, textiles, clothing, leather, wood) represented nearly three fifths of all industrial employment in the Nord in 1954; this region alone employed over half of the miners in France, and over a quarter of the textile workers.[15]

The Paris Region occupies an exceptional position with respect to industrial employment. It represents only a small part of industrial employment in regressive sectors, and it accounts for a considerable share of employment in fast-growing sectors. Thus, the Paris Region is "the privileged development pole of the French economy." [16] Nevertheless, the evolution of its industrial employment has been only slightly greater than the national average because of the strongly negative character of the regional component, a consequence of high costs and decentralization policy.

Of all the regions with a growth of industrial employment in excess of the national average, only one, Franche-Comté, benefited primarily as a result of the structural component. In other words, the growth of industrial employment has resulted for the most part from specifically regional factors. It is particularly noteworthy that most of these regions with high growth rates—for example Picardy, Lower Normandy, Center, and to a lesser extent Burgundy, Champagne, and Upper Normandy—are located relatively close to the Paris Region. Again it is evident that decentralization policy has tended to be of most benefit to areas near Paris, though it may also have been significant in the above-average growth rates of Rhone-Alps, Pays de la Loire, and Poitou-Charentes.

Tertiary employment in France increased by 11.2 per cent from 1954 to 1962. In general, the regional pattern of growth in this sector has been only slightly influenced by structural factors, though it has been strongly influenced by specifically regional factors. Lorraine's growth rate, about seven percentage points above the national average, is the highest and represents in part an effort to compensate for its still insufficient absolute status, especially with regard to provision of services. Growth of tourism and development of industry have induced higher than average growth in Rhone-Alps and Provence-Riviera, while the Center has benefited from the deconcentration of certain activities from the Paris Region. Higher than average tertiary employment growth in the Paris Region has been fostered by industrial decentralization, which has liberated both space and people for tertiary uses. "Less and less industrial, more and more tertiary, the Parisian pole not only will continue to grow, but even threatens to find in this conversion the sources of a new dynamism." [17]

Among the regions with low growth rates for tertiary employment are Burgundy, Champagne, Picardy, Upper Normandy, and Lower Normandy, all of which are in relatively close proximity to the Paris Region. This would indicate that the regions which have benefited most from industrial decentralization are also those which are affected most adversely by the attraction of tertiary activities in the Paris Region. In fact, one of Beaud's major general conclusions is that the importance and rapid growth of tertiary activities in the Paris Region, "favorized at the same time by industrial decentralization and by current tendencies in modern economics, have provoked, through backwash effects on neighboring regions, a check on the growth of their tertiary employment." [18]

In general, analysis of the structural and regional components of recent employment change indicates that while the twenty-one program regions are too many, there is sufficient diversity to warrant more disaggregation than obtains in the threefold division of East, West, and Paris.

Beaud suggests a division into eight regions, whose more or less homogeneous characteristics are summarized in Table 6.10. As indicated there, the Paris Region benefits from its structural composition; it has little agriculture and a large share of growth industries. Because of decentralization policy the regional component is unfavorable for industry, but partly as a consequence of this, tertiary activities are favorably placed.

Surrounding the Paris Region is the "Parisian Rim" (Center, Burgundy, Champagne, Picardy, Upper Normandy), whose average structural nature is reflected in the neutral influence on employment change of the structural component. In terms of the regional component, however, the region has benefited from industrial decentralization policy, but has been unfavorably affected with respect to tertiary employment by its closeness to Paris, whose influence in this regard may be somewhat overestimated by Beaud.

The regions of the Massif Central (Auvergne, Limousin) are in an unfavorable position concerning both structural and regional influences. Their generally low rank with respect to numerous demographic and economic variables was clearly seen in the earlier sections of this chapter. It is evident that the problems posed by the economic development of the Massif Central are the most difficult of any area of France.

The Southwest (Aquitaine, Midi-Pyrenees, Languedoc) suffers from structural problems similar to those of the Massif Central, including the importance of the agricultural sector and the presence of industries in decline. The effect of the regional component, however, has been somewhat more favorable, especially in relation to the picture in the Massif Central.

Table 6.10

Influence of structural and regional components
on employment in groups of Program Regions

Groups of regions	Types of employment	Influence of structural component	Influence of regional component
Paris Region	Total employment	1	4
	Industrial employment	1	5
	Tertiary employment	3	2
Paris Rim	Total employment	4	3
	Industrial employment	3	1
	Tertiary employment	3	4
West	Total employment	5	3
	Industrial employment	4	2
	Tertiary employment	3	4
Massif Central	Total employment	5	4
	Industrial employment	3	5
	Tertiary employment	3	5
Southwest	Total employment	5	2
	Industrial employment	4	3
	Tertiary employment	3	2
Southeast	Total employment	2	2
	Industrial employment	3	2
	Tertiary employment	3	1
East	Total employment	2	4
	Industrial employment	4	2
	Tertiary employment	3	4
North (Nord)	Total employment	4	3
	Industrial employment	5	3
	Tertiary employment	3	4

Source: Michel Beaud, "Une analyse des disparités régionales de croissance,"
R.E., XVII (January, 1966), p. 87.

Note: Rankings of Influence read as follows:

1 = Very favorable influence   3 = Weak influence   5 = Very unfavorable
2 = Favorable influence   4 = Unfavorable influence   influence

The Southeast (Rhone-Alps, Provence-Riviera) has benefited from
both its structural and its regional situation. Among its advantages

are its very favorable climate, its proximity to Switzerland and the wealthiest part of Italy, its position on the axis linking the North Sea and the Mediterranean Sea, industrial traditions, plentiful hydroelectric power, and the development of numerous public and private research activities.

The East (Alsace, Lorraine, Franche-Comté) benefits from a favorable structural component, but has a negative regional component for the evolution of total employment. Employment in agriculture in the East has decreased more rapidly than the national average, whereas industrial employment has increased by only slightly more than the national average. Because of its close proximity to rapidly expanding regions of Switzerland and Germany (Baden-Württemberg), the East is under constant pressure with respect to modernization of its industry.

Finally, the large proportion of industrial employment in the Nord accounted for by stagnating or declining industries has already been discussed. Its industrial structure is the most unfavorable in France, and the regional influence is not pronounced in either direction. It is evident that industrial conversion is a particular necessity to the future growth of this singular region.

In general, Beaud's regional divisions seem basically sound and of obvious usefulness in the formulation of regional policy. Moreover, they are similar to those made by the European Economic Community's study group of regional experts in 1961.[19] It will be recalled from Chapter 2 that this report defined nine principal regions in France on the basis of social as well as economic criteria. In the two sets of groupings four regions are identical: Paris, Nord, East, and the Massif Central. The principal difference in the two groupings is that the EEC report distinguishes between the Southeast (Burgundy, Rhone-Alps) and the Mediterranean Region (Provence-Riviera, Languedoc). Thus, Burgundy is detached from the Parisian Rim (termed the Paris Basin by the EEC), and Languedoc replaces Rhone-Alps as an associate of Provence-Riviera.

I definitely favor Beaud's classification. Rhone-Alps and Provence-Riviera are large, progressive regions along a common natural transportation route and should be treated in a similar fashion with respect to regional policy. The EEC's grouping of Burgundy with Rhone-Alps is difficult to justify on either demographic or economic grounds. Burgundy's recent population growth rate is only half that of France as a whole, and its median age is 34.2 as compared with a national value of 32.9. For each of the industrial and commercial indices considered in Table 6.3, Burgundy ranked lower than its population rank. A similar situation obtains with respect to such variables as housing construction and bank credit outstanding for all major sectors of economic activity. In contrast, Rhone-Alps compares very favorably with national patterns in these as well as other respects.

Similarly, it is more appropriate to include Languedoc with the regions of the Southwest, as Beaud does, than with Provence-Riviera, as the EEC does. Although Languedoc represents a transitional area, its problems are more closely related to those of the Southwest than its advantages are to those of Provence-Riviera.

The Future Evolution
of Regional Employment

Regional policy must, of course, take account not only of past sectoral and regional employment trends but of future conditions which might alter the technical and geographic evolution of national industry. Thus, the National Commission for *Aménagement du Territoire,* through its Work Group Number Two, has attempted to project employment growth trends by region to 1985. This study begins by distinguishing among three types of industrial branches, those where employment is expected to decrease, those where employment is expected to increase moderately, and those where it is expected to increase rapidly. The various branches are classified on the basis of a coefficient (i) relating projected employment in 1985 to employment in 1962 (for all branches combined $i = 1.16$).[20]

Group I includes all branches where employment is expected to diminish during the given period, i.e. where $i < 1$. Group II includes branches of modest expansion, where $1 < i < 1.3$. Finally, Group III is characterized by rapidly growing branches ($i > 1.3$).

Work Group Number Two developed the perspectives for regional industrial employment primarily by relating the values shown for Group I to those shown for Group III for the respective program regions, i.e. each region was given a coefficient $X = i_I / i_{III}$. The most favored regions were taken to be those for which $X < 1$; the least favored, those for which $X > 2$; and regions in a more or less average situation those for which $1 < X < 2$. Thus, on this basis, three program regions have distinctly unfavorable employment prospects; they are Nord, Lorraine, and Languedoc. Those in a relatively favorable situation are Paris, Pays de la Loire, Center, Upper Normandy, Picardy, Champagne, Alsace, Franche-Comté, Rhone-Alps, and Provence-Riviera. The remaining eight regions are in the average category.

Beaud has prepared a more detailed study of future regional employment trends using the same regional-structural analysis as he applied to changes in employment from 1954 to 1962.[21] However, whereas the study just discussed projects employment trends to 1985, Beaud takes a shorter-term approach—his perspective is 1970.

Beaud utilizes forecasts for agricultural, industrial, construction, and tertiary employment in 1970 established by the National Institute for Statistics and Economic Studies for the various program regions. In general, these regional employment perspectives give a total employment picture in terms of, in Beaud's words, "a 'mix' which is difficult to analyze, of projects and forecasts, of projections of past tendencies and of promises of desired change. Such are the 1970 perspectives which we are going to submit to the test of regional-structural analysis." [22]

Using the same method, Beaud's results show that there are few changes to be noted between the 1954–62 evolution and that anticipated for 1962–70. The only really notable changes would be an aggravation of the unfavorable situation in the North and an amelioration of that in the Massif Central. Similarly, few changes are anticipated with regard to the structural component. The Paris Region will remain particularly favored in this regard, while the West, the Massif Central, and the Southwest will continue to be at a relative disadvantage. On the other hand, the regional component of total employment change indicates that the position of the Paris Region, the East, and the Massif Central should become less unfavorable, but that in the North and Southwest more unfavorable. The Southeast, the Paris Rim, and the West should remain about the same. However, Beaud argues that these anticipated changes seem difficult to justify. For the Paris Region this would imply, for example, that decentralization policy will be relaxed or that there will be a relaxation in the inconveniences resulting from the region's growth.[23] Nevertheless, Beaud may underestimate the attractiveness of the external economies offered by the Paris Region in spite of these potential checks to expansion. It will be recalled from Chapter 2 that the past tendency has always been to underestimate the extent to which the Paris Region has grown. In addition to questioning the Paris forecast, Beaud also doubts that the regional component will improve in the Massif Central, or that it will deteriorate in the Southwest. Mild doubt also is expressed regarding its improvement in the East.[24] In the light of available evidence, these observations seem well taken.

As to industrial employment, the results point to a continual slowing of growth in the Paris Region in favor of the regions of the Paris Rim. The situation in the North, the East, and the Southeast should remain about the same, while that in the Massif Central, the Southwest, and the West is expected to improve. The structural component is expected to move from negative to positive in three regions: the Paris Rim, the Southeast, and the Massif Central. The regional component is expected to deteriorate in the Paris Region because of decentralization policy, and in the North, because of the bad psychological effects of both past and present difficulties and the preference of many managers for regions with a more agreeable climate. Otherwise, this component is characterized by stability, with the exception of the Massif Central. This region, which deviated on the negative side from the national average by six percentage points during the 1954–62 interval, is supposed to have a regional component that is three percentage points on the positive side in the 1962–70 forecast. Beaud correctly states, "One may ask oneself if this evolution does not reflect more the optimism or the hopes of organizations having participated in the work of forecasting than a reasonable possibility." [25]

It may finally be noted that the regional-structural approach is useful not only for descriptive analysis but as an aid in giving greater specificity to regional policies and their control. In the case of a region with a strongly negative structural component, for example, the problem is basically one of conversion to modern sectors and professional readaptation. The extent to which success is being achieved in this regard may be measured by the extent to which the value of the structural component approaches zero. Similarly, regional goals may be fixed and progress verified in terms of the regional component. The difficulties underlying a strongly negative regional component are generally more complex and more difficult to grasp than in the structural case. They may include geographic disadvantages, inefficient firm structures, insufficient transportation and communication means, a population structure dominated by older persons, mentalities resistant to economic or social change, or some combination of these and other relevant factors. In any event, remedies may be sought which conform to the diagnosis, and the accuracy of the diagnosis and efficacy of the remedies may be judged by the extent of improvement in the regional component over some specified time period. Of course, in regions where both structural and regional components are negative, both of these types of responses may be employed simultaneously.

It must be emphasized, however, that regional-structural analysis in itself does not provide an adequate basis for rational regional planning. Its greatest usefulness is in planning for individual regions, but it does not attempt to provide answers to the problem of efficiency with respect to interregional resource allocation, largely because it does not incorporate the notion of opportunity cost.[26] It is a valuable complement to, but not a substitute for, the more general model developed in Chapter 1. Therefore, before discussing specific regional policy proposals, it is necessary to examine more closely the relative priorities which characterize regional public investment needs.

7

The Need for
Social Overhead Capital
in Lagging Regions

In Chapter 1 it was argued on the basis of theoretical and empirical considerations that the principal difficulties of lagging regions are the result of inadequate social overhead capital. This does not mean that lagging regions do not also need expanded economic overhead capital, or that social investment may not be needed in more prosperous regions. The question is one of emphasis. Although lagging regions may be relatively deficient in both social and economic overhead, the most pronounced deficiencies generally relate to social overhead. Moreover, given the recent evidence on the contribution of social overhead, especially that for education, to economic growth it would follow that opportunity cost considerations would favor concentrating social investment in lagging regions where needs are greatest and where the relevant facilities are the least well developed. This chapter examines the extent to which these propositions are applicable to problems of economic development in lagging regions of France.

154

SOC Deficiencies
in Lagging Agricultural Regions

The evidence presented in Chapter 6 clearly shows that, with the exception of certain industrial areas characterized by a predominance of stagnating or declining sectors, the regions in greatest economic difficulty are those which are the most agricultural. Moreover, the difficulties experienced by agricultural regions are qualitatively different, since for the most part the essential problem is one of stimulating the initial growth of a modern economy, rather than of converting an already industrial region from one type of activity to another.

Claude Delmas has pointed out that as the heir of generations which have had only very limited sums of money, but also as a person concerned with securing the subsistence of his family, "the French peasant has for a long time put only the excess of his production into commercial markets, and he still is often repelled by producing primarily to sell. He is at the same time a man of tradition, indeed, of routine. Any break with custom appears to him to be an adventure. Vocational and technical training seem to many a useless luxury." [1] Thus, "the real problem is posed in terms of education of the rural masses," and "the essential aspect of the rural problem is less in the technical domain than in the human domain." [2] Similarly, the Economic and Social Council has often noted the importance of agricultural education as well as existing deficiencies in its availability. [3]

Jules Milhau has argued on comparative grounds that the major difficulties of France's lagging agricultural regions are not so much technical as social. He maintains that poor soil and severe climate have often been overestimated as explanations for the economic history of various regions. The sand of Israel is not particularly rich, and natural agricultural conditions are far from ideal in such places as the Swiss mountains, the area around the Zuyder Zee, or Jutland. Nevertheless, because of the quality of human effort, productivity has been high enough in these cases to enable the populations to attain relatively high living standards. Thus, Milhau concludes, with reference to the situation characteristic of a large part of France, that "it is in people and in their works that it is necessary to look for the real obstacles to the economic development of a region." [4]

A large part of the blame for the lack of investment in human capital in the provinces is placed on the overconcentration of intellectual and professional facilities in Paris. Faucheux maintains that too often the provinces have been regarded only as a source of manpower for the utilization of the "thinkers" in Paris. For most professors, scientists, financiers, technicians, engineers, managers, and skilled workers, "promotion means Paris; the provinces mean exile and stagnation." To redress the balance, "it is not a question of material investment, but of qualitative investment in people." Therefore, decentralization should be carried out with "greater emphasis on the areas of teaching, research, and administration in the largest sense, which in the end commands all industrial decentralization relating to quality. In this domain nearly everything remains to be done." [5]

Gravier also emphasizes the intellectual domination of Paris. For example, he points out that in 1962, 55.2 per cent of all engineering diplomas given by "establishments of higher technical education" were delivered in Paris. The Paris Region accounted for 48.6 per cent of France's 139,400 engineers and 43.8 per cent of the nation's 350,600 technicians. A survey conducted in 1963 indicated that 72 per cent of all persons engaged in scientific research worked in the Paris Region; another 11 per cent worked in Rhone-Alps, and only 17 per cent in the remaining nineteen regions. [6]

At the local level, on the other hand, subsidies and loans have permitted considerable improvements in economic overhead capital, especially in the matter of electrification and water supply. However, the provision of sociocultural investments has been much less satisfactory, and in the great majority of rural communes they are nonexistent. This difference results both from the greater ease of obtaining outside financial help for providing economic overhead capital and from a certain lack of interest in social investment on the part of many local authorities. [7]

It is evident that a necessary condition for economic development is a willingness on the part of the population in question (or at least a significant part of the population) to act in an economically rational manner. [8] Insufficiencies in this regard in much of rural France cannot all be blamed on the dynamism of the Paris Region. Nevertheless, much of the lack of adequate economic motivation in rural areas can be attributed to government policy. An excellent historical analysis of this phenomenon recently has been made by Jean Pautard, who traces many of the difficulties of France's agricultural regions to two basic areas of past public policy. The first concerns an official desire to maintain a large population in agriculture in the face of rapid technological change, while the second relates to inadequacies of social overhead in the regions in question.

After 1882 government protectionism tended to limit the transformation of the structure of French agriculture, whereas such change became increasingly necessary as a result of mechanization. During the 1880's the state regarded with satisfaction the increase in the number of small, individually-owned exploitations. As late as 1929, one could still find explicit official statements that the future prosperity of French agriculture depended on the maintenance of a large population attached to the soil. Indeed, it was not until 1960 that government policy officially admitted that a large number of small exploitations would have to disappear, and that there would have to be a consequent diminution of agricultural population. Practical means to further the realization of this revised position were not provided until 1962, with the creation of the Fund for Social Action and Amelioration of Agricultural Structures. The fund is intended to facilitate the diversion to other activities of farmers whose lands are too small in area to be feasible, and to facilitate the retirement of persons who are too old to undertake a new type of job.[9]

The glaring lack of social overhead capital in many agricultural regions in the middle of the nineteenth century was another major handicap to the transformation of agricultural structures in these areas. With the growth of industry and the mobility made possible by the introduction of the railways some regions were characterized by large-scale movements of population away from farms to the cities; in other regions, however, migration was checked by a high degree of illiteracy. During the decade of greatest migration, 1852–62, the number of male agricultural workers in the Paris Region declined by 35 per cent; in the Northeast (which here means the departments of the Meuse, Haute-Marne, and Côte-d'Or) they diminished by 32 per cent. In contrast, the corresponding values for Brittany and Limousin were, respectively, 22 per cent and 15 per cent. Similarly, between 1862 and 1892 the amount of cultivated surface in the Paris Region increased by only 2 per cent, while in the Northeast it declined by 3 per cent; on the other hand, the cultivated surface increased by 27 per cent in Brittany and by 25 per cent in Limousin. The greater exodus from agriculture in Paris and the Northeast is not to be explained by relative living standards in agricultural areas, since the average daily salary in these regions was, respectively, 1.66 and 1.56 francs, whereas the comparable values for Brittany and Limousin were only 0.84 and 1.21 francs. Moreover, differences in population pressure are also inadequate to explain out-migration in these cases, since the number of workers per hectare was considerably higher in Brittany and Limousin than in the Paris Region and the Northeast; in 1862 these values were 28.5 and 17.8 in the former regions, and only 11.1 and 8.9 in the latter. Thus, farm-to-city migration was not the result of a push from rural areas, but rather a consequence of the attraction of urbanization and industrialization.[10]

Why then was migration from agriculture greater in areas such as Paris and the Northeast, where rural life was relatively more rewarding, than in areas such as Brittany and Limousin, where rural living standards were relatively low? Geographical proximity is of course one explanation, but education seems an equally important factor. In the middle of the nineteenth century the illiteracy rate in the Paris Region was 23 per cent and in the Northeast, 11.6 per cent. In marked contrast, the corresponding values for Brittany and Limousin were 62.9 per cent and 68.3 per cent, respectively. Thus, regions with relatively poor education standards were in a sense forced back on themselves at a time when the structures of agriculture in other regions were being altered by mass out-migration.[11] In general, therefore, the central government in effect discouraged economic development in lagging agricultural regions by officially promoting a large agricultural population and by failing to provide the social overhead investment needed to give the populations of lagging regions an awareness of alternative opportunities, as well as the intellectual equipment to take advantage of them. Moreover, the regional disparities which became evident a century ago are basically those which may be observed today.

Although illiteracy has now practically disappeared, and although general education is vastly improved, professional training in agriculture has until very recently been nearly nonexistent. Even as late as 1955, 97 per cent of the French population engaged in agriculture had not received any formal professional training. "Insufficient technical knowledge of farmers is a bottleneck to regional development emphasized by agronomists. It is much more severely felt with regard to technical progress in biology and chemistry than with regard to mechanization." [12] This is well illustrated by the data shown in Table 7.1. The three categories of schools listed there represent progressively higher levels of professional training. Even though productivity, as measured by milk production per cow, has increased over time for each category as a result of greater mechanization, relative productivity at any given time is related to degree of professionally relevant education. "The productivity obtained is the result of sustained efforts concerning the selection, feeding, and hygiene of the cattle; the efficacacy of these efforts is logically a function of their technical level. The substitution of the reaper for the scythe and of the tractor for the horse absolutely does not impose such a developed technical competence." Moreover, the application of biological and chemical knowledge, which is particularly checked by lack of professional education, involves "the forms of progress most needed by regions characterized by small farms." [13]

Table 7.1

Relationship of agricultural education
and productivity in selected years

Category of schools attended by farmer	*Milk production per cow (liters)*		
	1918	*1928*	*1938*
Commune school	4.013	5.434	5.604
High School	4.769	5.971	5.828
Technical school	5.400	6.000	6.317

Source: Jean Pautard, *Les disparités régionales dans la croissance de l'agriculture française* (Paris: Gauthier-Villars, 1965), p. 143.

Land Reform
and SOC

A great deal of emphasis has been placed on land reform as a major solution for problems of lagging agricultural regions. Edward Higbee, for example, has emphasized that the smallness of French farms makes for high costs and inefficiency:

The problems of the French farmers are deep-seated, lying in the very nature of the country's agricultural system. France is a nation of small farmers. Over 21 per cent of the population still makes its living from the land, and 79 per cent of the farms are under 50 acres; 56 per cent are less than 25 acres. Despite the diminutive size, only about half the land on the average farm is cultivated; the rest is in permanent pastures and woods. It takes 2,100,000 commercial farms to feed France's 47 million people. By contrast, the 185 million Americans are fed by 2,400,000 commercial farms, averaging over 300 acres each and worked by only 6 per cent of the population.[14]

In 1961, France's 86 million acres of cultivable land were divided into 76 million cadastral lots. This means that the average farm was composed of about thirty lots, sometimes lying far apart and thus causing loss of time and difficulty in using machinery. The problem of fragmentation also is often tied to a highly uneven distribution of the farm population. The government has been trying to rectify this by means of land reparceling. It is thought that 34.6 million acres must be consolidated to create farms better suited to modern methods. Before 1941 fewer than 1 million acres had been consolidated, but from 1942 to 1961 reparceling projects covering 12.3 million acres were initiated, and 7.4 million acres of consolidation were completed.[15] By 1964, projects totaling 15.4 million acres were undertaken, with 10.7 million acres of consolidation completed. For France as a whole, the surface which remained to be reparceled in 1964 amounted to 60.8 per cent. However, there was considerable variation among the various program regions. In only four regions were consolidations over half completed. These were the Paris Region, with 12.5 per cent of the total surface to be regrouped remaining to be acted upon, Upper Normandy (38 per cent remaining), Picardy (46 per cent remaining), and Champagne (about 50 per cent remaining). At the other extreme, five regions had over 85 per cent of the surface to be regrouped still to be acted upon. These regions were Pays de la Loire, Limousin, Aquitaine, Midi-Pyrenees, and Languedoc. In general, the regions which have accomplished most with respect to reparceling are the Paris Region and those around it, whereas the task remaining is greatest in the regions of the West and Southwest.[16]

The essential point, however, is that land reform will not provide adequate solutions to problems of regional development where the fundamental difficulty is lack of investment in the quality of human effort. Indeed, there is considerable evidence that small farms do not necessarily imply noneconomic operations, if the quality of human resources is high. For example, in Table 6.2, value added per hectare (column 7) is highest by far in Nord, whose productivity in this regard is over twice the national average. The value for Nord in terms of value added per worker (column 5) is the second highest among all regions and nearly twice the national average; normally, however, Nord also ranks first in this category. During the nine-year period from 1954 to 1962, Nord ranked first in worker productivity six times.[17] Yet the average farm size in Nord is only 16.7 hectares, even less than the national average of 16.9 hectares. Only 3.8 per cent of the cultivated area is accounted for by farms of over 100 hectares, whereas the comparable national value is 11.7 per cent. Similarly, only 18.8 per cent of the cultivated area in Nord is accounted for by farms of over 50 hectares, compared to the national figure of 29.2 per cent.[18] Moreover, natural conditions in this region are not particularly favorable. Rainfall is sufficient but warmth, and more especially sunshine, are lacking. The soil is of variable quality, but originally it was not fertile and was difficult to work.[19] With regard to Nord, Livet maintains that:

> It certainly has few inherent qualities which could be easily found. To be sure, modern techniques are utilized for the most part. The number of tractors is important, borrowing and investments are above average, and fertilizers especially are widely used in abundance—the region accounts for 6.5 per cent of the total tonnage. But history and economics together affirm that here *it is, in the final analysis, the attitude of people which has determined the picture.*[20]

Livet remarks that the Flemish peasant in the Nord is less quick, less ardent, and less flexible than his counterpart in the South, but he is also more regular in his effort, more serious, more tenacious, and more severe. The high productivity of the Fleming is evident in numerous instances, but whether it be sugar beets, wheat, barley, milk, or apples, he tends to orient his activity toward the commercial market. There also is considerable concentration in the Nord of industrial cultures which furnish products of high quality and high value, for example tobacco, hops, chicory, and flax. In southern regions, on the other hand, there is a greater tendency to utilize crops on the spot; they are mostly consumed by local urban populations or processed by firms in or near the region of origin. Although this involves lower transportation costs and avoids the uncertainties of distant markets, it often tends to reduce initiative and to result in a certain sluggishness. "If it is necessary to draw from the Flemish example lessons of highly productive tenacity, it is also necessary to agree that French agriculture must have wider ambitions and must substitute for the closed future of regional markets the broader possibilities of international traffic." [21]

It must be noted, however, that even in the South one may find instances where human resourcefulness has succeeded in overcoming conditions unfavorable to agriculture. The Vaucluse is a case in point. In 1962, this highly agricultural department had 27,500 male agricultural workers on 143,000 hectares of cultivated land. This is equivalent to 19 workers per square kilometer, whereas the French average is 7.5. Although no other department had so dense an agricultural population, no other had a more moderate decline in male agricultural employment between 1954 and 1962; the diminution in the Vaucluse was 8.9 per cent while the national average was 19.1 per cent. Thus the most densely occupied land also was that which best maintained its peasant population, contrary to what might have been expected. The agriculture of the Vaucluse is "intensive, erudite, has been oriented for a long time toward supplying urban markets, and has constantly adapted to fluctuations in demand." [22] Moreover, "this living and dynamic milieu" has benefited from the creation of numerous nonagricultural activities which nevertheless have been induced by agriculture. These include food-processing plants, container manufacturing, chemical fertilizer and weed-killer factories, and a large number of commercial and transportation undertakings. Although the number of industries without apparent links to agriculture is in fact quite low in the Vaucluse, its nonagricultural employment increased by 16 per cent between 1954 and 1962; the corresponding value for all of France was 9 per cent. Since 1936 the population of the Vaucluse has increased by 23 per cent, as against a French average of 12 per cent. With the exception of one mountainous canton, all of the department's cantons have been characterized by more or less substantial population growth, including a positive balance with respect to migration. Although a plentiful water supply has been a definite asset to the Vaucluse, Gravier argues that "even in the nonirrigated rural zones of Apt and Ventoux, where population density does not exceed 25 persons per square kilometer (versus 100 to 150 in the plain), arrivals have been for the most part more numerous than departures. It is the entire Vaucluse which is now a zone of attraction by virtue of water and sun, but *especially because of the ingenuity of people."* [23]

Livet maintains that, in general, natural factors have ceased to be the primary influence in the progress of French agriculture; rather it is the human factor which is decisive. In the present situation, "it is necessary to judge a farm less by its size than by its capacity to adapt, to react, to organize—in a word, by its dynamism." [24] Thus, he concludes that

> the highest revenues per hectare are obtained from the small tenures of the Eastern Pyrenees and the Vaucluse . . . and the French champions in gross revenue are to be found, as we have seen, in the small farms of Flanders.
>
> It may be noted in passing that the farmers of Holland and Belgium, whose capacities are guaranteed by a half-century of rural success, draw sufficient resources from farms whose size is less than the average French farm of 14 hectares. [25]

The evidence from various regions that small farms and high rural population densities are not necessarily incompatible with a prosperous peasantry may, of course, be overemphasized. In particular, too great an emphasis on this phenomenon may be tied to the traditionally conservative French attitude toward agriculture in such a manner that out-migration may be discouraged. However, to argue that improvement in the quality of human resources through investment in social overhead should receive greater official attention, especially in relation to land reform programs (whose importance to many regions, for example Brittany, cannot be denied), still implies a common assumption on the part of all parties concerned, namely, that it is desirable to increase agricultural productivity. Here is one of the numerous instances in economics where attempts at improving the lot of individual units may in fact have the opposite effect for the whole; obviously the "farm problem" is a result of higher over-all productivity (and inelastic demand), and continuing improvements in productivity will only aggravate the difficulties of structural change in agriculture. Clearly, any long-run solution to these difficulties must face up to the issue of out-migration.

SOC and Out-migration from Lagging Regions

One of the principal difficulties for regional policy with regard to lagging agricultural regions is the desire for higher productivity, higher per capita incomes, and very limited out-migration. The last issue is primarily responsible for this inconsistency in general aims.

Brittany, for example, ranks sixth among the program regions in total population, but second in per cent of population employed in agriculture, eighteenth in average farm size, and seventeenth in value added per worker (see Table 6.2). Whereas in France as a whole 34 per cent of cultivated surface is in farms of less than twenty hectares, in Brittany the corresponding amount is 61 per cent.[26] The small and often scattered plots characteristic of farms in this region present an obvious need for a rational regrouping of plots. The number of hectares which still need to be reparceled has been officially estimated at 1.4 million.[27] It is clear that Brittany's population is too large in relation to existing resources (given the goal of high living standards), and that pressures for out-migration will be increased by land reform measures which inevitably will reduce the number of farms in this region. Yet official statements have made it clear that out-migration will be strenuously resisted.

The principal aim of policy proposed in the regional plan for Brittany is "to progressively reduce Breton emigration to the level of a normal outflow of demographic surplus by creating within the region new employment possibilities and by raising the average standard of living." [28] This result can be obtained, it is argued, by more effective and more intensive utilization of land and sea resources, and by a "massive injection" of industrial capital; the central government is called upon to contribute to the realization of these objectives by all the means at its disposition. The main difficulties with this approach are not hard to spot. Without probing into the meaning of a "normal outflow" of population, it is difficult to see how any substantial improvement in employment opportunities or living standards could be expected from more intensive utilization of natural resources already subject to greatly diminished returns. Moreover, the issue of the most rational utilization of capital from a national viewpoint is not raised. Brittany has not been in a position to offer the external economies available to private firms in intermediate regions, and as a consequence it has not succeeded in attracting much industry, even with the help of the decentralization incentives provided by the government. Nevertheless, nearly a decade after the publication of the program of regional action for Brittany one still finds the same themes being echoed. For example, M. Gilbert Grandval, then Minister of Labor, told an audience in Lorient in 1965 that Brittany (and especially the subregion of Lorient) was "abnormally" underequipped with respect to industry. More industry was needed, he maintained, because "it is necessary to check and even bring to a halt the emigration of Bretons." [29]

Reluctance to admit a need for out-migration from lagging agricultural regions is not confined to a few special cases such as Brittany but is often part of the general approach to regional resource allocation. The official policy until very recently attempted to preserve the maximum possible number of small farm units. The Fourth Plan, while admitting that labor mobility is necessary in an expanding and changing economy, still defined the nation's objective with respect to regional policy to be the limitation of migratory movements to a "reasonable rate" in regions characterized by net out-migration. In particular, the Plan stated that

> the public authorities wish to combat the depressing effects which too great a number of departures would have on the economy of certain regions. Their concern is to maintain in these regions an active population sufficient in number and quality to permit profitable exploitation of existing resources and to encourage modernization of structures and development of productivity.[30]

How the maintenance of a population larger than that which would obtain under "natural" conditions would encourage modernization or increase productivity is not discussed, nor is the possibility that out-migration might well increase the marginal product of labor in the regions concerned.

Although the Fifth Plan, as will be seen in Chapter 9, is more realistic in its approach to population movements, this by no means reflects unanimity of official opinion. For example, one legislative report regarding the preparation of the Fifth Plan defined the objective of regional planning to be the development of each region "in a fashion which permits its population to live as well as it would elsewhere through a better utilization of its resources."[31] It is difficult to read any real meaning into this statement since it implicitly denies any role to resource mobility; and it is obvious that with given populations and given resources living standards will certainly continue to vary from region to region, no matter how well the resources of less privileged regions are utilized.

Resistance to population movements from relatively less-developed regions also is frequently found in the writings of professional economists. Jules Milhau, for example, maintains that the natural possibilities of regions characterized by out-migration often are underestimated. He argues that scientific and technical progress undoubtedly will create wealth in areas whose potential natural-resource endowments have not yet been fully exploited. Moreover, he states that because of population growth it will eventually be necessary to put back into use agricultural land which at present is being abandoned. Therefore, "if the maintenance of a minimum population appears as a cost to the nation . . . we believe that this cost should be viewed as a reasonable expenditure by a collectivity concerned about its permanent interests."[32] Milhau's arguments, of course, are highly questionable on economic grounds. They are given in the context of a discussion of rational land use, but rational decisions concerning location of economic activity cannot be based on discoveries which may or may not be made at some undetermined date in the future. Moreover, even if demographic forces should necessitate returning to cultivation land now being abandoned because of productivity increases in agriculture, this will come about through the operations of the same market mechanism that is now creating out-migration pressures. There is no economic reason for the social costs of maintaining an unnecessary agricultural population, or at least no reason which could not also be applied to other sectors of the economy. Of course, the broader sociological implications associated with out-migration should not be ignored. Alain Prate has pointed out that as a result of migration

numerous workers are passing their lives far from their regions of origin, sometimes separated from their families for long years and living in alien areas and climates. In strictly economic terms, the growth of agglomerations which are already too large imposes heavy costs on society. . . . The objective to be attained is thus clear: as M. Marjolin has declared several times, it is industry which must, insofar as possible, be brought to the workers and not the workers to the industry. Full employment . . . should not only be sought at the national level, but also within the regional framework.[33]

However, two major qualifications may be made with respect to this position. In the first place, it is difficult to imagine how full employment in any country may be attained without significant out-migration from lagging regions. In other words, checking out-migration and attempting to achieve full employment in lagging regions with labor surpluses involve mutually inconsistent ends. A second, related qualification concerns the types of regions involved in Prate's comments. He implicitly assumes that there are only two kinds of regions, those represented by congested agglomerations and those in a state of relative stagnation. This enables him to assume that the social costs of bringing industry to poorer regions would be less than the social costs involved in the migration of workers and the increase in congestion of large agglomerations. This might well be true if there were only two basic types of regions. However, if it is feasible to distinguish congested, intermediate, and lagging regions, as was done in Chapter 1, then the issue of the social costs of increasing urban congestion is not a necessary objection to out-migration from lagging regions, since population movement may be channeled to intermediate regions.

In any event, the social costs of migration inevitably are related to the preferences of the individuals concerned. In the French case, it already has been noted that given a choice of region in which to live and comparable resources, the areas least attractive in terms of personal preferences are those that are highly urbanized and industrialized, for example the Paris Region, Flanders, the Artois, and the Lyon region (see Chapter 2). In contrast, lagging regions of the West and Southwest such as Brittany, Lower Normandy, Languedoc, Pays de la Loire, and Auvergne are considered attractive. In each of these cases, the proportion of the total French population living in the region is equal to or less than the proportion preferring to live there. Since these are areas of high out-migration, it therefore is probable that there are numerous persons who would like to return to their native regions.[34] This also is indicated by another survey which showed that

86 per cent of provincial migrants living in Paris strongly backed the government's decentralization measures.[35] In a still more recent survey made for the Délégation à l'aménagement du territoire et à l'action régionale by the French Institute of Public Opinion, the following question was posed: According to you, should most emphasis be placed on creating factories in areas where there is a population surplus, or on facilitating the movement of surplus population and its reception in industrial centers?

Seventy-one per cent of the respondents (excluding inhabitants of the Paris Region, which was not included in the sample) favored the former alternative, while only 15 per cent favored the movement of people; 14 per cent were undecided. Respondents were also asked which of these two possible solutions appeared to them the easiest to realize. In this case, 51 per cent of the sample indicated the movement of factories to areas of surplus population, 25 per cent indicated population migration, and 23 per cent expressed no opinion.[36] In general, emphasis on mobility of nonhuman resources is much preferred to emphasis on population mobility, though many persons favoring the former alternative obviously do not believe that it is the most easily accomplished, since there is a drop of twenty percentage points when the question is posed in these terms. Nevertheless, the relative feasibility of enterprise transfers or creations in regions with surplus populations is probably overestimated by the public in general. It already has been demonstrated that French migration patterns can be explained as a result of movements within a basically free market from largely agricultural regions to regions with higher living standards and greater economic opportunity. On the other hand, despite government intervention on behalf of industrial development in lagging agricultural regions, industry continues to be attracted for the most part to regions already well developed. Thus, in fact, migration would seem to be the easiest alternative to realize.

It is understandable that a resident of Limousin or Auvergne would prefer to work at a new factory in his own town rather than leave to seek employment in another region. However, this should not obscure the fact that if the factory in Limousin or Auvergne could produce more efficiently elsewhere, there would be a genuine, if less obvious, social cost from the viewpoint of the nation as a whole. But then, if government officials and even some economists fail to take account of foregone alternatives, it should not be surprising that this should also be the case for the average citizen.

It has been argued that investment in economic overhead capital should tend to be concentrated in intermediate regions where it can be combined with other factors potentially favorable to industrial location, and that lagging regions should benefit from relatively high investment in social overhead capital. Investment in EOC alone cannot be expected to attract significant private investment from other areas and thus halt out-migration. The relationship between social overhead and out-migration, however, is more complicated.

One possibility is that social overhead, particularly in the form of education, will train a sufficient number of qualified local workers to attract certain types of light industry and thereby put a brake on out-migration. Thus, the Economic and Social Council has suggested that light industries might be planted in rural zones of France, as has been done in Germany and Switzerland. But it finds that while such decentralization has become technically feasible, given the relatively low equipment cost of these enterprises, it is likely that "this interesting initiative will immediately run into the impossibility of engaging qualified local personnel. Such a situation bears witness to the necessity of an effort in the matter of technical education in the underdeveloped regions." [37] However, there is still the problem of knowing how to orient technical training. For example, the regional plan for Poitou-Charentes emphasizes the need for more social and cultural investment and professional training to attract industry, but points out the difficulty in organizing professional training before it is known precisely what types of firms will be established.[38]

In general, then, SOC investment in lagging regions will result in two contrary tendencies, the one involving the attraction of firms seeking qualified labor and the other involving out-migration of persons with skills and training which can best be put to use in more highly industrialized regions. The extent of out-migration therefore will depend on the extent to which industry is in fact attracted and the time lag involved in this process, and on the extent to which persons prefer to live in their own region despite economic disadvantages. There is also the possibility that if growth is initiated, numerous persons who left the region may return, bringing with them skills acquired in more advanced regions. Faucheux points out that many young people would be quite willing to leave Paris for provincial regions if they could find employment there, or if facilities were available to give them the necessary skills to work in specific provincial centers.[39]

In any event, SOC investment in lagging regions will not necessarily check out-migration in the short run, and it may possibly even encourage it. Nevertheless, rational public investment policy should not be confused with attempts to stabilize regional populations, at least insofar as economic policy aims at increasing welfare from a national point of view. However, as has been argued, if problems of lagging regions are not amenable to rapid solutions in the short run, initial emphasis on SOC investment still offers the most feasible policy in the long run. This proposition must now be examined with specific reference to France's program regions and their needs within the context of national planning.

Regional Investment Priorities:
Views at the Regional Level

In the preparative stages of the Fifth Plan, the regional *préfets* and the Regional Economic Development Commissions of the twenty program regions (excluding the Paris Region) were asked to specify the priorities which should be given to various types of public investment in their respective regions. Table 7.2 attempts to classify the orders of priority given to various undertakings in the program regions. The values shown for each region are those determined by the Section on Regional Economies of the Economic and Social Council and are based on the reports of the relevant *préfets* and commissions. Before considering the significance of these data, however, it is necessary to qualify them.

Comparing regional priorities is frequently difficult because the very notion of priority is not always clear. In some cases it may refer to an increase in physical volume relative to some base period, and in others it may refer to a greater financial effort. In addition, the priorities stated for any given region may or may not take into account existing projects which benefit a number of regions. For example, the development of river basins in the Southwest has an important influence on the economies of Aquitaine, Midi-Pyrenees, and Languedoc. In any case, the numerical classifications shown in Table 7.2 should not be taken for exact indicators of relative priorities because of the

Table 7.2

Classification of regional public investment priorities
on the basis of reports of regional *préfets*
and Regional Economic Development Commissions

Projects

Region	Highways	Other Transportation	Telecommunications	Housing	Urban equipment	Street maintenance	School & university equipment	Scientific research	Accelerated professional training	Cultural equipment	Sports equipment	Agricultural & rural equipment	Sanitary & social equipment
ace	1A	1	1B	5	3	3A	2	—	2A	2B	6	4	7
uitaine	2	2A	2B	3	3A	3B	1	1A	1B	1C	1D	4	5
vergne	1	—	1A	—	3	3A	5	—	4	—	—	2	—
ttany	2	—	2A	1	2B	—	3	—	3A	—	—	2C	1A
rgundy	4(1)	(1A)	5	1	2	2A	3	—	9	6	4	8	7
ıter	3	—	4	1	1A	2	1B	—	5	2B	2A	2D	2C
ampagne	4	4A	4B	1	1A	4C	2	—	3A	2A	3	3C	3B
ınche-Comté	7	7A	—	1	2(3)	1A	3(2)	—	4	2A	2B	6	5
ıguedoc	1A	3B	3C	2A	1D	3A	2B	1C	1B	2C	3	1	2
ıousin	2	2A	5	1	1A	3A	4A	—	4	—	7	3	6
raine	2(1)	2A (1A)	2B	3	3A(2)	—	1	—	1A	—	—	4	4A
li-Pyrenees	3	4	5	—	2	3A	—	—	—	—	—	1	—
rd	(1)	(1C)	(5)	(4)	(1A)	(1B)	(3)	(3A)	(2)	—	—	(5A)	(2B)
ver Normandy	1	—	1A	2	2A	2B	3A	—	3	3B	—	4	—
per Normandy	3(1)	(1A)	3A	1(4)	4	—	2	2A	—	(3A)	2B	5	—
s de la Loire	3(4)	(4C)	3A (4B)	2A	2	—	1	1A	1B	—	6(3)	4	5
ardy	3(5)	(5A)	3B	2	2A(3)	3A	1	—	—	—	—	4	—
tou-Charentes	2(5)	2A	6(5A)	1B (1A)	(1A) 1	—	4A(2)	—	3	—	5	1(2A)	4(6B)
vence	1	11	3	4	2	2A	5	—	6	10	9	7	8
one-Alps	1	—	1C	2	1A	1B	2A	—	2C	2E	2D	2B	—

Source: Avis et rapports, Ve Plan, p. 54.

Note: The numbers indicate the priorities of undertakings or groups of undertakings. For a given ıup of undertakings, each constituent project is arranged in hierarchic order by means of a letter B, C, D). The values in parentheses give the opinion of the Regional Economic Development Comısion if it differs from that of the *préfet*. In the case of Nord, the *préfet* stated no priorities.

delicate procedure involved in elaborating these divisions; in particular, ranking does not in itself express the magnitude of differences in the need for various types of investment.

It also should be noted that conformity of opinion between the *préfets* and the Regional Economic Development Commissions in most regions is a result of varying circumstances. In some cases it represents a temporary lack of means for complete studies by the newly created commissions. In most cases, however, the commissions have worked closely with the *préfet* and other public officials, as well as with the private Regional Expansion Committees. Thus, the reports of the *préfets* were established for the most part in close consultation with a wide range of interested local parties.[40]

Before we consider the significance of the rankings shown in Table 7.2 it should be pointed out that certain categories do not clearly fall under either SOC or EOC, as defined in Chapter 1. Such is the case for "urban equipment" and "agricultural and rural equipment." Housing is clearly in the SOC category but may be distinguished from social, educational, and cultural activities. With these exceptions, then, it may be said that the first six columns of Table 7.2 show EOC categories, while the last seven show SOC.

It is not surprising that in the two most rapidly growing regions, Rhone-Alps and Provence, EOC activities have higher priority than SOC activities. I have argued elsewhere that one of the important distinctions between SOC and EOC is that consumers generally have a more immediate demand for EOC and they want it in close proximity to their places of work or residence. Establishment of SOC facilities is more readily postponed, and SOC demand can be more easily satisfied in other areas. For example, roads and utility services generally are wanted immediately and on the spot, whereas schools and health and recreation facilities tend to be more readily postponed or sought out in other areas. This means that where population is growing, demand for EOC will be greater than for SOC, and governments will tend to provide EOC before SOC.[41] It also is pertinent to note that the rapidly growing regions of Alsace, Nord, and Upper Normandy also tend to put top priority on EOC investment. Indeed, of the seven most rapidly growing regions, in only two, Franche-Comté and Lorraine, do the *préfets'* reports not clearly favor EOC investment on balance. Moreover, even in these two regions it cannot be said that priority is given to SOC. In the case of Franche-Comté the top priority is given to an EOC item, while in the case of Lorraine the report of the Regional Economic Development Commission puts emphasis on EOC. The high priorities given to accelerated professional training in Lorraine and Nord reflect that, despite relatively rapid population growth, both regions need substantial industrial conversion and worker retraining.

The regions of the West and Southwest vary considerably in their respective priority rankings. Aquitaine, Languedoc, and Pays de la Loire tend to emphasize SOC undertakings; Auvergne, Limousin, and Lower Normandy tend to emphasize those of an EOC nature; Brittany, Center, Midi-Pyrenees and Poitou-Charentes do not particularly emphasize one or the other.

Thus, for all regions taken together there is somewhat more emphasis on EOC projects than on SOC projects. However, the greatest relative emphasis on EOC tends to be found in the more developed and faster-growing regions, whereas the greatest relative need for SOC tends to be found in the lagging regions of the West and Southwest. The reports of Aquitaine and Pays de la Loire consider education to be " 'the priority of priorities,' especially for professional training and higher technical education. Numerous reports insist on the training of the agricultural labor force and, in particular, feminine workers (Languedoc, Center, Lower Normandy, Auvergne)." [42]

To what extent are these views consistent with those of the populations of the respective program regions? Considerable information in this regard is provided by recent survey data.

Regional Investment Priorities: Public Opinion

French public opinion data indicate that it is not possible to distinguish any significant difference between SOC-EOC priorities in lagging regions, on the one hand, or intermediate regions, on the other. However, it is probable that here again public opinion may not be as accurate a reflection of real differences in regional needs as the findings of scholars or the officials and local representatives consulted in the preparation of the Fifth Plan. Evidence in this regard is apparent within the context of the survey in question.

In addition to being asked to name the needs of their respective regions which they felt to be most pronounced, the respondents were asked to state the advantages their regions enjoyed with respect to future economic development. The most frequent responses, in order of importance, were the value of cultivable land and of forests (60 per cent of the adult male respondents), beauty of the countryside and touristic resources (52 per cent), quality of workers in agriculture (38 per cent), abundance of young persons (37 per cent), quality of industrial workers (31 per cent), mineral and energy resources (26 per cent), quality of schools and universities (21 per cent), industrial potential and reputation (21 per cent), value of transportation means (19 per cent), existence of large, prosperous cities (18 per cent), and richness of the region in capital (14 per cent).[43] Generally speaking, the provincial Frenchman has considerable faith in the quality and possibilities of the agricultural base of the country. The number of responses in favor of the quality of the land also shows that it is not farmers alone who share this confidence. "In a word, for the French of the provinces as a whole, France is, above all, a bountiful land peopled by men of quality." [44] This attitude is particularly noteworthy in view of responses to the following question: In general, what appears to you to be the greatest obstacle to the development of your region, excluding, of course, things such as altitude, terrain, and other factors about which nothing can be done? The most frequent responses were lack of capital (15 per cent), insufficient industrial potential (15 per cent), agricultural crisis (14 per cent), and incompetence or unconcern on the part of public authorities (14 per cent).[45] In other words, while there is considerable confidence in the nation's agricultural resources, it is also true that agricultural crisis is listed as a principal obstacle to regional development. As has been pointed out, the effects of high agricultural productivity on marginal producers are probably not thoroughly understood by a large segment of the population.[46] Thus, in frustration it is natural to blame public authorities for inherent economic difficulties. It is also important to note the number of nonresponses to the question concerning obstacles to development. On average, three employed men out of ten did not believe that there were any major impediments to regional growth, while in certain regions this figure was four out of ten. As the survey commentary points out, the belief that there are no important barriers to increasing prosperity can only serve as a source of political discontent when problems of growth do appear.[47]

It is evident, at least in the case of France, that public opinion as such would not be an adequate guide in selecting regional investment priorities. Moreover, it also is doubtful whether public opinion concerning goals can be effectively utilized in planning public investment priorities, even where the latter are not based on public opinion but on more or less expert analyses and findings. The chief problem here is that people generally favor increasing agricultural productivity but oppose out-migration. This contradiction could be resolved if lagging regions could attract sufficient industry, but, as we have seen, movement of firms to lagging regions generally has not been pronounced in the past, even with government incentives; moreover, there is no compelling reason to believe that this situation will be changed in the immediate future, at least in the absence of artificial and noneconomic, hothouse, industrial development, an unlikely prospect within the French framework.

French public opinion indicates that the population as a whole is especially sensitive to the need for more SOC facilities, though in broadly regional terms there is no significant variation in the regional EOC-SOC composition of total public investment needs. It is interesting to note, however, that those lagging regions which tend to emphasize the relative importance of EOC requirements put particular emphasis on agricultural and highway needs. But amelioration of agricultural needs would probably result in a greater labor surplus, while improvements in highways would provide better means for out-migration.

In summation, then, the analyses and judgments of scholars and specialists clearly indicate that the problems of lagging regions are closely bound to lack of benefits accruing from SOC investment. Thus, it may be said that the propositions advanced in Chapter 1 concerning SOC investment in lagging regions generally were confirmed by these students of French experience. The degree of conformity of opinion with the SOC aspects of the relevant model increases as one moves from the often contradictory views of the public, to the views of regional authorities and economic leaders, to the findings of specialists and scholars. Finally, if a good case can be made for expansion of SOC in lagging regions, it nevertheless is also useful to examine the difficulties involved in attempting to induce growth in lagging areas through EOC investment. The case of Lacq is particularly instructive in this regard.

Difficulties of Inducing Growth
Through EOC: The Case of Lacq

Problems of creating economic growth in a lagging region through EOC investment are well illustrated by the case of Lacq, in the Lower Pyrenees of Southwestern France. Exploitation of a large natural gas find at Lacq was begun in April 1957 with a daily production of 1 million cubic meters. Output subsequently was regularly increased until it reached a rate of 20 million cubic meters in 1961. In all, thirteen wells have been drilled, with an average depth of over 4,000 meters. The network which transports the crude gas from the wells to the treatment plant is entirely underground. The plant itself occupies 2,200 hectares and is built above the gas layer. It is the only plant of its type in Europe and its desulfurization installations are the most important in the world. In the Southwest, the gas is transported via two interconnected networks of pipelines, the one built originally for an exploitation at St. Marcet and the other constructed especially for Lacq. For the rest of France, a pipeline network of more than 2,000 kilometers has been constructed, starting at Lussagnet.[48] The industrial complex of Lacq now includes a thermal electric center of the Electricité de France (three groups of 125,000 kw.), which in turn furnishes power to the aluminum factory at Noguères, the most important in Europe. In addition, plants have been constructed for the manufacture of acetylene, ammonia, methanol, polyethylene, and nitrate fertilizers.[49]

The distribution of the gas of Lacq, as of 1961, was as follows: enterprises of the Lacq complex utilized 16.8 per cent; other chemical industries, 1.2 per cent; public distribution, 23.5 per cent; industry, for energy, 25.5 per cent; thermal electric stations, 31.5 per cent; carburetant, 1.5 per cent. In other words, 18 per cent (represented by the first two categories) has been used as primary input, and 82 per cent as a source of energy.[50]

The regional distribution of the gas has been as follows: Southwest, 38 per cent; Paris Region, 28 per cent; Center-East, 23 per cent; and West and Center-West, 11 per cent. In the Paris Region, the gas is used for domestic consumption only.[51]

At the outset there was great hope in the Southwest that the discovery at Lacq would provide the means to induce industrialization of the region. Indeed, as Aydalot points out, "the complex of Lacq

responds perfectly well to the definition that F. Perroux has given of
propulsive industries (assymetric effects, rate of growth superior to the
national average)." [52] Even the program region of Poitou-Charentes,
some several hundred kilometers away from Lacq, stated in its regional plan of 1957 that it was in large part basing its future industrialization prospects on Lacq gas. It maintained that "the energy
handicap of the Center-West will be eliminated by bringing new resources into this region: the natural gas from the Pyrenees and the
electricity from stations operating on the basis of this energy source." [53]
A British study of regional development in Europe, published as
recently as 1962, stressed not only the opportunities presented by the
Lacq find, but also treated its regional significance as a development
pole as a virtually accomplished fact. Noting that Brittany's industrial
development has been disappointing because investment there has
tended to be scattered among a large number of small projects, it
contrasts it with "a remarkable development of industry in south-west
France around the natural gas field at Lacq and the nearby oil fields
at Parentis. The production of a plentiful and cheap source of power
has quickened the whole tempo of activity in the region. . . ." [54] Elsewhere the study states that "the development of natural gas has
already revolutionized the economy of parts of south-west France." [55]

In fact, however, the effects of the Lacq complex on regional employment have been quite modest, contrary to original hopes and
despite the creation of some induced industries. The induced expansion has been limited to one valley near Pau and its immediate
surroundings. In all, this area comprises only seven cantons and 1,080
square kilometers. The population of the area increased from 111,000
to 145,000 inhabitants between 1954 and 1962, largely because of net
immigration of 29,000 persons. Thus the Lacq complex is in essence
a local phenomenon, which has done little to modify the over-all
economic situation of the Southwest.[56] In this regard, Raymond
Guglielmo has remarked,

> It remains to be seen if the indicative planning of liberal econ-
> omies is capable of resolving the problem of the industrialization
> of depressed rural regions. The "Cassa di Mezzogiorno" has not
> succeeded in creating the basis for regional industrial develop-
> ment in southern Italy. Indeed, the only new industries which
> have located in these regions are extractive industries or highly

automated basic industries (petroleum refineries, chemical plants) which employ few persons and are scarcely capable of producing the multiplier effect which people sometimes expect, as is illustrated by the example of Lacq, whose complex remains isolated in the countryside.[57]

The failure of the Lacq complex to induce more widespread regional growth has frequently been blamed on government policy. Coront-Ducluzeau argues that by not utilizing all or most of the gas in the Southwest, and instead distributing it to numerous regions, a major chance was lost to create a development pole which would have had a positive influence on the whole Southwest.[58] Although the Paris Region has received slightly over one quarter of the gas, but none for industrial uses, Professor Lajugie complained that while the gas should have served as the basis for the development of the Southwest, it was not used for this purpose because public policy "led it as quickly as possible to the gates of Paris. To bring the gas of Lacq to Paris is to bring the water to the mill. It is to favor the overconcentration of the Paris Region and goes counter to regional development policy. . . . I believe it is the perfect example of a lost opportunity." [59] Similarly, Leroy finds that "the gas of Lacq, which, it had been hoped, would animate a region without industry, is going to be dispersed over a large part of the nation. . . . Its rapid exhaustion (one anticipates its intensive exploitation over thirty years) will not correspond to a lasting enrichment of the region." [60] Such attacks on government policy could be expanded at length, and on the surface they seem quite justified. However, the problem demands closer consideration.

The Lower Pyrenees, or more generally, the Southwest, has a number of factors favorable to its economic development. These include the regeneration of the forests of the Landes, the introduction of hybrid corn, irrigation in Languedoc, potentially favorable tourist attractions, and the aircraft and space industry centered in Toulouse.[61] The infrastructure is that of a developed region; there are two important ports (Bayonne and Bordeaux), adequate rail and highway facilities, and at least a minimum necessary level of air service. Moreover, the tertiary sector is quite important, owing to tourism, the commercial activity of Toulouse and Bordeaux, and the influential banks and navigation companies of Bordeaux. The Southwest also possesses two good universities, one at Bordeaux, the other at Toulouse.

Nevertheless, the Southwest has a number of handicaps, many of them deriving either from the area's eccentric geographic position or from deficiencies with respect to certain social variables amenable to influence by increased SOC investment. The region's principal industries (hats, footwear) are of the traditional variety. They generally are quite vulnerable, with old equipment, rigid prices, and rates of profit insufficient to allow for investment in more modern facilities. Agriculture, which provides a large proportion of regional income, is backward in relation to the rest of France. The decline of the wood and vineyard sectors, which created considerable prosperity even up to the 1930's, has been particularly felt, especially since they have not been replaced by more modern activities. There are few contacts with Spain even though it is relatively close, and the comparative isolation of the Southwest from the rest of France is disadvantageous to heavy industry.[62] Finally, "individual dynamism, which could have mitigated certain drawbacks and fostered indispensable conversions, is absent. It is noteworthy in this regard that the universities of Bordeaux and especially of Toulouse prepare many jurists and literary students, but relatively few engineers." [63]

Turning more specifically to the development opportunities presented by Lacq, it is first necessary to consider to what extent expansion might have been induced in other sectors if public authorities had decided to limit utilization of Lacq's gas to the Southwest. In the first place, the very nature of such an operation would have practically excluded any possibility for vertically inducing regional industrialization, since it would have required relatively little intermediate consumption. Prospects for horizontally inducing other activities would seem more promising. Natural gas has two possible industrial uses, one as a source of energy and the other as primary input in the chemical industry. As a source of energy, the possibilities for inducing industrialization must take account of two basic considerations: the importance of energy costs in the value of the outputs of various industries, and the extent to which these industries are growing. The importance of energy consumption has been estimated for various sectors of French industry on the basis of interindustry relations in 1956. The sectors with relatively high purchases of energy as a proportion of the value of the final product (at market prices) were aluminum (16.3 per cent), electricity (15.3 per cent), steel products

(14.7 per cent), mineral chemical products (11.6 per cent), glass (10.0 per cent), construction material (9.7 per cent), organic chemical products (9.3 per cent), and synthetic fibers (6.4 per cent).[64] However, looking at the other side of the coin, if these estimates give some indication of the relative extent to which leading energy-consuming industries might be attracted to a site such as Lacq, it must also be recognized that even for these sectors nonenergy expenditures, which could well lead to localization in other areas because of other criteria, account for between 84 and 93 per cent of total outlays. As Aydalot points out, distance from primary materials, narrowness of the market, labor-force characteristics, the nature of the industry, and the weight of the product are all factors capable of posing obstacles to location at the source of energy.[65] Even in instances where gas is used as a primary input by other industries, for example the chemical industry, laboratory facilities frequently pose a problem to locating at the source of the gas. For example, the nationalized Aquitaine Petroleum company, which exploits the Lacq gas, found that because it was difficult to communicate with Paris, a technical library costing 500,000 new francs had to be created at Lacq. Even so, a documentation center had to be maintained at Paris because of gaps in the Lacq library. In addition, it was necessary to establish a complete inventory of basic chemical products at Lacq in order to avoid breaks in the execution of experimental programs while waiting on orders placed in Paris. In the face of so many inconveniences and precautions, "it could be imprudent to create important laboratories far from major intellectual and economic centers." [66]

The chemical industry in the Lacq complex is part of a rapidly growing sector, and as a result it is potentially capable of inducing further industrialization through technical polarization. The Lacq gas can be treated to produce butane, propane, sulfur, and other products, which in turn could be used to produce synthetic rubber, synthetic fibers, glues, varnishes, plastics, glass, and numerous other items. The principal problem now is whether the Lacq complex will continue merely to produce, for example, a variety of acids, or whether horizontally induced production of fibers and even cloth will also become significant. Here again, regional savings and regional initiatives could play a big part. Antoine de Tavernost remarks, "It is all the more regrettable to find an insufficiency of investment in the Southwest since it is a region where important capital exists." [67]

Nevertheless, despite the potential advantages which Lacq represents for the Southwest, it is necessary to view government policy in this regard from a national perspective. When the decisions concerning the rate of utilization of the gas of Lacq were taken, France's energy deficit was considerable and represented a heavy charge on the balance of payments. Thus, it was decided to amortize the find rapidly, over a short, thirty-year period. This in itself would have been sufficient to deprive the Southwest of a monopoly on the gas; it accounted for only 2 per cent of France's energy consumption and could not possibly have absorbed the entire output in the given time period. Of course, it might have been assumed that the structure of industry would evolve over time owing to induced investment, thus permitting eventual utilization of all the gas within the region. However, given the considerable uncertainties involved, it probably was correct to avoid the risks this course of action would have entailed.

In any event, the distribution of the gas of Lacq also had to be decided on the basis of comparative costs. Transport costs vary according to the power of delivery and the rate of utilization. Therefore, a large user located at a distance of 600 kilometers would not have to pay a higher transport charge than a small user in the Southwest located at 150 kilometers from the source.[68] In sum, then, although the government accorded some small price rebate advantages to firms in the Southwest, it was apparent that

> Under these conditions the Southwest could only expect a substantial price advantage from a comprehensive policy of the public authorities. The latter, however, had put the national interest before that of the Southwest in deciding the rate of utilization of the gas. In the area of pricing the national interest once more found itself opposed to the regional interest: in the perspective of France's entry into the Common Market, the concern to lower industrial energy costs became an imperative tending to extend to all of France the price advantages which would have benefited the Southwest. . . .[69]

Finally, Aydalot has found that in many respects the establishment of the Lacq complex in the Lower Pyrenees bears comparison with the dualist economies often characterizing underdeveloped nations in which large petroleum or other firms have located. In each situation the dominant firm or group of firms behaves largely as a monopolist, exploiting local resources as quickly as possible to amortize initial investments, and acting independently of the needs of the area where it operates. The firm's financing is assured in the developed country (region) where it has its headquarters (Paris). The firm's balance of payments is highly positive; profits and depreciation allowances are sent to Paris, and the firm has a propensity to invest outside the region, in favor of the financial center of the developed country (Paris). Contacts with the underdeveloped economy (the Lower Pyrenees) are rare and the total wage bill is relatively low. A large part of the personnel come from the developed country (over half the labor is from outside the Southwest). The personnel who have come from outside the country do not live in the towns of the local population, but in a city constructed especially for them (Moureux, which was built for incoming Lacq employees and which has little contact with the surrounding culture). Indeed, in addition to these similarities the less developed region may be at a greater disadvantage than the less developed country in at least one respect: it does not have the ability to tax the large firm.[70]

Of course, this negative picture overemphasizes the similarities. Aydalot holds out the possibility that in the long run it will be easier for a propulsive firm to integrate its activities with those of a lagging region in a developed country, and thereby constitute a genuine development pole, than would be possible in an underdeveloped country, where the dualist economy is likely to persist for a long time. In either case, however, the transition to a spatially integrated development pole "resides essentially in the capacity for response of structures" [71] in the societies concerned. This in turn depends on the quality of human effort, both physical and mental, and on the degree of motivation to behave in an economically rational manner, both of which are more open to influence through investment in SOC than investment in EOC.

The case of Lacq well illustrates the difficulties involved in trying to induce self-sustained growth in a lagging region through EOC, even when the government is necessarily compelled to locate the EOC facility in such a region. Indeed, considerations of rational resource allocation from a national point of view have led the government to direct most of the EOC benefit stream to other regions. Moreover, one of the principal barriers to the Lacq complex becoming a development pole for its region has been the more or less traditional attitude of the indigenous population. Thus, while the advantages more EOC brings to a lagging region are undeniable, their effectiveness also depends on the degree to which SOC investment has developed the region's human resources.

8

Public Investment
in Intermediate Regions:
The Need for
Economic Overhead Capital

In Chapter 1 it was argued that EOC investment can make its greatest contribution to the national economy in intermediate regions, that is, in regions which are not congested but which offer a large number of actual or potential external economies to private firms. The proposed creation of a major North Sea-Mediterranean development axis in eastern France, centered on the Rhone-Alps program region represents this sort of advantageous EOC investment. However, although the East best shows the conditions, needs, and opportunities which are associated with an expanding intermediate region, it also is necessary to consider the case of the Nord, an intermediate region characterized by relative stagnation in its dominant sectors and sharing some of the problems confronting lagging regions. These two situations are examined here in turn.

Eastern France
and the Rhine-Rhone Axis

With the advent of the Common Market, considerable interest has been aroused in France over the possibilities for creating a major central European development zone by providing an unbroken waterway from Marseille to Rotterdam. Although certain variations have been proposed, the basic axis would follow the Rhone north from Marseille, join the Saône at Lyon, and then proceed by a complex system of canals to the Moselle Valley, which in turn would provide the final link with the Rhine and the North Sea.

A number of French projects have already contributed to the economic development of portions of this potential axis. The first was the establishment, in 1932, of the Compagnie nationale du Rhone (CNR) for the purposes of constructing hydroelectric facilities, improving navigation conditions, and extending irrigation projects in the Rhone Valley. The CNR was organized as a branch of the French National Railway under the tutelage of the Ministry of Public Works and Transportation, but from the outset certain departments, communes, and chambers of commerce and agriculture have been allowed to hold shares.[1]

In no other Mediterranean country is there a river with the abundance of water found in the Rhone; nor is there any river which penetrates so far into the interior of the continent. Nevertheless, its hydrography poses numerous difficulties. In particular, floods tend to form shoals, the river bed slopes sharply toward the sea, currents are rapid, and silt accumulates in the delta. Thus, the efficacy of linking the Lower Rhone to Marseille by canal has real value only insofar as the Rhone can be made navigable for larger vessels as far as Lyon. The principal difficulty in linking Marseille and Lyon by water has been presented by the section between Lyon and Arles. The CNR has undertaken a number of multipurpose river development projects in this area, including those at Génissiat, Donzère-Mondragon, and Montélimar. Up to the present, the hydroelectric aspects of river development have been emphasized. Once fully equipped, the installations of the CNR will provide 7.5 billion kilowatt hours of the potential 15 billion which the Rhone could furnish. Nevertheless, navigation and irrigation prospects for the valley have also been considerably enhanced. Types of agricultural products and methods of cultivation will be altered as a result of irrigation to the benefit of the region's farmers. Yet despite these evidences of progress, the work of the CNR could be considerably enhanced if more funds were placed at its disposal.[2] As the company's director, M. Tournier has pointed out,

> The scantiness of present financial means only permits the Rhone to be developed at a very modest rate. If we could devote to these undertakings not, as now, some twenty billion [old] francs per year, but five times more, we would no doubt see the realization of what for the moment is only a hope, that is to say, the creation along the developed Rhone of industries capable of giving to its traffic the importance of which the founders of the CNR dreamed, and we could envisage its link-up with the Rhine as a close reality.[3]

Another important EOC project on the Lower Rhone was undertaken in 1955 by the Lower Rhone-Languedoc Development Company, under the leadership of Philippe Lamour. This program aims at irrigating 617,500 acres in the departments of Hérault, Aude, and Gard over a fifteen-year period. Actual work was begun in 1957 and is expected to eventually benefit 600,000 persons. The main canal runs from the Rhone just above Arles to the Aude River, 150 miles away. The construction of secondary underground canals and sprinkler irrigation systems permits 1,000 gallons of water to produce the same results as 5,000 gallons under the old gravity irrigation system. The use of chemical fertilizers and scientific breeding along with irrigation is expected to eliminate the chief weather problems and stabilize production conditions. In addition, the project includes market organization, renovation of rural housing, technical assistance to farmers, and agricultural engineering surveys. The latter are designed to establish best soil use and to aid in reparceling of land under the best conditions. A voluntary conversion project envisages a changeover of 420,000 acres of chronically overproduced vineyards. A canning factory also has been set up on the spot with the aid of French and American capital, the latter from Libby Foods.[4]

Meanwhile, work has been pushed forward on the northern sector of the potential Rhine-Rhone axis. After six years of construction and an investment of nearly one billion new francs, the Moselle River Waterway was inaugurated in 1964. This project widened the Moselle and provided locks which made the river navigable for large barges, thus giving Lorraine's steel mills easy access to the coal of the Ruhr

Valley. The importance attributed to this undertaking by France is indicated by the fact that although nine tenths of the channel flows through German territory, France paid two thirds of the total cost and, incidentally, renounced all claims to the Saar.

Although these various projects are important in their own right, they are, even in their ensemble, still far from constituting the kind of European-scale enterprise advocated by proponents of the Rhine-Rhone axis. The arguments which have been presented by this group are numerous.

Trintignac, for example, maintains that such an axis would result not only in drawing through France traffic which would otherwise circulate outside the country, but would attract substantial industry. The waterway "would play the role of a veritable economic stimulant, multiplying employment and business revenues, attracting new industries, favoring in a general manner industrial deconcentration." [5]

Similarly, Boudeville finds that a Moselle-Saône-Rhone axis should be developed across twenty-three departments of seven program regions. This would have the advantage of creating regional units of a dimension more in harmony with the nine regions envisaged by the European Economic Community (or the eight proposed by Beaud). Boudeville [6] and Lamour [7] both see the Rhone as a link between industrial Europe and overseas countries.

In this context the central position ascribed to Lyon has been particularly noteworthy. The regional plan for Rhone-Alps defines the principal objective of the region as the development around Lyon of an economic complex sufficient to offset the attractive force of Paris. Lyon merits this role, it is maintained, by virtue of "its industrial, commercial, and financial power, its long intellectual tradition, and its site as a crossroads in the middle of a well-articulated and harmoniously diversified region, with scattered, active secondary nuclei." [8] With the development of the Rhine-Rhone project, Lyon would be at the intersection "of this great North-South Eurafrican axis and the East-West transversals which lead from the Atlantic ports toward Turin, Geneva, and Milan," and would thus "occupy a geographic position in the Common Market superior to that of Paris." [9] Of course, it might be expected that the regional plan prepared by Rhone-Alps would emphasize the importance of Lyon, but more objective evidence in this regard is not lacking.

Lyon is, after Paris, the principal regional center of France. The Lyon agglomeration included 887,640 inhabitants in 1962, an increase of 18.5 per cent over 1954. But its influence extends beyond the Rhone department to all eight departments of the Rhone-Alps program region, whose dynamism was indicated in Chapter 6, and even to portions of the departments of Haute-Loire and Saône-et-Loire.[10] The case for Lyon's future is summarized by Gravier in the following terms:

> Lyon, supported by Grenoble and Saint-Etienne, is the only metropolis which can, in the medium run, efficiently balance Paris in most domains. Commanding a great central European axis, dominating a region of over four million inhabitants, well placed to extend its influence over all the Southeast part of France, this urban trinity already groups 13 per cent of the country's science students (against 28 per cent in Paris) and trains 16 per cent of the engineers. Grenoble, whose attractiveness to managers is well known, is the only provincial center where one has been able to locate an Institute of Scientific and Technical Nuclear Studies. The "strategy" of *aménagement du territoire* should thus direct a priority effort toward the structural improvement and qualitative equipment of the Rhone and Alpine metropolis, so that it can become the "French Milan," that is to say, a pole of international influence.[11]

Nevertheless, it must be emphasized that whether or not attention is concentrated on development in terms of Lyon or the Rhone-Alps region as a whole, the need to provide a balance to the influence of the Paris Region is a major problem even within the Rhone-Alps region itself. Recent studies have shown that in many respects Lyon does not fulfill the role of a dominant metropolitan center. This is especially true in such crucial areas as decision-making power in financial matters and investment choices. Many cities of Rhone-Alps have their most important economic relations with Paris, where most decision-making centers are still concentrated. Moreover, the growth of such cities as Grenoble and Annecy seemingly has not been dependent on Lyon to any significant extent. It therefore has been argued that for public policy to make Lyon a privileged growth pole would only complicate matters by adding an intermediate stage to the mechanisms linking the rest of Rhone-Alps to Paris.[12] This problem is discussed in more detail in Chapter 10, where efforts to create a series of *métropoles d'équilibre* throughout France are discussed. However, it should be noted here that regional policy in this instance should not be regarded as a means to fortify existing relationships, but rather as a means to make them more rational from a national point of view. The relevant issue in this context is not so much whether Lyon is or is not to be the locus of the development of Rhone-Alps, but whether it is not best for the nation to decentralize much of the economic activity now concentrated in the Paris region, and whether the future of Rhone-Alps itself is not best assured by its assumption of a more independent role with respect to Paris, and a more international role with respect to its own economic orientation. These issues in turn are related to the nature of public policy concerning the development of the Rhine-Rhone axis.

If the development of the Rhone and much of the Saône is an obvious necessity to those who advocate a Rhine-Rhone axis, the route, or routes, by which the Saône should be linked to the Rhine is a matter of considerable debate. Three principal routes, one having two variants, have been proposed. The first would pass across Lorraine, linking St. Symphorien to Toul, whence the Moselle River Waterway would lead to the Rhine at Coblenz. This would require developing the Saône, the Canal of the East, and the Moselle over 270 kilometers, with sixteen locks and two inclined surfaces. The second route would be a branch of this and would require developing the Meuse over 284 kilometers between Toul and Givet and include the installation of thirty-three locks. From Givet this system would pass through a series of existing canals in Belgium to Antwerp. A final alternative would be to construct a channel to the Rhine via Alsace. In this case the route would lead from St. Symphorien to Mulhouse and the present Canal of Alsace. However, two different paths have been proposed for this channel; the first would follow the Doubs River, and the second, the Saône and the Canal of Montbéliard.[13]

In addition to the problem of selecting an appropriate route or set of routes is that of whether to make the channels large enough to accommodate the standard 1,350 ton international barges, or to expand them to accommodate ships of 3,000 tons. For the first of these two alternatives, the respective costs for the three basic routes would be as follows: Lorraine route, 1.2 billion francs; Meuse route, 1.1 billion francs; Alsatian route, .9 billion francs. If channels are to be made large enough for bigger ships, then the respective costs would be: Lorraine route, 1.3 billion francs; Meuse route, 1.15 billion francs; and Alsatian route, 1.25 billion francs. It will be noted that if all of the routes were developed, the smaller channel would cost 3.2 billion francs and the larger channel 3.7 billion francs. Because this difference is relatively narrow, many technicians have come out in favor of the latter alternative,[14] and it is the one which in fact has recently been adopted by the government.

Studies of routes, costs, traffic potentials, comparative returns, and other aspects of the Rhine-Rhone project have been carried out for over ten years by numerous organisms, including the Commission for Linking Major Waterways, special committees of the Fifth Plan, the National Commission for *Aménagement du Territoire,* the DATAR, and the North Sea-Mediterranean Study Group. In general, the case for the undertaking may be summarized in seven points.

First, the creation of a Rhine-Rhone axis would enhance the value of the considerable investments already realized on the Moselle, the Rhine, and the Rhone. Second, only a project of this magnitude would permit the French economy to sustain competition from other members of the Common Market, since only this project can adequately tie France to the industrial heart of Europe. Third, the axis would constitute an essential aspect of regional development policy, since it would provide Lorraine, Alsace, Lyon, and Marseille a unique opportunity to offset the attraction of the Paris Region. Fourth, rapid growth of traffic tends to reduce competitiveness among different modes of transportation. At present rates of growth, the demand for transportation will double in fifteen years; different means will therefore detract from one another less and complement one another more. Fifth, the effort on behalf of the Rhine-Rhone axis would compensate in large part for deficiencies inherited from the past. France invests two times less than Germany, five times less than Belgium, and six times less than the Netherlands in navigable waterways. At present, waterways for large ships stop at the French border. Sixth, transport costs for heavy materials favor waterways. Over the same distance, the tariffs at present applied to metallurgical products by the railway are four times what would be charged on a waterway built for larger ships. Even under the worst conditions, a waterway would cut transportation costs for such commodities in half. Seventh, development of waterways is not only a transportation question but is vital for supplying water to industry, which today often needs water as much as, in an earlier period, it needed coal.[15]

The arguments against the Rhine-Rhone project may be summarized under five main points. First, the expected advantages may not be sufficient to justify the investment costs proposed. Second, the evolution of traffic is unfavorable to water transportation, as pipelines replace petroleum vessels. Moreover, the prospective implantation of a steel and port complex at Fos, near Marseille, does not offer favorable prospects for Lorraine; in fact, steel from Provence might even cut into Lorraine's present markets if the waterway is realized. Third, heavy merchandise is becoming less important while light industry, usually of a precision nature, is becoming more important. The latter frequently needs expensive inputs, but these are generally not heavy or cumbersome. Light industries often are more attracted by sun than by water. Fourth, certain categories of heavy merchandise can benefit from changes in railway tariffs, and not only from the French network. In 1964, for example, the French National Railway and its German counterpart reduced charges on coke and iron for Lorraine by 30 to 40 per cent. Fifth, the granting of large sums to develop a North-South waterway in the East would deprive the regions of the West and Southwest of needed projects and accentuate disparities between the East and the West and Southwest. This would run counter to basic regional policy, whereby public investment would play an inducing role in the West and Southwest but assume an induced role in the East (see Chapter 9).[16]

The problems posed by the issue of the Rhine-Rhone project and what route or routes it might take finally reached a point where further research and debate could yield little new economic or technical evidence. This situation was reflected in Boudeville's remark that "Sterile disputes impede growth and should, under the arbitrage of the central government, be replaced by measures of cooperation or compensation." [17]

In fact, the Fifth Plan marks the beginning of official approval for equipping the Rhine-Rhone axis. Following the *First Report of the National Commission for Aménagement du Territoire,* the *Report on the Principal Orientations of the Fifth Plan* points out the natural advantages offered by the series of river valleys extending from the Mediterranean to the Rhine. The prospects for this linear region are enhanced by the high degree of urbanization and industrialization already found in certain of the valleys, but an integrated axis demands further EOC investment, especially in the areas of urban equipment, industrial zones, and transportation infrastructure. As to the Rhine-Rhone project, "it appears that the essential problem is not to determine whether to achieve a large waterway linking the Rhine basin to that of the Rhone, but to know when economic development will justify one or another given investment." [18] Thus, while development of the axis is approved, the execution of specific stages of its equipment is tied to immediate economic need and to the question of financial feasibility. In this respect, the report seems to adopt a policy of emphasizing the induced, rather than inducing, role of the relevant EOC expenditures.

The Fifth Plan itself states that for the regions of the East, the principal aspect of regional policy "consists in making the North Sea-Mediterranean economic axis a reality by progressively developing its urban equipment, by creating industrial zones, and by constructing transportation infrastructure." [19] In addition, specific projects are designated for completion during the period 1966–70.[20]

In principle, then, the government has decided to carry out the Rhine-Rhone project by developing two parallel routes to the Rhine in northeastern France, one via the Moselle and the other via Alsace. For the immediate future, however, the undertakings specified in the Fifth Plan will tend primarily to benefit Lorraine. The work required to make the Rhone navigable for large ships has turned out to be more difficult than was originally believed, and the government therefore maintains that it would be pure waste at this time to construct a canal from Alsace to the Rhone. On the other hand, the Moselle branch has immediate utility, since it already links the North Sea to Lorraine's steel complex.[21]

The decision to emphasize the Moselle branch, at least for the time being, has stirred considerable reaction in Alsace, where a major Rhine-Rhone waterway has long been regarded as a necessary means "to permit Alsace to exercise with maximum efficiency its role as a crossroads of navigable waterways in the framework of the Common Market." [22] The principal fear in Alsace, therefore, is that "the canalization of the Moselle threatens to cause the port of Strasbourg the loss of part of its present traffic." [23]

Given these views, it is not surprising that the Fifth Plan's stipulations concerning the Rhine-Rhone project have aroused anxiety in Alsation economic circles. The president of the regional chamber of commerce and industry has already argued that the consequence will be to accentuate "the risks of attraction of the local economy toward powerful industry situated across the Rhine in Baden-Württemberg," and M. Pflimlin, mayor of Strasbourg, has evoked "the grave and irreparable damage that the absence of the indicated river link will involve for Alsace." [24] The Alsations can also make a case for themselves on the basis of one of the most thorough studies, from an economic viewpoint, yet made of the Rhine-Rhone proposal. This report, prepared by a group of experts under the presidency of André Boulloche, found that the Alsatian branch appeared economically justifiable with a large margin of security; using a rate of discount of 6 per cent, the report maintained that this branch would be clearly profitable if the annual rate of growth of traffic was greater than 3.5 per cent. However, conclusions regarding the other proposed routes were more guarded. It found that the investment outlays required for the Moselle route would not be entirely compensated by direct benefits, though it did point out that concomitant external economies would probably make the operation justifiable. A similar finding was set forth for the canalization of the Meuse.[25]

Given the complexities of estimating both the direct and indirect costs (including opportunity costs) and benefits associated with the execution and timing of alternative Rhine-Rhone routes, it is certain that choices will be influenced to some extent by political as well as economic and technical considerations. Nevertheless, within the context of the present study at least two main points merit emphasis.

First, in terms of the analysis developed in Chapter 1, the areas of Eastern France under discussion here are clearly intermediate regions, and their primary public investment needs lie in the area of EOC projects. Gravier points out that with the advent of the Common Market one increasingly sees the old term "Lotharingia" employed to designate the large central European zone marked out by the Rhine and Rhone basins; within this complex of international relationships are five French program regions: Lorraine, Alsace, Franche-Comté, Burgundy, and Rhone-Alps.[26] In general, the importance of EOC needs in these regions is clearly indicated by the reports of regional *préfets* and

Regional Economic Development Commissions (see Table 7.2). More-over, the debate over the Rhine-Rhone proposal has not been an issue between EOC and SOC projects, but has rather concerned the best mix of EOC projects. Indeed, the Rhine-Rhone axis is amenable to development by rail, highway, and pipeline infrastructure, as well as by water resources. The government's interest in comparing the alternative costs and benefits of competing undertakings in spite of considerable pressures for one or another waterway system has been well taken, though the danger of inaction in the face of difficult choices is always present. This tendency may, however, be related to the second point which should be emphasized, that is, the issue of interregional opportunity costs.

Given the relevant budget constraint, the government probably is correct in more or less limiting public investment in the East to projects demanded by immediate economic needs. In other words, the government has tended to regard public investment in the East as an induced, rather than inducing, form of economic activity. (Of course, induced public investment will induce other activities even if this is not its principal aim.) This approach in turn allows diversion of more funds to developing lagging regions, through excess capacity of public overhead capital.

If the East, taken as a whole, corresponds closely to the notion of an expanding intermediate region with considerable potential for continued growth, the case of the Nord is more complex, since this region is much closer to the lagging range of the regional spectrum. Regional needs and appropriate regional policy measures therefore deserve special consideration.

The Nord: An Intermediate
Region in Difficulty

The Nord was one of the first French regions to participate actively in the industrial revolution of the last century. It benefited to a great extent from its geographic position, which made it a natural link in the transportation axis joining northern Europe to England.[27] During the first half of the last century the textile industry played the role of a propulsive industry in this region. Although few technical innovations were made by French entrepreneurs, they were quick to adapt those made abroad.[28] Fresh impetus was given to the development of the

Nord by the discovery of coal in 1847. Production of coal rose rapidly, reaching a level of 28 million tons, or two thirds of total French production, by 1900. However, despite these early advantages, the roots of the region's recent difficulties are already discernible in the last century. Coal producers showed no interest in merging with steel firms or in profiting from the growth of the steel industry in Lorraine after 1890. The Nord also adopted a strongly protectionist stance with respect to coal. Moreover, the urbanization which accompanied industrialization was characterized for the most part by providing minimum housing—often hovels, caves, or company dwellings—for workers. "Education, sanitation and housing lagged well behind the French average, and infant mortality was higher in the city than in the country, unlike the rest of France. Here was little of the civilizing urbanity which Lerner and Gorden consider fundamental to growth or, apart from Lille, of the intellectual vigor sought by Gravier." [29]

Today the Nord has 3.7 million inhabitants, of which 2.3 million are in the department of the Nord and 1.4 million in Pas-de-Calais. In an area representing only 2 per cent of the French total, this program region accounts for 8 per cent of total population and 8.7 per cent of national production. However, the industrial structure of the region is that of its past; textiles and coal still constitute its economic base. Recently, 16 per cent of persons employed in the Nord worked in the textile sector and 12 per cent in extractive industries; the corresponding values for France as a whole were 7 per cent and 2 per cent.[30] Thus, the Nord is heavily specialized in declining industries. The ratio of employment in combustible mineral solids in 1985 to that in 1962 is estimated to be 0.31, while the corresponding figure for textiles is 0.73.[31] Although the Nord is one of the fastest-growing regions in terms of population, its total employment is expected to decline by 1 per cent between 1962 and 1970.[32] It is in fact the only region whose total employment is not expected to increase during this period. As Table 6.10 shows, the structural component of change in total employment from 1954 to 1962 was unfavorable with respect to total employment and very unfavorable with respect to industrial employment. In addition, the regional component shows no positive influence on total, industrial, or tertiary employment. Regional-structural analysis also indicates that the relative position of the Nord will deteriorate with respect to total, industrial, and tertiary employment between

1962 and 1970. Thus Beaud concludes that "the fears that we wish to express do not concern the insufficiently industrialized regions of the West, but the old industrialized regions of the Nord" and, to a lesser extent, Lorraine and Alsace.[33]

One of the principal difficulties associated with the structure of the Nord's industry is that raw materials and semifinished products, which it produces in great quantities, generally are finished, perfected, or combined with other inputs in other regions. In other words, the Nord lacks the manufacturing industries to complement its production of coal, steel, and cloth.[34] Moreover, the basic industries in which the Nord specializes do not require the labor skills which are needed in later stages where value added is greater. Consequently, the Nord is characterized by a relatively unskilled and low paid labor force.[35]

If the workers of the Nord have had little opportunity to acquire skills on the job, it also is true that lack of SOC has greatly hindered development of the area's human resources. The region's industrialization was accompanied by very dense population concentrations in "cities" constructed with only immediate economic need in mind and without reference to even minimum considerations of urbanism or hygiene. Lack of health and social equipment is still reflected in a high infant mortality rate, and the average level of schooling in the Lille area remains one of the lowest in France.[36] With respect to the comfort and equipment of housing, the Pas-de-Calais ranks eighty-seventh among France's ninety departments.[37]

Although all types of SOC are needed in the Nord, education and vocational training are particularly necessary if conversion and diversification of industry are to be achieved. Thus the plan for the region emphasizes that

> schools of all kinds are numerically insufficient to respond in a satisfactory manner to the general needs of the region and, in particular, to those of its economy. The level of professional qualification of the labor force, as a direct consequence of this lack, does not attain the national level.[38]

Similarly, the president of the Nord's Regional Expansion Committee has urged that "if there exist zones for priority urbanization, why should there not also be zones for priority education? This is the *sine qua non* condition for any policy of inducement worthy of the name." [39] The Fourth Plan noted the Nord's abnormal lack of vocational and technical training facilities and pointed out that "its insufficiently skilled labor force has indeed been one of the principal obstacles to the economic modernization of the Nord down to the present day." [40] The *First Report of the National Commission for Aménagement du Territoire* also states that the "lack of technical training given to young workers certainly constitutes the most serious obstacle to the creation of new industrial activities" in the Nord.[41] Finally, the Fifth Plan states that regional policy in the Nord "must contribute to conversion and diversification of industry. The difficult employment problems which are present. . . demand recognition of priority for vocational training through creation of a center for training advisors and sections for vocational education for adults." [42]

However, Beaud fears that the Fifth Plan does not sufficiently emphasize the effort required in the Nord, with its concomitant problems of human sacrifice and distress: "such conversions pose very difficult problems, not only technical, economic, and financial, but also psychological, social, and human; not only for heads of firms, workers, and trade unions, but also for local authorities and the total population." [43]

Without in any way minimizing the difficulties of industrial structure which characterize the Nord, it still should be recognized that this type of region has advantages lacking in a lagging region which has never experienced industrialization. It was shown in Chapter 7 that agricultural productivity, per worker and per hectare, is higher in the Nord than in any other French region. Pottier has shown that agriculture in close proximity to development axes, which concentrated population, industry, and commerce, benefited relative to that in other areas because of greater involvement in the dynamics of modernization and technological progress. This process operated not only in the Nord, but also around Paris and in the East.[44] If its climate is dreary, the geographical location of the Nord remains a positive factor and should become more so as European economic integration progresses. If the labor force generally is unskilled, it at least is accustomed to the work discipline of modern production systems; its inflexibility should be subject to correction by adequate vocational training. Indeed, the most difficult problem may be not so much conversion of the labor force as conversion of entrepreneurial mentalities. For example, Gendarme finds that in the textile sector entrepreneurs have lost much of the dynamism characteristic of the nineteenth century. Whereas they were once quick to convert from wool and linen production to cotton mixed fibers, they have been notably hesitant to adapt to production of artificial fibers, which now constitute the principal competition for the Nord's textile output.[45]

In general, an older industrial region in need of substantial conversion, such as the Nord, can justifiably claim that it has significant potential advantages which, in combination with increased EOC investment, can provide a realistic basis for attracting new industry on comparative cost grounds. However, the Nord also shares with lagging regions a need to reorient labor from stagnant sectors of the economy —agriculture in the one case, coal and textiles in the other—to activities with greater prospects for growth. In this regard the Nord and similar regions have need of considerably expanded SOC investment. Moreover, this SOC need is not just a question of retraining workers, but of upgrading the whole level of the region's urban amenities and health and education standards. Only in this way can the region compensate for past neglect, which has served to make many parts of the Nord, to use Gravier's term, "poles of repulsion." [46]

The pronounced need for both EOC and SOC investment in the Nord has been reflected in public investment policy toward the region. The principal project to benefit the Nord has been the creation and development of a large-scale port and steel complex at Dunkirk. Although completely destroyed during World War II, Dunkirk's harbor facilities have been steadily expanded in the past two decades. A particularly important step was taken in this regard in 1956, when local political authorities decided to construct a new $14 million ore harbor, a move concomitant with a decision by the giant steel firm Usinor (which produced 17 per cent of French steel in 1962) to concentrate future investment in Dunkirk. The recently completed ore harbor has 4,400,000 square feet of water space and can easily accommodate 45,000 ton ore carriers; it also has a four-mile-long breakwater, a half-mile berthing quay, and completely modern harbor services. It is now the leading ore-receiving port in France. In all, the Dunkirk port complex has about 500 acres of water surface area, five and a half miles of quays, and sufficient facilities to handle 16 million tons of annual shipping traffic. This makes Dunkirk the third ranking port of France. Meanwhile, Usinor has constructed a new integrated steel complex on a 1,200 acre site west of the city. In 1963 its annual capacity was 700,000 metric tons, but future expansion is expected to raise this figure to 6 million tons within a decade. Expanded port and steel facilities have been accompanied by many other new enterprises, including firms engaged in shipbuilding, refining, export-import trade, storage, and diverse types of manufacturing.[47]

Although a majority of the capital for the construction of Dunkirk's ore harbor was put up by the local chamber of commerce, the central government and a number of nationalized industries have cooperated closely in the development of the over-all infrastructure of the area. This has been in keeping with the Fourth Plan, which provided that in addition to the implantation of the steel complex and the development of manufacturing industries in Dunkirk, "public investment policy will be oriented to favor . . . the economic transformation of the region."[48] Toward this end the Plan provided for the creation of a canal between Dunkirk and Valenciennes capable of handling the 1,350 ton barges which are standard for Europe's international waterways. The general purpose of this project is to extend the influence of Dunkirk's vigorous economic growth and to attract new industry to "this large transverse transportation axis."[49] The canal is expected to provide Dunkirk with important markets in the industrial areas of Valenciennes and Lille, to which the main canal will be linked by a spur. There also is the prospect that this waterway eventually will be linked up with the Sambre and the Meuse, providing a direct water route between Dunkirk and Strasbourg. Railway electrification is expected to reinforce the attractiveness of this transverse axis, which, it is hoped, "should become the great axis for regional industrialization, sustained at the center by an interregional capital—Lille, core of an urban-industrial agglomeration of 700,000 inhabitants—and in the south by Arras, whose privileged position on the Paris-Lille line constitutes a valuable advantage."[50]

The Lille agglomeration receives specific attention in both the Fourth and the Fifth Plans. The Fourth Plan states that the creation of new industrial activities in the Nord should be accompanied by redevelopment of the region's old cities. The Lille agglomeration is singled out in this regard, especially for housing and transportation.[51] The Fifth Plan notes that as a result of consultation with regional authorities, priority will be given to the renovation of urban agglomerations and to improved transportation. In this regard it stipulates that particular attention will be given to the Lille-Roubaix-Tourcoing *métropole d'équilibre* (see Chapter 10), which will benefit from the creation of a new business center, development of its university, and improvement of streets and expressways. Finally, in addition to providing for a regional development axis based on EOC investment, and for renewal of the Lille area with respect to both EOC and SOC, the Fifth Plan, like the Fourth, emphasizes the necessity for SOC equipment to adapt workers' skills to the needs of expanding industrial sectors.[52]

Summary
and Conclusions

In Chapter 1 it was argued on the basis of general theoretical and empirical considerations that it is useful to distinguish three types of economic regions and three corresponding types of public investment policy. In Chapter 2 it was shown that the Paris Region corresponds closely to the notion of a congested region, and that public policy has been correct in limiting its growth to a level below that which would have obtained if the public sector played only a passive, induced role in response to private investment. In the preceding chapters it has been shown that, taken as a whole, the regions of the West and Southwest correspond to the concept of a lagging region. The relative importance of SOC needs in these areas has been clearly indicated.

In this chapter the East, and in particular the program region Rhone-Alps, has been considered a good illustration of an intermediate region. The relative importance of EOC investment to this region has been emphasized by regional authorities and scholars, as well as in government policy. However, the latter has been correct in specifying a relatively induced, rather than inducing, role for public investment in this region. It is true, of course, that development of the Rhine-Rhone axis is viewed as a means to induce higher levels of growth in the East, but opportunity cost considerations have led the government to develop this axis at a modest rate so that more funds may be diverted to lagging regions. In a sense, therefore, it may be said that public investment is staying only one step ahead of private investment in the East for the sake of staying three steps ahead in lagging regions. If human resources were perfectly homogeneous and perfectly mobile, it no doubt would be rational to reverse this policy. However, since residents of lagging regions generally prefer to remain where they are for noneconomic reasons, migration involves considerable social costs, even if they are not reflected in the cost calculations of private firms. Moreover, migration frequently is not feasible in any event because SOC deficiencies in lagging regions have limited the development of human resources and thus lowered the possibilities of employment in other regions. On the other hand, these arguments should not be used to discourage migration; at the margin there always are persons willing and able to migrate, especially if this alternative is not explicitly or implicitly shrouded by misguided public policy.

Finally, the Nord has been examined as an area with many of the attributes of an intermediate region, but also with a basic characteristic of lagging regions, namely, a pressing need to find employment in expanding sectors for labor leaving declining activities. In this situation public policy calls for a balanced SOC-EOC response, which in fact is the course being followed by the French government in the Nord.

Thus, the general assumptions and conclusions of the policy model developed in Chapter 1 have been supported by evidence concerning relative regional needs within the French context. Although a number of specific policy measures have been examined in this regard, it nevertheless is necessary to consider more generally the means and ends which orient French regional planning efforts.

9

French Regional Policy in the Fourth and Fifth Plans

The Hacketts have correctly pointed out that the turning point in the history of regional development in France was the application of the Fourth Plan.[1] This does not mean that regional economic policy was not important before then, but it tended to be limited to loosely coordinated decentralization measures which restricted the growth of the Paris Region while attempting to attract industry to critical areas by means of equipment subsidies, tax benefits, and similar devices. Only with the Fourth Plan, and still more with the Fifth, has a real effort been made to establish a coherent regional policy within the framework of the national Plan; regional objectives have been formulated with wider consultation and greater care, and the regionalization of the government budget has made it increasingly possible to measure the extent to which these objectives are supported by concrete action.

202

Regional Policy
and the Fourth Plan

Since regional policy means essentially government policy, greater attention to regional development problems was given impetus by the priority which the Fourth Plan accorded to social investments of the type generally undertaken by the central government or local authorities. Indeed, the projected increase for investments of this nature (50 per cent) was the greatest for any type of activity, and the Plan stated that this choice marked the beginning of an "inflexion of the structure of final demand." [2] In Wickham's words, the intention of the Fourth Plan was "generally to raise the standard of public facilities to a level adequate for the transition towards the future disquieting heights of an affluent society (the word was not printed, but J. K. Galbraith may be something of a spiritual father of the French 4th Plan)." [3]

With respect to regional policy the Fourth Plan emphasized that government action should be viewed within the framework of the national Plan. Its objectives should not be limited to insufficiently developed regions, but should rather aim at over-all expansion. However, a distinction was made with respect to the induced versus the inducing role of public investment. The induced role was prescribed for regions where economic growth is proceeding spontaneously and vigorously. In this event, government policy consists in developing infrastructure, educational facilities, financial means, and other public forms of economic participation at a rate required by this expansion. In other words, public investment should follow the natural evolution of the economy, avoiding lags on the one hand and on the other massive aid or spectacular projects designed to significantly speed up growth. However, this does not preclude measures to favor industrial conversion in localities where regression may be contrasted with the general expansion of the region.[4]

In less-favored regions, "the action of the government must change its character and become a policy of inducement comporting more audacious anticipation and more important forms of aid." [5] However, the Plan maintained that the efficacy of such investment would be curtailed if it took the form of a general sprinkling of outlays and projects over a given region. Here the influence of French regional economic theory will be noted, since what was called for were "well chosen points of application" which could become "genuine growth poles exercising a propulsive influence on their environment and inducing especially the creation of a network of secondary poles." [6]

In addition to these two types of situations, the Plan also noted the existence of regions where concentration of industry and population "threaten to take on excessive proportions." In this event, it emphasized the necessity for induced public investment to associate itself with the positive aspects of growth and dissociate itself from the negative aspects. "Checking growth indiscriminately, in abstraction of the complementary effects among regions, would be damaging to the nation as a whole." [7]

Thus, the Fourth Plan distinguished among three types of regions, which correspond fairly well to the intermediate, lagging, and congested types defined in Chapter 1. It did not, however, explicitly consider questions of opportunity cost or the differing emphasis which should be accorded differing types of public investment in different types of regions. Nevertheless, a deliberate choice was made to limit unbalanced growth through excess public overhead capital in intermediate regions in favor of promoting unbalanced growth in lagging regions.

With respect to migration, the Fourth Plan aimed at limiting population movement resulting from lack of employment opportunities "to a reasonable rate," though it made clear that this did not mean that every Frenchman would be guaranteed a job in his present locality—a guarantee which "would create an intolerable rigidity in a dynamic economy." [8] Three areas were singled out for special attention because of the deficiency of available jobs resulting from the evolution of industry, commerce, and services in relation to the number of demands for employment resulting from immigration, natural population increase, and modernization of agriculture. These were Brittany, the Massif Central, and the Nord. The entire Southwest was also mentioned as a problem area in these regards. The Plan's effort to limit, if not preclude, migration was complemented by measures to attract industry to these regions. In addition to public investments, the government would also favor the industrialization of certain regions through favorable tariffs for energy and transportation, a policy which was instituted specifically for Brittany. To benefit the West and Southwest the Plan also specified five special zones for conversion—Montpellier,

Limoges, Bordeaux, Nantes-St. Nazaire, and Brest—the first four of
which had this status prior to 1962. These zones were favored by particularly generous investment subsidies. An effort was called for to
have civil and military administrations favor the West in choosing locations. Public and private firms were encouraged to locate in the West
plants which would produce light and highly elaborated products. This
type of industry would not be hampered by the high transportation
costs resulting from the area's geographical situation. The government
also expressed its intention to promote activities with an important
multiplier effect. The plan was careful to point out, however, that a
major educational effort would be required to prepare workers, and
especially young people coming from rural areas, for industrial employment in the West. Indeed, a great deal of attention was given to
the general need for increased "intellectual investments" in the West,
both to attract industry and to modernize agriculture.[9] The Plan also
specified that

> Because of the employment disequilibrium which is present there,
> the West of France is in the first rank of regions where a policy
> of inducement must be carried out. A complete halt to out-
> migration in this area could only be obtained if 90,000 extra
> nonagricultural jobs—that is to say in addition to those whose
> creation is now anticipated—were created between 1960 and
> 1965. . . . Public authorities will take all necessary measures to
> encourage and to orient new industrial implantations in this direc-
> tion, as well as to promote the concomitant development of the
> tertiary sector. The industrialization of the West is one of the great
> tasks which the Fourth Plan proposes to the ambition of the
> nation.[10]

In general, the major innovations of the Fourth Plan with respect to
regional policy methods included making forecasts and setting objectives by region for employment and investment, and the introduction
of the regional sections. In fact, however, the manner of preparation
of the regional sections (see Chapter 4) and rates of investment in key
social categories both fell short of original expectations. Obvious deficiencies in the regional planning aspects of the Fourth Plan were
already apparent in late 1963, when the Economic and Social Council
remarked,

> Concerning private production and investment, the insufficiency
> of statistical sources at the disposition of regional organisms,

in particular the Regional Expansion Committees, and also their unequal and sometimes incomplete consultation, have prevented the formulation of complete over-all region-by-region forecasts. Up to the present the regional sections have only been able to regionalize the objectives of the national Plan without really altering these objectives.[11]

The council went on to recommend that the regional sections include not only public investment but private investment and details concerning the creation of new employment. It also regretted that the conditions under which the Fourth Plan was prepared and executed did not permit the regional sections to have the forecasting character they should have. Finally, in view of experience under the Fourth Plan, it recommended that the Fifth Plan involve a real confrontation between national needs and regional objectives.[12]

The special effort which the Fourth Plan marked out for increasing the absolute and relative importance of the public sector had been especially tied to regional policy. Indeed, the Plan stated that the process of regionalization "has been pursued for those public investments which exercise the greatest stimulating effect on the regional economy. Thus, investments from 1962 to 1965 in transportation, education, scientific research, vocational training, and urban equipment are the principal categories of outlays to serve as the object for examination by region." [13] However, it was these categories which, taken as a whole, most notably failed to realize the progress anticipated.

For the period of application of the Fourth Plan the annual growth rate of GNP was 5.1 per cent, somewhat less than the 5.5 per cent rate which had been forecast. The latter figure probably would have been attained were it not for stabilization measures which particularly affected growth in 1965. Stabilization measures also adversely affected private investment, which increased by 5.9 per cent per year instead of the anticipated annual rate of 7.3 per cent.[14] With respect to public investment, two sectors more than fulfilled the expectations of the plan: funds authorized for transportation were 110.4 per cent of the planned amount, while the corresponding value for postal services and telecommunications was 103.1 per cent. On the other hand, expenditures in the categories of education, housing, culture, and urban equipment were considerably below the amounts projected.[15]

Expenditures for educational equipment were 91.9 per cent of the originally programed amount of 12 billion francs.[16] As early as 1964, the Economic and Social Council, which at that time estimated that the percentage of plan realization would be 91.6 per cent, decried the effort which was being made in this regard. It pointed out that despite the accomplishments of the Fourth Plan in education, which accounted for a little over one third of all public investment from 1962 to 1965, not only were the realizations inferior to the amount stated in the Plan, but the planned investments were themselves less than the minimum needs set forth in 1960 by the Commission for Educational Equipment. Thus, the council maintained that by 1966 it would not be possible to accommodate the children who would be entering the lower grades without resorting to classes too large for adequate teaching. This was all the more regrettable, the council pointed out, because if these needs were not satisfied the economic future of the country would be compromised. "If during these years not enough importance has been attached to the economic return from education, this is because it cannot be expressed in numbers; it nonetheless is a reality." [17] A similar argument could be made for cultural investment, which amounted to only 81.8 per cent of the amount originally programed for execution under the Fourth Plan. A still lower percentage of realization was that for urban equipment: 78.6 per cent.[18]

The effort made with regard to urban equipment and housing represented the biggest shortcoming of the Fourth Plan. Only 74,300 dwelling units were constructed from 1962 to 1965, whereas 145,000 had been projected. Slum dwellings which should have been replaced at the rate of 50,000 apartments per year were replaced in fact at a rate of 20,000 per year. At this rate it would take one hundred years to carry out the urban renewal projects now needed. One reason for this lag was that the government did not extend 38 per cent of the credits originally anticipated. Water purification facilities for towns and cities were constructed at a rate which left an already bad situation equally bad after the Fourth Plan. Facilities provided for parking and urban mass transportation also were insufficient; in general, traffic problems increased rather than decreased. Here again, the government extended only 86 per cent of the credits which had been planned.[19]

In general, proponents of vigorous regional policy expressed little enthusiasm over the results of the Fourth Plan. Although the regional aspects of the Plan seemed relatively impressive at face value, the manner in which consultations were carried out at the regional level, together with failures to realize Plan objectives in sectors of special interest to regional development, combined to create a great deal of skepticism concerning the government's true intentions with respect to regional policy matters. A source of special concern has been the obvious priority given to the international prestige of the franc over issues of internal expansion, including regional development measures.[20]

More specific complaints have also been made. For example, one of the leading figures in the formulation of the regional sections for Franche-Comté has asked if the objectives of the Plans and the facilities available for their realization are not diverging. This point was brought out particularly with reference to the last two years of the Fourth Plan. Thus, he maintained that "in many regions . . . it may be estimated that the last regional section gave only 20 to 40 per cent of the credits which would have been necessary to respond to the most evident needs, and that this poverty has been felt most in the most essential areas, such as housing, education, and agriculture." He concludes, "we provincial populations ask ourselves if we should continue to cultivate the hopes inscribed in our regional plans and harvest the disappointments of the regional sections." [21]

Finally, the high priority given to the development of the West in the Fourth Plan obviously left much to be desired in practice. The *First Report of the National Commission for Aménagement du Territoire* pointed out, in guarded language, that "The policy of inducement has been begun by the Fourth Plan; despite some important operations, it has not given sufficient results. Certainly a 'time for response' is needed for the economy to register the effects of initiatives taken during these last years in favor of the regions of the West. The Fourth Plan has undertaken a task; the Fifth Plan will take it to the point where it will become self-sustaining." [22]

Preparation of the Fifth Plan: The National Commission for *Aménagement du Territoire*

The important reforms in the institutional structure for French regional planning and in regional planning procedures which were made in the light of deficiencies in the Fourth Plan were discussed in Chapter 4. As a consequence of these measures, the regional aspects of the Fifth Plan have been prepared with considerably greater care in regard to both consultation at the regional level and formulation of regional goals within the context of the national Plan.

It will be recalled that in 1963 the functions of the *aménagement du territoire* section of the Ministry of Construction were transferred to a new agency attached to the General Planning Commission. This new agency, the National Commission for *Aménagement du Territoire,* was charged with synthesizing the objectives of regional planning and those of the national Plan. The First Report of the National Commission, which appeared in 1964, was prepared within a general long-term perspective, but it also provided the basis for elaborating the more specific regional objectives of the Fifth Plan. The latter task was undertaken only after extensive consultation with other interested organisms, for example the modernization commissions, the DATAR, local authorities, and the Regional Economic Development Commissions.

The First Report pointed out that if past trends continue geographical disparities in France will be accentuated rather than reduced. Economic activity will be oriented primarily toward regions whose urban-industrial environment assures the most favorable conditions for increased productivity, whereas in other regions, especially in the West, the Southwest, and the Massif Central, modernization of agriculture and industrialization will evolve more slowly and in some cases even regress. To remedy these disparities it is not sufficient to rely on the "natural mechanisms" of the economy, which may in fact only aggravate the problem. Firms' localization decisions take account only of the costs which immediately affect themselves, not of long-run social costs. In consequence, it is the task of regional planning to re-establish the true cost of each individual action. The orientation of regional policy therefore should be accompanied by significant progress in the analysis of costs and in particular their geographic aspects. Only in this way can rational decisions be made with respect to public policy concerning taxes, credits, subsidies, and the location and nature of public investments. Moreover, regional policy should assume an open economy, subject to the pressures of international competition. The localization of activities which would be unfavorable to the development of external exchange because of high production or transportation costs should be avoided. On the contrary, regional policy should contribute to the competitive aspect of the French economy. Thus, necessary agricultural and industrial conversion should be prepared for well in advance of the time when external pressures would force a sudden and painful transformation.[23]

Of particular interest is the First Report's rejection of the notion that regional policy should aim at reducing population movements to a minimum. In contrast to the Fourth Plan's emphasis on limiting migration to a "reasonable rate," the First Report states that

> many persons consider that *aménagement du territoire* should tend to create, in each region, a sufficient number of new activities to assure internal equilibrium of labor availabilities and needs. Such a policy of development given a 'closed population' would weigh heavily on over-all economic growth, and would threaten to bring on more or less long-run stagnation. . . . Social and economic development is inseparable from mobility, that of persons as well as that of capital, and from diffusion of information and the knowledge which accompanies it.[24]

The long-term perspective of the First Report concentrates on the interval to 1985 and deals with the "three basic tendencies" which are expected to dominate the next two decades: economic growth, the opening of national frontiers, and urban concentration.

Although no particular rate of economic growth is projected, it is anticipated that technological progress will continue to bring about substantial increases in per capita income. Consumption per capita will be two and one-half times the present level. It is probable that technological innovation will remain "less autonomous" than in the United States; it will be necessary not only to make up for present deficiencies, but to exploit these developments in such a fashion as to promote better management and a more rapid diffusion of the most productive techniques. The France of 1985 will have a population of around 60 million inhabitants, with a lower average age than at present. The proportion of the population in agriculture will be about half of what it is now, whereas new employment will have been created in industry and especially in the services sector. The number of factories should be double the present number and the number of dwelling units should have increased by about 50 per cent. New industry will continue to be attracted by the external economies available in already industrialized regions, but a number of factors may permit the orientation of a substantial part of this growth toward regions now insufficiently developed. Industrial expansion increasingly involves the fabrication of more and more elaborated products and the use of complex machines; moreover, the cost of these products includes a larger quantity of labor and a lower fraction of primary inputs and transportation. Thus, choice of location will be less and less influenced by considerations of distance and material factors, but it will at the same time be increasingly influenced by human factors. In particular, activities such as precision instrument making and research will tend to locate in urban centers which are not only economically active but which have a lively intellectual life and possibilities for cooperation with a university. All of these phenomena, which will have an increasing influence on choice of location, indicate the type of preconditions regional policy must foster in areas where substantial increases in industrialization are desired.[25]

The opening of national frontiers to international competition is expected to be of greatest benefit to the regions contiguous to the heart of the European Economic Community, which constitutes a highly industrialized "Lotharingia." These regions benefit from a dense consumption market, considerable possibilities for specialization, and relatively low transportation costs. Thus, the Common Market will bring about increasing concentration in favor of the most advanced sectors and firms and those found for the most part in the most industrialized "central" regions of the Community. In France this tendency already is seen in the orientation of investment with respect to the Paris Region and the regions of the North and the East. In consequence, peripheral regions such as those in the West and the Southwest of France will encounter greater difficulties in their efforts to industrialize, and pressures for out-migration will increase. In view of this, the European Economic Community has advocated special measures in favor of less-developed regions whose future is further threatened by the progressive realization of the Common Market. Of course, increased competition also makes more imperative conversion and modernization measures in the frontier regions of Alsace, Lorraine, and especially the Nord.[26]

The First Report makes numerous recommendations concerning the third of the basic long-run tendencies it considers—the increasing urbanization of France. However, detailed examination of this important aspect of French regional policy is reserved for Chapter 10.

After discussing the essential long-run trends of the French economy, the report proposes four principal domains for future regional policy: the industrialization of the West; the growth of the already industrialized regions of the North and East; the problems of rural areas; and, finally, the balance between Paris and urban agglomeration in the provinces, an issue which will be taken up in Chapter 10.

Agricultural employment in the regions of the West (Lower Normandy, Brittany, Pays de la Loire, Center, Poitou-Charentes, Limousin, Auvergne, Aquitaine, Midi-Pyrenees, and Languedoc) is expected to decrease by one million persons by 1985. Even if half of the new jobs created in France between 1962 and 1985 were located in the West, this area would still have a higher proportion of its employed population in agriculture and a lower proportion in industry and services than the French average. However, it seems unlikely that the West can attract this high a percentage of new employment. The recent trend shows that the West, with 37 per cent of the nation's population, accounted for 23.8 per cent of total industrial employment in 1954 and 23.7 per cent in 1962. If past tendencies continue, the West will have only 25 per cent of the new jobs created between 1962 and 1970, and the number of workers leaving the area during this period will be around 250,000. In view of this situation, the report recommends that the Fifth Plan pursue inducement policies designed to accelerate the industrialization of the West; decentralization of the Paris Region is to be encouraged as a complementary means to achieve this end. In particular, the installation of activities with a strong stimulating effect on the whole economy should be encouraged—industries such as precision products and research, which already are represented in the aerospace industry in the Southwest. Heavier industry should be oriented toward port complexes, though the report leaves open the question of which of these activities should be located in what ports. In general, it is proposed that policy for the West aim at locating 35 to 40 per cent of new French employment in the area during the period of application of the Fifth Plan; otherwise, a mere continuation of past trends would be contrary to the very spirit of a policy of inducement on the part of the government. Given past trends, the net increase in industrial employment in the West from 1966 to 1970 would be 70,000. The objective of a 35 to 40 per cent share of new employment for the West during this period will require an extra 40,000 jobs, or a total net increase of 110,000. This goal is proposed as a working hypothesis for modernization commissions in the preparation of the Fifth Plan. Beyond the Fifth Plan, this percentage could be increased progressively, though in the period up to 1985 there will continue to be substantial out-migration toward the Paris Region and the West will remain strongly agricultural. For the long run, the report proposes a strengthening of decentralization measures and a more pronounced orientation of public investment in favor of the West, though spectacular projects which would have only limited effect on the present social and economic structure of the area should be avoided.[27]

With regard to the already industrialized regions of the North and East, the report emphasizes the necessity for conversion and modernization to meet the increased international competition which will be the essential characteristic of the Common Market. A special effort at adaption is urged for the Nord, while the situation in the Southeast, on the other hand, is considered to be relatively good. The economic development of the East, it is maintained, should be organized around a privileged infrastructure axis following the principal valleys, and public investment should be concentrated on transportation, development of industrial zones, and modernization of urban equipment. The focus is placed on the Rhine-Rhone axis, with respect to rail and highway facilities as well as water resource development. In addition, however, the cities of Annecy, Chambéry, Grenoble, and Nice are recognized as foci of rapid economic growth not directly attached to the Rhine-Rhone axis, and public investment in these centers is advocated as a means to intensify further the progress already being made.[28]

The First Report concludes with a lengthy discussion of certain broad problems and prospects related to the spatial location of economic activities; the nation's urban hierarchy; transportation, education, and research; and finally the conservation of France's natural resources. In the light of this analysis the report emphasizes three main areas which should be acted on during the Fifth Plan.

First, since rapid modernization in agriculture induces an accelerated evolution of rural life, it will be necessary to pursue several objectives simultaneously in this regard. The displacement of more than 500,000 agricultural workers from the primary to the secondary and tertiary sectors will have to be assured between 1966 and 1970. Land

structures and farm equipment will have to be adapted to a new distribution of agricultural activities. For zones of dispersed population,
a sufficient network of transportation, educational, and health facilities
must be maintained, and complementary activities such as handicrafts
and tourism encouraged. Second, the increasing urbanization of France
must be guided in a systematic fashion and efforts to deconcentrate
Paris continued. Finally, the industrialization of the West, one of the
main objectives of the Fifth Plan, will be pursued. Emphasis will be
placed on the development of light industry by making the region more
attractive to industry, especially through providing centers for vocational training, and by government aid.[29]

Preparation of the Fifth Plan:
The Principal Orientations

In 1962 a law was passed which stipulated that before the government sent its general directives for the preparation of the Fifth Plan
to the General Planning Commission, it should submit to Parliament a
bill outlining the principal options, or orientations, which would govern
the formulation of the Plan within a regional planning framework. This
innovation was motivated by a concern to discuss and debate the
principal guidelines before detailed studies gave the Plan its definitive
form. Thus, in 1964 a *Report on the Principal Orientations* was submitted to Parliament. It served as a basis for discussion and had the
character of a study on general choices, though it was not, of course,
the Plan itself. In particular, it made no mention of individual projects,
even of major importance. A Law of December 22, 1964, gave official
approval to the report.

The report recalls that for the Fourth Plan, regionalization took
place only after the Plan had already been approved by Parliament.
For the Fifth Plan regionalization would begin sooner so that interested
parties at the local and regional levels could participate fully from the
outset of the Plan's preparation. After parliamentary debate on the
general orientations, the modernization commissions and the Regional
Economic Development Commissions would be consulted directly concerning the elaboration of the Plan itself. The regional and sectoral
approaches would be combined, and after final approval of the Plan
the procedure for regional sections would be carried out as under the
Fourth Plan.[30]

The report points out that the spontaneous localization of economic activities does not always conform to the pattern which would be preferable from a social viewpoint. However, if there is general agreement that in consequence it is necessary to have a regional policy, the consensus is less general concerning the specific content of this policy. One approach would be to create maximum expansion in already advanced regions and transfer a part of the gains thus obtained to less developed regions. However, the real problem is to induce self-sustaining growth in the lagging regions, rather than to put them on the dole. At the other extreme would be a policy which attempted to halt all interregional migration of workers within a few years. This approach, though, would threaten the growth of propulsive regions, reduce over-all economic growth, and seriously weaken France's competitive position in the international marketplace. Thus, a compromise should be found between regions benefiting from a policy of government-induced economic activity and regions where public policy is designed to accompany growth, i.e. where government investment is more induced than inducing. This distinction is made not to divide the nation, but to prevent its division as a result of increasing disparities.[31] In view of these considerations, the principal orientations for the Fifth Plan in the domain of regional planning are presented under eight headings.

First, the integration of the French economy into the Common Market will accelerate the evolution of agriculture. The population employed in agriculture will continue to decrease by about 120,000 persons per year, but in conditions differing considerably according to region. In the East, the past exodus from agriculture has already resulted in a situation where many areas are approaching the threshold of the population technologically necessary to maintain efficient production. Moreover, surplus labor in rural areas of the East has a relatively easier time finding employment in industry. In the West, on the other hand, there remain 2.5 million farmers, or two thirds of all the persons in France employed in agriculture. In 1962, the West had 35 per cent of all employed persons in the agricultural sector, whereas the corresponding value for the East was only 15 per cent. Outmigration from rural areas helps to solve the problems of agriculture but it is by no means sufficient. In the West especially, there is a great need to rationalize land patterns by reparceling plots. The modernization of agriculture also requires an accelerated effort with regard to education and vocational training. Insofar as possible, the education and technical training given to rural young people should be sufficiently flexible to permit them either to enter agriculture or to find employment in industry or services. The modernization of agriculture, finally, should avoid transformations which would result in an irremediable deterioration of rural space. Tourism, conservation measures, and other activities may be substituted for traditional cultivation where the latter is no longer competitive.[32]

The second major orientation of regional policy should be to promote the industrialization of the West. In this regard, the report adopts the goals, and indeed for the most part the very language, of the relevant findings and recommendations of the *First Report of the National Commission for Aménagement du Territoire.*

Third, the effort to develop the West should impose no drag on the growth of the North and the East. Here again the orientations are taken directly from the *First Report of the National Commission for Aménagement du Territoire.* The major objectives are to place these areas in a better position for meeting the competition of the Common Market and to carry out necessary conversion and modernization in zones experiencing difficulties.[33]

Fourth among the principal orientations is the modernization of Paris, which receives greater emphasis than in the First Report. Until recently, the realization of major urbanism and equipment projects had been nearly halted in Paris since the economic crisis of 1929. Progress with respect to transportation, parking facilities, telecommunications, and new business centers has been much more marked in other major European cities than in Paris. Therefore, the Paris Region is below the level of its European counterparts and the living standards are inappropriate for its own inhabitants. To improve living conditions in the Paris Region it is necessary both to limit its growth and to provide a coherent program for public investment. The first of these aims should be promoted by a continuation of regulations controlling the location of economic activity in the region and, even more, by efforts to increase employment opportunities in other parts of France. Among the major investment projects needed are public transportation facilities and infrastructure for automobile traffic. A principal objective should be not just to speed up the movement of people, but rather to encourage a more rational redistribution of activities and residences, so that the number and length of journeys to work may be reduced. It also is essential to reform the pricing of public services in the Paris Region. Users of public services, especially in the area of transportation, should pay a tariff which covers not only operating costs but the investment costs necessary to improve service quality and to give users a degree of comfort corresponding to their needs and their purchasing power. This will allow government subsidies now being used unjustifiably to be applied to alternative undertakings.[34]

Because increased foreign trade is accelerating the evolution of both agricultural and industrial activities, which must adapt to conditions of the international market by partial or total conversions, the fifth major orientation concerns specific actions in certain zones. The work on the Fifth Plan must include studies on what activities can be prepared in advance for zones in need of conversion; too often in the past conversion operations have been carried out in a climate of uncertainty and lack of cooperation which has retarded their fulfillment. Measures for conversion will be facilitated by better education and training of the labor force; the accent should be on general, basic education and training of a type that will permit more flexible professional readaptation.[35]

The sixth general orientation concerns development of a hierarchy of urban centers, which will be considered in detail in Chapter 10.

Seventh, the development of the nation's transportation network must be carried out in the perspective of new centers of population and economic activity. For example, transportation policy should be coordinated with urban development policy. The rate of construction of automobile expressways should be increased, though construction of highways of all types which would bring about significant improvement in traffic movement should be given serious consideration. In particular, the creation of a series of four-lane highways in the West could contribute to induced growth of economic activity.[36]

Finally, the planning commission for water and other commissions dealing with problems involving water resources will cooperate in preparing a plan for investments in this domain. It is particularly important to overcome past neglect of urban and industrial water pollution and flood control.[37]

Before being submitted to Parliament for final approval, the principal orientations for the Fifth Plan were examined by the Economic and Social Council, as required by law. Unfortunately, the council was given only a brief period to prepare its opinions. Its report was presented on October 28, 1964, but the Prime Minister had submitted the options to the council only a month earlier, on September 23. In addition, the council was presented a single set of orientations, and it thus was unable to examine and compare alternative options. Despite these limitations, the Section on Regional Economies prepared a report which was critical of a number of aspects of the orientations relating to regional policy.

With respect to specifically regional problems, the Section argues that the present system of government financial assistance to firms locating in lagging regions constitutes only a minor aspect of the over-all financial effort needed for regional development. The reforms made in this regard in 1964 were valuable in that businessmen now know in advance the exact advantages they may expect to receive, and aid has been concentrated in areas of greatest need, namely, in the West, Southwest, certain parts of the Center, and Corsica. Nevertheless, it remains difficult for firms to obtain long-term credit to expand or modernize their installations, and government aid does not concern research facilities. In general, it takes too long to obtain investment credit, interest is too high, and the collateral required is excessive.[38]

A vigorous regional policy, the Section maintains, requires transportation facilities adapted to modern needs; more housing construction activity to permit greater labor mobility and make up for past neglect; implementation of a genuine tourism policy; more rational utilization of the natural resources of each region; and the creation of regional economic study centers to analyze regional problems and to train qualified specialists in regional economics and other aspects of *aménagement du territoire*. The Section further urges that the government indicate the nature and volume of investments it intends to devote to such major objectives as the modernization of agriculture, development of the Rhine-Rhone axis, and the modernization of Paris. With respect to private investment, a number of reforms are urged, including diversification of the mechanisms for obtaining medium- and long-term credit; increased possibilities for personal credit; greater capital participation on the part of public and quasi-public institutions in the SDR; and the favoring of lagging regions in the redistribution of funds centralized in the Caisse des dépôts.[39]

Regional Policy
and the Fifth Plan

Following parliamentary approval of the principal orientations, decentralized planning efforts were undertaken in accord with the legislation of March 14, 1964. Thus, the contents of the Fifth Plan take account of the reports prepared by the regional *préfets* on the potentialities and needs of their respective regions, and of the advice of the Regional Economic Development Commissions formulated on the bases of these reports.

As with the other aspects of the Fifth Plan, regional policy is influenced by the necessity for making the French economy more competitive, the principal preoccupation of the Plan. In particular, regional objectives take account of the changes which were made in the principal options. These are summarized in Table 9.1; they are, according to the Plan, on the whole favorable to regional policy. Accelerating productive investment will favor decentralized expansion, which lagged in 1964 and 1965 because new plant construction fell off. Increasing the level of housing construction will benefit all regions. On the other hand, the public equipment objective has been somewhat lowered because of the requirements of monetary stability. Nevertheless, this sector continued to have the highest rate of increase during the Fifth Plan.[40]

Like the *Report on the Principal Orientations*, the Fifth Plan itself emphasizes that a practical compromise must be found between ex-

Table 9.1

Annual economic aggregates projected for 1970
(in billions of 1960 francs)

Variable	Orientations	Plan
Gross national product	433	432
Productive investment	53	56
Inventory change, balance of trade, etc.	12	12
Resources available for consumption and general uses, including	368	364
Household consumption	300	294
General uses, including	68	70
Government consumption	9	9
Military purchases	14	15
Housing	24	26
Public equipment	21	20

Source: *Ve Plan*, p. 18.

penditures intended to induce growth in lagging areas and outlays designed to accompany growth in more progressive regions. It reasserts in this regard the need to adapt regional social and economic structures to conditions of increased competition.[41]

The Plan points out that several factors will accentuate problems posed by population mobility. One is the increasing youthfulness of the labor force, since it is young adults who most often migrate. Despite the longer time which young people are spending in school, the number of workers less than twenty-five years old will increase by more than 500,000 during the Fifth Plan. Moreover, there is an increasing tendency to migrate on the part of highly skilled workers in the tertiary sector, whose movement reflects a search for higher living standards and social advancement.[42]

The third major concern of the Fifth Plan, in addition to increased international competition and labor force mobility, is the need for more public equipment. The accent is placed on the necessity for increased infrastructure investment in urban agglomerations and the need for development of newer, more rational urban structures. Charges for public services should be adjusted to correspond to their true cost; water supply, public transportation, and parking are singled out for special mention in this regard. In addition, local finances should be better adapted to the burden borne by the communes. In larger agglomerations this means proceeding rapidly to a greater harmonization of resources and expenditures among the communes of the same agglomeration, taking account of disparities in receipts and the public overhead facilities available. More generally, the distortions which exist in the area of local business taxes must be reduced. Industrial decentralization policy sometimes is countered by the greater financial resources available to communes which already have a great deal of economic activity. Finally, such devices as Zones for Priority Urbanization will be employed more extensively in an effort to control rising land prices, which, if they continue to increase at the rate of the past fifteen years, threaten to compromise the realization of necessary public investment and housing programs.[43]

Within the context of these general considerations, the Fifth Plan adopts the eight major orientations outlined in the *Report on the Principal Orientations* with reference to regional policy. However, it goes further by giving each one a more specific context.

In the domain of agricultural modernization, emphasis is placed on structural change in agriculture, which in turn calls for a continuing policy of land reparceling, especially in the West, the Southwest and the Massif Central. However, change in land-use patterns cannot be dissociated from training and education. A special effort to develop agricultural education will be carried out in Aquitaine, Brittany, and Lorraine, and measures will be taken to encourage out-migration by the excess agricultural population in the West. The Plan also provides for programs in rural areas for public overhead capital, reforestation, creation of national parks, and development of rural centers to give greater accessibility to public services.[44]

The general goals proposed for the industrialization of the West in the *Report on the Principal Orientations* are adopted in the Fifth Plan, even though the studies made by the modernization commissions and the Regional Economic Development Commissions indicate that their realization will be difficult in a number of regions. However, at the end of the second year of the Plan a comparison will be made of the results obtained up to that point and the rate of growth of industrial employment which would be required for 35 to 40 per cent of all new jobs in France to be located in the ten regions of the West. If necessary, the government will then undertake a general review of all the measures being used to stimulate development in the West.[45]

Regional policy for the Nord and Lorraine emphasizes the need for conversion and diversification. With these ends in view, priority is given to vocational training. The process of modernization in the Nord will be carried out with the aid of urban renewal and improved transportation, focusing on the *métropole d'équilibre* Lille-Roubaix-Tourcoing. In the East, the Rhine-Rhone axis will receive urban equipment, industrial zones, and transportation infrastructure in keeping with the growth of that area (see Chapter 8). Specific projects are outlined for urban areas along the Rhine-Rhone axis, as well as in other parts of the East. These projects are almost all of an EOC nature and tend very much to emphasize transportation facilities.[46]

Where the *Report on the Principal Orientations* spoke of modernization of the Paris Region, the Fifth Plan substitutes modernization of Paris and development of the Paris Basin, thus putting the problem in a broader context. Following the Strategic Plan for the development of the Paris Region (see Chapter 2), the Fifth Plan emphasizes the need to create new towns. During the Fifth Plan land reserves should be acquired for long-term regional needs. For the new towns to be begun during this period government investment aid should be extended so that they can be sufficiently equipped to have a degree of economic autonomy heretofore lacking in suburban residential developments. The creation of new towns implies that a number of automobile expressways be undertaken very soon; several projects of this nature are specified in the Plan. Emphasis also is placed on other expressway construction, including a peripheral highway around Paris to be completed in 1971 and improvements in public transportation. The financing of the modernization of Paris should, insofar as possible, be based on service charges which reflect all of the corresponding costs. Services which are difficult to measure in terms of individual benefits should be financed by the District of the Region of Paris, since it would be "unjust and antieconomic" if the strongest of France's regions did not directly support a substantial part of its own modernization. Finally, in order to limit the number of persons migrating to Paris from the provinces, the growth of other cities in the Paris Basin should be encouraged. In particular, this includes Rouen, Le Havre, Orléans, Reims, and Amiens. The Basin's valleys, especially that of the Lower Seine, should constitute privileged development axes. The development of eight *métropoles d'équilibre* will also serve to limit the population pressure on Paris (see Chapter 10). [47]

The *Report on the Principal Orientations* called attention to the particular efforts at adaptation which would be required in certain zones. The Fifth Plan describes the measures which should be undertaken in this regard for zones which are only lightly industrialized or which are dominated by a single activity, rural zones, and the regions of Languedoc-Roussillon and Corsica.[48]

Provision of improved transportation and communications facilities during the Fifth Plan is related to the development of a structured urban hierarchy. Thus, an effort will be made to increase accessibility between the cities at the top of the hierarchy and the regions situated within their zones of influence. Moreover, each major region should be easily accessible by highway, rail, air, and telecommunications. Because of present traffic intensity in the North and East, construction of automobile expressways will primarily benefit these areas. The principal project in this regard will be a Dunkirk-Lille-Paris-Lyon-Marseille

expressway scheduled for completion in 1970. Since construction of
expressways in the West and Southwest would not be feasible economically, even under a policy of excess public overhead capital capacity
in these areas, emphasis will be put on widening, straightening, and
otherwise improving existing roads. Major projects of this type are
scheduled for the Bordeaux-Toulouse-Narbonne and Tours-Bordeaux
routes, as well as the north and south coasts of Brittany. If agreement
can be reached with the British government on the construction of a
tunnel under the English Channel, this undertaking will also be inscribed in the Fifth Plan. With respect to air traffic, the Plan calls for
the equipment of a maximum of some twenty airports, with special
attention to that of Nantes on the Atlantic coast and Lyon in the East.
Telecommunications facilities will be improved throughout the country, both to make up for present deficiencies and to help induce
increased economic activity in the regions of the West.[49]

Finally, the Fifth Plan points out that water resource deficiencies
have been aggravated in recent years in the most industrialized and
most densely populated regions. Urban-industrial growth and increased
irrigation have accentuated the gap between needs and resources and
have increased problems of pollution. In response, public policy efforts
will be oriented in three directions: construction of purification plants
in urban communes (investments amounting to 1.1 billion francs) and
for industry; projects to increase available water supplies; and projects to provide protection against sea and river flooding. Priority will
be given to the Nord, Lorraine, and the Paris Region, where water
problems are the greatest.[50]

The first step of the application of the Fifth Plan is the government's
budget for 1966, which represents a transition from the Fourth to the
Fifth Plan. This budget was not formally regionalized at the time of
its preparation because Parliament had not yet voted on the national
objectives for the new Plan. Nevertheless, the work of the National
Commission for *Aménagement du Territoire,* the Regional Economic
Development Commissions, and the regional *préfets* provided a basis
for its basic orientations in matters concerning regional policy.

The report on the regionalization of the budget for 1966 tends to
emphasize recent growth in regions of the West, rather than their continuing deficiencies in relation to other regions. For example, construction permit data show that the industrial surface authorized for the

West in 1954 was 65 per cent of the surface authorized for the Paris Region. In 1964, on the other hand, this value was 350 per cent. In Brittany alone, the surface authorized in 1954 was only 3 per cent of that authorized for the Paris Region, whereas the proportion had risen to 40 per cent in 1964. In recent years industrial energy consumption has risen at a more rapid rate in the West than in France as a whole. Similarly, using 1960 as a base, turnover taxes on businesses in 1964 had an index value of 166.5 for the West and 160.0 for France as a whole (using 1954 as a base, the growth in the West was inferior to that in the entire nation). However, data on variables such as taxes on personal income, low-tension electricity consumption, and household savings indicate that while living standards have risen at a somewhat higher rate in the past few years in the West than in the rest of France, progress has not been as great as for industrial growth. It also is important to note that statistics for such broad geographic divisions as the West, the East, and the Paris Region mask substantial differences within the West. Thus, disparities between Aquitaine and Limousin, or Brittany and Midi-Pyrenees, are sometimes more marked than differences between the West and the East taken as a whole.[51]

To reinforce decentralization policy in favor of areas to the west and south of Paris emphasis is placed on the promotion of development poles, or axes, which have already given evidence of growth. These include Orléans, Tours, Le Mans, Rennes, the Lower Seine Valley, the Paris-Lyon transportation axis, and, to a lesser extent, the Paris-Bordeaux axis. Although the Seine Valley and the Paris-Lyon axis are not in the West, they add to the evidence that "transportation infrastructure has constituted an important factor in industrial location and specialization in the past ten years."[52] It is further pointed out that development of industry along these axes is only one part of the complex relations making up an economic axis, which involves interdependent financial exchanges, labor movements, and interindustry transactions. These phenomena are best seen in the Rhone axis; and more generally, "this interdependence is, in the actual state of things, more advanced in the regions of the East than in those of the West."[53] Indeed, one is struck by the fact that EOC investment has been instrumental primarily in creating development axes in the intermediate regions of the East (as well as in the intermediate region of Upper Normandy, which benefits from the Seine axis), whereas in the West the growth poles which are cited are relatively isolated centers of activity not too distant from Paris.

In general, the policy of industrialization of the West "should not be understood as a policy of regional equalization or of 're-equilibration,' but as an effort to aid . . . industrial sectors . . . in those zones where the site guarantees their economic viability." [54] The report on the regionalization of the budget outlines the direct and indirect forms of financial aid for industrial expansion. Direct financial aid includes subsidies for industrial development or adaptation, fiscal exonerations, and decentralization indemnities for losses due to material transfers. Indirect aids are available to facilitate the preparation and financing of industrial zones, and the provision of preconstructed factories, housing, telecommunications, and professional training.[55]

The Economic
and Social Council's Critique

The Economic and Social Council's critique of the Fifth Plan covers a number of general problems concerning regional policy, as well as difficulties of a specifically regional nature.

The council expressed its regret that it was obliged to examine the Plan before all of the reports of the modernization commissions were available for consideration (in fact most of the commission reports were not published before the middle of 1966). This procedure ran counter to what should be an essential feature of the planning process; that is, it should involve a synthesis, after arbitrage, of all of the studies and reports relating to the Plan. The council objected also to the elaboration of the Plan as a series of annual budgets whose content is not subject in any way to the advice of the council. This tends to dilute the Plan, which already suffers from too much emphasis on its merely indicative nature.[56]

Pointing out that if there exists any domain where the anticipations of a plan can be useful it is that of economic conversions, the council expressed its concern over the imprecision with which this area is treated in the Fifth Plan. Given the grave difficulties faced by a number of regions, the Plan should define more explicitly the practical means by which workers will be retrained and new activities created in places where establishments are to be closed.[57]

Despite the fact that the Plan allocates 2 billion francs more to housing than had been proposed in the *Report on the Principal Orientations,* the council points out that the new objective of an annual rate of construction of 480,000 dwelling units by 1970 threatens to become only a pious hope in the absence of greater government aid. In addition, the council notes that the Plan ignores the question of renovation of existing housing, which in many respects is a task as essential and urgent as new construction.[58]

In May 1965 the Commission on Educational Equipment for the Fifth Plan estimated that 43 billion francs would be necessary to satisfy France's educational needs; 32.8 billion francs, it held, would be the minimum that could be allocated. After the vote on the principal orientations, the government specified that a minimum of 25.5 billion and a maximum of 28 billion francs would be devoted to education. The minimum amount was finally chosen. Unfortunately, the credits thus made available for education are not sufficient to implement the diverse programs which have already been voted into law in this area, at least not within the time limits anticipated. Development of technical education and the prolongation of schooling at the secondary level are among the programs particularly affected.[59]

The council finds that the relative diminution of the central government's financial role with respect to public investments of local authorities may work to the detriment of regional development policy. Reforms to increase local revenues by price increases on public services and increased taxation will not go into effect until midway through the Fifth Plan. Moreover, despite revenue increases, the difficulties associated with loans already contracted by local governments will limit the possibilities for their undertaking new investment projects. In other instances, too, the Fifth Plan does not give enough attention to financial problems relating to regional economic development. It makes no mention of the SDR, whose activity needs to be given greater encouragement. At the national level, the redistribution of funds centralized in the Caisse des dépôts should take account of development programs in regions at a financial disadvantage.[60]

Another major concern of the council is the regional pattern of urban growth. As pointed out in Chapter 2, the council fears that the very existence of the Strategic Plan for coordinating the growth of the Paris Region tends to favor investment in Paris over urban centers which do not have such a plan. Thus, the Fifth Plan's proposal to provide similar urban plans for Nantes-St. Nazaire, Bordeaux, and Toulouse is held to be inadequate; other urban areas, especially other *métropoles d'équilibre,* should also have systematic schemes for future growth. Nevertheless, this does not imply that the council endorses without reservation the idea of developing *métropoles d'équilibre* to offset the growth of the Paris Region. However, consideration of the council's attitudes in this regard first demands more comprehensive description and analysis of this important recent aspect of French regional policy.

10

The Urban Hierarchy and the Policy of Métropoles d'Equilibre

The Urban Hierarchy

It was not until about 1930, one hundred years after England and fifty years after Germany, that the population of France became urban in the majority. From 1936 to 1946 the urban population, i.e. persons living in agglomerations with at least 2,000 inhabitants, remained practically stationary. By 1954, it amounted to 25,463,000 persons, or about 60 per cent of the total population; in 1962 it had risen to 29,225,000 persons, or 63.3 per cent of the total population. If present trends continue, urban population will represent 67 per cent of the total in 1971 and 72 per cent in 1986. Before 1954 the rate of expansion of the Paris Region was higher than that of provincial agglomerations. Now, however, the latter are growing at about the same rate as Paris, and many are growing much faster.[1]

228

The trend toward greater urbanization has become one of the major preoccupations of French regional policy. On the one hand, the objective of limiting the growth of Paris has made it necessary to concentrate on orienting urban growth to alternative locations. On the other hand, the notion of development poles has served to focus attention on developing a few provincial agglomerations which would in turn constitute a stimulating force within their respective spheres of influence. One of the earlier expressions of these concerns is found in an article by Pierre Bauchet. He argued that basic administrative, social, health, and educational activities which depend on public authorities should be assured to all French citizens at a distance not greater than 200 miles from their residences. "Experience shows that these functions attract and reinforce one another in the same center, and that they develop badly in isolation." The absence of major provincial centers to provide these services results in individuals demanding them in Paris, which induces in the capital a multitude of tertiary activities. In consequence, "the transfer of these activities—business headquarters, study laboratories, insurance, publishing—empties the provinces of managers and other leaders and overcrowds the capital." In response to this situation, the government should undertake to provide necessary infrastructure in the provinces, taking account of comparative population and commercial importance of cities, and of administrative needs. However, the necessity to group essential public activities limits the number of centers in which public overhead capital should be concentrated. Thus, the government must choose a few agglomerations where "it will create those functions which depend on it in order to attract and hold tertiary activities in the regions. In France, five or six of these centers should be designated." [2]

Although it has appeared for some time that the harmonious development of a provincial urban structure should be an integral part of regional planning, the problem of an appropriate system of classification has been undertaken systematically only in the last few years. At the time of the creation of the program regions the multiplicity and diversity of existing administrative divisions demonstrated the lack of rationality in France's urban network.[3] As a result, planning authorities have attempted to establish an urban hierarchy in terms of functions performed by urban centers. Thus, Bloch-Lainé states that in France, as elsewhere,

The whole of the territory is polarized by the urban network. It appears as the juxtaposition of zones of influence which are defined in relation to the center from which they receive services and directives. The cities which provide these functions of animation and command are themselves tied to one another, according to the importance and variety of their equipment, by chains of subordination. This hierarchial system constitutes the *armature urbaine*. Because it governs the distribution of population and activities, it can be one of the essential elements for a long-run strategy of *aménagement du territoire*.[4]

Using this functional approach to the study of the urban hierarchy, a research group associated with the General Planning Commission has determined a set of eight *métropoles d'équilibre,* which together constitute the highest level of the hierarchy. In the relevant studies of the French hierarchy, the influence of a city depends on the intensity as well as the rarity of the functions it performs. These two factors are in turn related to total population, employed population, or population specialized in various given activities. The equipment of urban centers has been examined in relation to five types of activities: tertiary; commercial; banking and financial; services; and cultural, artistic, and sports equipment. Tertiary importance has been measured by the absolute and relative importance of employment in tertiary activities. Commercial equipment has been examined in terms of number of wholesalers in eight types of nonfood commercial activities, as well as twenty-seven types of special or "rare" commerce. Banking and financial importance has been evaluated according to agencies or district offices of four large national banks, the sales of large firms with headquarters in the cities in question, and the presence of a regional stock exchange. The study of equipment in "services" has taken account of twenty-two "rare" professions, administrative equipment, and higher education, medical, and hospital considerations. The study of cultural, artistic, and sports equipment has taken account of activities in these spheres, as well as the number of local events of an international nature.[5]

To complement the analysis of the intrinsic equipment of cities, the importance of their exterior influence has also been examined. In this regard Le Fillatre has studied the exterior influence of cities in terms of the number of workers who work outside of a given city for branches of firms whose headquarters are in that city.[6] In addition, Hautreux has studied the attraction exercised by cities as shown by telephone communications, railway passenger traffic, and population migration.[7]

On the basis of a synthesis of these studies, the *First Report of the National Commission for Aménagement du Territoire* defined the "large provincial agglomerations which exercise a true directing role in the economic and social life of a regional or multiregional zone of influence, thus avoiding all generalized recourse to the capital." [8] These *métropoles régionales* (the report avoids the more generally used and more value-laden term *métropoles d'équilibre* in favor of this more analytic term) include Lyon and Marseille, clearly at the head, followed by Bordeaux, Lille, Strasbourg, Toulouse, Nantes, and Nancy.

In addition to defining the superior level of the urban hierarchy, the First Report also specifies a number of cities which belong to the intermediate level of the hierarchy. Whereas Paris and the eight *métropoles d'équilibre* are clearly detached in importance from other French cities, no clear break exists among cities at the intermediate level. Nevertheless, ten "regional centers" are distinguished from among other urban centers at this level because they offer more numerous and varied services over a larger area; this group consists of Grenoble, Rennes, Nice, Clermont-Ferrand, Rouen, Dijon, Montpellier, Saint-Etienne, Caen, and Limoges. Besides the regional centers, the intermediate level includes three other groups of cities. The first is formed by twenty-four cities having an incomplete regional function, the second by twenty-five cities which are for the most part the main centers of relatively well-equipped departments, and the last includes a large number of small cities corresponding to subprefectures, even if they lack an administrative function.[9]

The base of the urban hierarchy consists of towns and rural centers characterized by increasing concentration resulting from the transformation of rural life. This process is accentuated by an augmentation in the consumption of services by farmers, and by the development and spread of individual means of transportation. At the beginning of the present century primary education was possible in nearly all communes, but present needs, particularly with respect to secondary education and vocational training, require more concentration of equipment in rural centers; the investment needed to overcome the basic causes of rural inadaptation is not compatible with dispersion.[10]

Having distinguished the principal levels of the French urban hierarchy, the First Report proposes some general guidelines for policy concerning the urban network. First, to provide a counterweight to Paris the eight *métropoles régionales* should receive priority for public investment in culture, research, higher education, specialized hospital equipment, administration, transportation, and other public overhead capital characteristic of the urban hierarchy's superior level. It is emphasized that this action will be fruitful only if it provides each agglomeration with a sufficiently complete range of services and activities. It would be illusory to expect important benefits if the normal functions of a large agglomeration are dispersed among a number of centers of lesser importance, often distant from one another and incapable of constituting a coherent cultural and economic entity. The efforts of the central government to equip the *métropoles régionales* adequately must be accompanied by active cooperation at the local level, especially in such matters as the formation of intercommunal groups to coordinate mutually beneficial undertakings and in accepting the need to carry out renovation operations which are often onerous and unpopular. New urban structures better adapted to automobile traffic are necessary to make services more accessible, and insufficiencies in such areas as water supply and purification must be overcome.[11]

The number of *métropoles* chosen for development must, according to the First Report, necessarily be few. The qualitative and quantitative gap separating the Paris Region from other French agglomerations imposes a considerable effort if disparities are to be reduced. Moreover, expensive projects such as hospital centers and airports can be economically justified only if they are assured of a sufficient number of users; similar considerations also hold for private investment projects. The cities which at present are capable of constituting *métropoles* by virtue of the degree of development and influence they already have attained are all located around the periphery of France and correspond to the eight cities at the superior level of the urban hierarchy. However, for policy purposes, the eight *métropoles* are more broadly defined in most cases than single cities. The reason is that certain polynuclear urban areas are beginning to appear, largely as a result of increasing use of automobiles. For the moment, these areas for the most part still lack cohesion because their internal relations are inadequate and because their residents do not, psychologically, feel themselves part of a common community. Nevertheless, the longer-run perspective which must be adopted for regional policy dictates that it is not agglomerations as they now exist that should constitute the frame of reference, but rather agglomerations as they will appear as a consequence of the effort at restructuration. In this sense, the period up to 1985 should see the following agglomerations equipped to fulfill the role of regional *métropoles:* Lille-Roubaix-Tourcoing, whose influence covers the Nord; Nancy-Metz-Thionville in Lorraine; Strasbourg, whose proximity to Germany should give it an increasing influence in the Rhine region; Lyon-St. Etienne, whose influence covers the non-Mediterranean Southeast; Marseille-Aix-Rhone Delta in the Mediterranean Southeast; Toulouse, whose influence extends over the program region Midi-Pyrenees; Bordeaux, whose influence sphere includes Aquitaine and Poitou-Charentes; and Nantes-St. Nazaire in the West. A parallel though less general effort also should be made to develop agglomerations which, by virtue of their own growth or their geographic location, have an important role to play in the near future and strong potentialities for eventually becoming regional *métropoles.* However, the First Report does not attempt to specify what cities are worthy of priority in this regard.[12]

The First Report envisages that the development of cities in the intermediate level should be closely associated with the growth of the *métropoles,* especially through the establishment of rapid and convenient transportation between the latter and cities within their spheres of influence. However, research carried out by the commission shows that the various regions are very unequally endowed at the intermediate level with regional centers which can relay the influence of the *métropoles.* The situation is quite good in the areas where Paris, Lyon, and Marseille exercise a preponderant influence. On the other hand, other areas are characterized by quantitative and qualitative deficiencies in cities with a regional function. For example, the Southwest has two *métropoles,* Toulouse and Bordeaux, but despite their extended influence it is imperfectly relayed. Brest, in Brittany, could be a regional center for an area with over a million inhabitants but it is not at present equipped for such a role. On the whole, the characteristics and roles of cities at the intermediate level need further study; planning will be facilitated when studies, which have already been begun in some program regions, are available for the entire country. In particular, it is necessary to define as soon as possible the policy which should be pursued concerning the organization of cities circling Paris at a distance of some hundred kilometers. These urban centers— Amiens, Rouen, Chartres, Orléans, Troyes, and Reims—should become key sites for the economic development and urbanization of the Paris Basin. In addition, policy in this regard should be established in terms of the principal transportation axes which follow the valleys of the Seine and the Oise, and to a lesser degree, the Marne and Yonne.[13]

At the lower level of the urban hierarchy, where small cities serve as links between the countryside and larger cities, it is appropriate to encourage concentration both to assure better quality of service and for technical and financial reasons. To improve regional policy at this level two complementary kinds of studies will be carried out. The first will be theoretical and inductive and will concern hypotheses relating to optimal dimensions of facilities in relation to users, distance, and other criteria; the second will be based on direct observation of the norms used in cases where the present organization of services seems particularly satisfactory. Finally, all forms of cooperation and integration among rural localities should be strongly encouraged, and investment policy should favor rural organizations which have taken significant initiatives in these regards.[14]

Following the First Report, the *Report on the Principal Orientations* for the preparation of the Fifth Plan adopted the definition and *aménagement* of a hierarchic urban structure as one of the eight major objectives for regional policy during the last half of this decade. In general, the report emphasized the problems associated with urban growth and pointed out the need for a policy of urban investment appropriate to each level of the hierarchy. At the highest level, it is urged that

> the *métropoles d'équilibre* should offer advantages which can be compared to those of the capital in most domains. The weight of Paris, though it is adapted to the dimension of Europe, will continue to be excessive in the economic and social life of France so long as it is not balanced by the development of regional *métropoles* with sufficient population and activities. The

métropoles must be given priority in the provision of equipment characteristic of the superior level (culture, research, higher education, hospital equipment, administration, transport, etc.).[15]

Development of the nation's urban structure should also include the equipment of regional centers capable of relaying the influence of each *métropole*. In general, the role of cities at the intermediate level should be reinforced in all areas, but especially in regions where there are not a sufficient number of cities, quantitatively and qualitatively, with a regional function. The Southwest is mentioned as a case in point.[16]

Urban Policy and the Fifth Plan

The importance recently accorded to urban matters in regional policy is illustrated by the change in nomenclature on regional policy from "regional development" in the Fourth Plan to "regional and urban development" in the Fifth Plan. The Fifth Plan stresses the need to define more carefully the hierarchic urban structure of France, as well as to prepare specific development plans for individual cities. Principal attention is given to the *métropoles d'équilibre,* which are identical with the broadly defined agglomerations proposed by the National Commission for *Aménagement du Territoire*.[17]

The Plan insists on a number of new measures concerning the distribution of economic activities and equipment between Paris and other large agglomerations. More selective decentralization should be encouraged by several means: the restrictions governing the location of new activities in the Paris Region should be extended over a larger geographic area; public and quasi-public organisms should place more of their orders and seek more markets with firms located in the provinces, assuming that is economically justifiable to do so; and an effort should be made to assure that consumers of public services in the Paris Region pay charges sufficient to cover the true corresponding social costs. With respect to the tertiary sector, present measures to decentralize activities of the government or those under government control should be reinforced; services whose presence in the capital is not a necessity should be transferred to the provinces, and new extensions in the Paris Region should be permitted only if they are really needed. Decentralization of private tertiary activities should be favored by endowing the *métropoles d'équilibre* with renovated central cities and new business centers; a special effort should be made to attract activities which exercise a stimulating effect on social and economic development, for example research.[18]

Investment in public overhead capital during the Fifth Plan should take into account the need to renovate Paris and to develop the *métropoles d'équilibre*. With respect to the geographical distribution of new housing aided by the government, the proportion of the national total accounted for by the Paris Region will diminish relative to the Fourth Plan; conversely, the proportion to be constructed in the eight *métropoles* will increase. Mass transportation needs in Lyon and Marseille are to be the object of detailed studies concerning the feasibility of subway systems for these cities. If the relevant findings are positive, a start on these undertakings can be made before the end of the Fifth Plan. In addition, government aid will permit construction to begin on a number of new towns in the vicinity of Paris, Lyon, and Marseille. Higher education policy will aim at progressively reducing the proportion of students enrolled at the University of Paris. This figure was 41 per cent in 1954 and 33 per cent in 1964; the goal is to reduce it to 26.5 per cent by 1973. Research investment by the government will be substantially altered in favor of the *métropoles*. The proportion of such outlays destined for the Paris Region (including Orléans) during the Fifth Plan is from 35 to 40 per cent, that for ten large provincial agglomerations (including Grenoble and Rennes), 50 to 55 per cent, and that for other agglomerations, 10 to 15 per cent. The corresponding proportions during the Fourth Plan were 58 per cent, 22 per cent, and 20 per cent, respectively.[19]

Finally, the Plan makes several observations concerning the role of urbanism. In particular, it points out that urbanism should specify its planning doctrine and do so in a manner which can be translated into practical programs. The importance attached to this aspect of regional planning is illustrated by the Plan's statement that results of studies of France's urban structure "should guide the location of public investments over the territory." [20] Toward this end, programs for renovation and new construction will be prepared in cooperation with interested regional parties for all agglomerations with a population of over 50,000 persons. New urban agencies will be created to prepare "plans for *aménagement* and organization" or "strategic plans" more or less on the model of that for the Paris Region. With the exception of the Lyon-St. Etienne area, such projects still need to be undertaken in all of the large urbanized zones in the provinces. During the Fifth Plan, provincial agglomerations will receive more financial aid from the government to support the preparation of urban plans than will the Paris Region. Urban planning policy also calls for organizations which can coordinate and supervise the activities of the various communes which comprise each large agglomeration.[21]

It has been argued that "the policy of *métropoles d'équilibre,* designed to provide a balance to Paris, but especially to stimulate the regions where the *métropoles* are situated, now appears to be the keystone of the actions which, taken as a whole, today constitute *aménagement du territoire.*" [22] Whether or not this position overstates the case, the importance attributed to the *métropoles* already has been reflected in concrete terms in the regionalization of the budget for 1966.

In the matter of housing the 1966 budget provides for a special allocation of 7,000 dwellings to the *métropoles* apart from the dwelling units allocated by program region. These special allotments range from 400 units in Strasbourg to 1,300 in Lyon-St. Etienne, and they represent a substantial increase over the 4,000 units accorded to the *métropoles* in the last year of the Fourth Plan. In order to provide land for the growth of these agglomerations, or for the construction of related new towns, the Caisse des dépôts has purchased 2,350 hectares of land which will be held in reserve for these purposes. In addition, 90 million francs has been made available to a special National Fund for Land-Use Planning and Urbanism for the purpose of acquiring land at the periphery of new towns. Another special credit of 20 million francs has been opened for the creation of urban expressways outside of the Paris Region. The Fund for Intervention for *Aménagement du Territoire* will also accentuate its efforts on behalf of the *métropoles,* principally in the fields of expressways and water purification and supply. The *métropoles* also benefit from priorities for telecommunications and hospital investment. To these benefits must of course be added those concerning the provision of higher education and basic research facilities.[23] The increasing importance attributed to the *métropoles* demands that their nature and significance be examined more carefully from an economic, as well as demographic and cultural, viewpoint.

The
Métropoles d'Equilibre

Excluding Paris, nine of the eleven largest agglomerations in France are included among the *métropoles*. Those not a part of a *métropole* are Rouen and Nice, which rank eight and tenth respectively (again excluding Paris). Nancy ranks sixteenth and Metz twenty-second, but their combined agglomeration populations, as shown in Table 10.1, would put the Nancy-Metz *métropole* among the top ten urban units. Although the *métropoles* rank at the head of France's provincial cities, their combined populations are still less than that of the Paris Region. The combined *métropole* total for population in "industrial or urban population zones" was 5,737,373 in 1962, while that in the more narrowly defined agglomerations was 4,706,000. In 1962, the residential complex of the Paris Region included 7,814,000 persons, and the narrowly defined Paris Region (Seine and Seine-et-Oise) included 6,583,000 inhabitants.[24] Thus, Paris alone accounts for about 2,000,000 more persons than the eight *métropoles* combined, even though the latter are large in relation to other French cities.

Between 1954 and 1962 the total population of France increased by 8.1 per cent, while urban population increased by 15.6 per cent.[25]

Table 10.1
Population of the *métropoles d'equilibre*

	Industrial or urban zone[a]		Agglomeration		
Métropoles d'équilibre	*Numbers of communes*	*Population 1962*	*Numbers of communes*	*Population 1962*	*Percentage growth 1954–62*[b]
Lyon-St. Etienne	191	1,479,757	42	1,194,000	18.5
Marseille-Aix	22	934,700	9	879,000	16.4
Bordeaux	59	537,632	14	471,000	5.8
Lille-Roubaix-Tourcoing	89	873,247	57	780,000	8.4
Toulouse	21	365,927	2	336,000	21.0
Strasbourg	71	427,093	11	307,000	14.1
Nantes-St. Nazaire	48	512,376	12	383,000	14.1
Nancy-Metz	290	606,641	24	356,000	14.8

Source: André Lewin, "Caractères originaux des métropoles d'équilibre," *Urbanisme*, No. 89 (1965), p. 27.

[a]Includes "dormitory" communes, industrial satellites, or communes situated along industrial or transportation axes closely tied to the respective agglomerations.

[b]Rate includes only that for the principal city of the agglomeration.

Most of the *métropoles* had growth rates (Table 10.1) which corresponded rather closely to the national rate of urban growth, though the rates for Lyon, and especially Toulouse, were notably higher, and those for Lille and Bordeaux markedly lower. Indeed, the growth rate for Bordeaux was lower than the over-all national average. It also is pertinent to note that for all agglomerations with over 100,000 inhabitants, eleven had higher growth rates than Toulouse, the highest-ranking *métropole*. These other agglomerations had growth rates ranging from 21.9 per cent in the cases of Toulon and Le Mans to 44.5 per cent in the case of Grenoble.[26] Thus, taken as a whole, the *métropoles* do not present a picture of dynamism in terms of demographic expansion.

In most respects the *métropoles* are characterized by pronounced deficiencies in relation to other large European cities. Cultural activities, for example, are of importance not only for local residents but also for the inhabitants of a city's entire zone of attraction. Lewin has pointed out that the "cultural poverty of the *métropoles,* and especially certain ones, is flagrant; the remedy must not consist only in organizing periodic spectacular activities . . . which sometimes exhaust all local possibilities in a few days: it is necessary to create and give life to a veritable cultural infrastructure." [27] Contrary to some of their large foreign counterparts, the French *métropoles* are rarely the headquarters for national administrations; rather, they are the seat of regional or departmental branches, though these may be fairly important. Although Strasbourg is the seat of the Parliamentary Assembly of the Common Market countries and for the Council of Europe, and although Lyon has recently been designated as the headquarters for the International Center for Cancer Research, an organization linked to the World Health Organization, these phenomena are exceptional. In the domain of banking and finance, "the eight *métropoles* taken together have a financial importance equal to about one tenth that of the Paris Region"; here again "one is far from the concentration of banking and financial means and centers of economic decision-making that are encountered in Milan, Frankfurt, or Dusseldorf." [28] As to commercial activity, Hautreux's analysis of the location of twenty-seven types of "rare" or special branches (for example, motor bearings, industrial cloth, laboratory glassware, air conditioners, exotic wood) showed that outside of Paris only Lyon provided all of the categories; Marseille had only nineteen; Lille, Bordeaux, Toulouse, Nantes, and Strasbourg had between eleven and thirteen; and Nancy, like Nice and Grenoble, had only from six to nine.[29] In general, therefore, it is evident that a considerable effort will be required to give the *métropoles* the status and functions corresponding to those of major provincial centers in other countries.

An undertaking of the magnitude implied in the policy of *métropoles d'équilibre* inevitably has provoked a significant amount of opposition, and a number of the arguments which have been urged against this policy have some merit.

One of the most frequently occurring objections is that concentration on developing a few major urban centers will only serve to drain the regions corresponding to the respective *métropoles* in much the same way that Paris has drained France as a whole. Pierre Bauchet, one of the earlier advocates of concentrating public overhead capital in a relatively few regional centers, also expressed the fear a decade ago that the growth of one part of a region may inhibit the growth of the rest of the region. He was specifically concerned with disparities between northern Lorraine, where Nancy and Metz are located, and the more thinly populated mountainous areas of southern Lorraine. The development of Lorraine, he maintained, "threatens to be characterized by growing disequilibrium. It is necessary to prevent the expanding north of the province from attracting men and capital, and from monopolizing important manufacturing industries on which employment of the population of the Vosges depends. One must take care that the most dynamic zone does not crush its environment." [30]

In a similar vein, Gravier warns against concentrating economic activity "in a few large agglomerations draining all the life from their surrounding regions by daily migrations over a long distance, then by permanent migrations which result in a chronic shortage of housing and public overhead capital in general"; in this event, decentralization policy would only serve to "reconstitute the impediments of Paris and to transform rural areas into lifeless agricultural ghettos." [31]

Edgard Pisani, then the Minister of Agriculture, told the Economic and Social Council in 1965 that while he approved of the principle of creating *métropoles d'équilibre* to compensate for the growth of Paris, there also is a need to organize rural life around centers having a vitality and diversity of activity sufficient to respond to the needs of the rural population. In this regard it will therefore be necessary to encourage a "discontinuous urbanization" of the countryside.[32]

The corollary to the fear that the *métropoles* will only serve to promote the conversion of the countryside into a desert is a concern that concentration of population in a few large agglomerations will result in the creation of external diseconomies such as those now so prevalent in Paris. This point, brought out by Gravier, has been raised in numerous writings. For example, the report of one parliamentary commission on the Fifth Plan agrees that it would be desirable to have regional *métropoles* with important government administrations, universities, business headquarters, banks, and decision-making centers. But it argues that if there is a proliferation of tertiary activities, this will in turn induce industrial employment. This is not necessarily desirable because, in the commission's view, "our large provincial cities are already on the way toward suffocation." [33] Indeed, it maintains that if the development of *métropoles d'équilibre* is accepted as national policy, their growth should be limited to "a certain diameter" so that they will not become overcrowded in the center, surrounded by a ring of dormitory communes, and, in general, the source of "a new disequilibrium between the regional capital and its environment." [34] In present cities and in their immediate surroundings, high land prices constitute a heavy handicap in the face of needs for housing, factories, parks, and green space (as is customary in the French literature, this phenomenon is attributed to "speculation" rather than to the rationing function of the price mechanism). On the other hand, the commission points out that this is not the case in a new city or in a rural environment:

> the land costs only the price of a field or meadow. In large cities, the work of new investment and renovation requires delays, studies, precautions, and complications such that its cost multiplies without end. In a new city or in a rural milieu, roads can be made easily with bulldozers and pipelines can be laid in virgin ground. While respecting French taste for a certain diversity and while adapting construction to regional style and the countryside, houses as well as factories can be mass produced and, in consequence, cost less than in any other location. . . .
>
> The new city and the natural utilization of the countryside—there is the grand orientation which is offered to our country. . . .[35]

However, this approach is oversimplified. Unless land is acquired at once, market forces will tend to raise land prices in areas under consideration for development. Land reserves might be acquired in advance of significant price increases, but this would be difficult on a large scale. Any contemplated construction project presumably would not be undertaken without considering alternative sites, and reserves cannot be purchased for each possible alternative. But once an area is even under study for an important development land prices will tend to rise. Moreover, housing developments cannot be undertaken without reference to the employment possibilities available to its residents. Under a system of indicative planning firms cannot be compelled to locate in close proximity to new towns; it must be feasible for them to do so on comparative cost grounds. Here again, the external economies available in or near already existing major urban centers would be more attractive to most firms. Provision of new external economies in the form of major infrastructure investment also would be more economically justifiable where there is a large or potentially large number of users; a given major highway clearly would be more economical if it served, say, Lyon, than if it served a town of 10,000 inhabitants.

In any event, the arguments that the *métropoles* will at the same time drain their surrounding regions and become overcongested themselves is not necessarily implied in the policy of promoting a few *métropoles,* since their development is linked to the notion of an urban hierarchy. In this context, the *métropole* is not isolated from its region but is a complement to the rest of the region's urban pyramid. As Guichard has emphasized, "the essence of the *métropoles* is not to have a big population, but to perform certain functions." [36]

Nevertheless there are other criticisms of *métropole* policy which must be considered. One is that promotion of a few large agglomerations is not called for, because since World War II the highest growth rates have been those of smaller cities. Thus, according to this argument, it is only reasonable to devote more investment to smaller cities, both because of needs created by their population expansion and because it would be of more general benefit than concentrating investment in only a few locations.[37] Moreover, insofar as urban growth policy should be responsive to public preferences, the results of a recent survey prepared for the DATAR lend support to those who favor giving relatively more attention to smaller cities.

Survey respondents were told that some persons think that in about forty years, seven or eight cities should have at least a million inhabitants, and that, more generally, the population living in cities will have at least doubled. Only 24 per cent of the respondents believed that this would be "reasonable"; 40 per cent held that it would be "not reasonable," while 17 per cent said that this would "constitute a folly." Similarly, 61 per cent believed that such a possibility should be "avoided at all cost," whereas only 14 per cent thought that it should be encouraged. These attitudes were very general, with women reacting about the same as men, and with young persons reacting about the same as older respondents. The major motives given by those who thought that the evolution described would be not reasonable or a folly were that the city is tiring, unhealthy, and inhuman (25 per cent), that housing would be still more crowded and that it would be necessary to invest too much (19 per cent), and that it would be better to decentralize (15 per cent).[38]

Public opposition to the growth of large cities was expressed in still another manner. Respondents were told that some persons believe that in France there are not enough cities with over 500,000 inhabitants, nor enough cities with from 100 to 500,000 inhabitants. They were then asked if they mostly agreed or disagreed with this viewpoint. With regard to the proposition concerning cities with a population of over 500,000 persons, only 18 per cent agreed, while 61 per cent disagreed (21 per cent had no opinion). On the proposition concerning cities with from 100,000 to 500,000 persons, 37 per cent agreed and the same number disagreed (26 per cent had no opinion).[39] Thus, "if the establishment of *métropoles d'équilibre* is to succeed, it will be necessary that public opinion understand that it is possible to live agreeably in the large cities of tomorrow. If the public is to realize this, it is necessary today to propose new models; and it is equally necessary that the public be willing to pay for their realization." [40]

Although public hostility to large cities may be based on an exaggerated view of the inevitability of the social costs which characterize the Paris Region, it is also clear that proponents of the *métropole* approach have so far failed to propose concrete alternative models for the development of more agreeable urban agglomerations. Some authorities have even questioned the possibility of preparing such models within the context of present *métropole* policy. For example, a recent study of the urban structure of the Rhone-Alps region questions whether the existence of a regional *métropole* is really necessary. Even if such a center is only vaguely defined as a city which provides sufficient services and functions so that its residents and those of its region do not have general recourse to Paris, it would remain true that Paris, rather than Lyon, is the real *métropole* of Rhone-Alps. Although Lyon is by far the largest city in this program region, many cities of the region have their most important economic relations with Paris, especially in matters of finance and investment decisions. Of course, it might be argued that this is precisely the kind of situation which a policy of *métropoles d'équilibre* aims at correcting. Nevertheless, there seems to be little indication that Lyon has contributed, or would contribute in the future, any substantial impetus to the growth of the rest of the region. The continuing prosperity and growth of Rhone-Alps is based on several autonomous centers of development, including, in addition to Lyon, St. Etienne, Grenoble, Annecy, Chambéry, Valence, and Roanne. Moreover, insofar as the growth of these centers is tied to relations with Paris, it might well only complicate matters to create a "false" *métropole* which would only serve to insert an intermediate stage between the region and decision centers in Paris.[41] Although the situation which characterizes Rhone-Alps may not correspond to that of slower growing regions, or to regions where growth is geographically less broadly based, this negative view of *métropole* policy is nonetheless highly significant because of the dominant place which has been ascribed to Lyon as a city with great potential for balancing the influence of Paris.

The choice of Nantes as a *métropole d'équilibre* for the West provides another example of the potential weakness of present urban policy. Gravier has effectively argued that a major error was made when Nantes was chosen as the site for a new university and for regional administrative headquarters. This apparently was done on the ground that Nantes, with 328,000 inhabitants, "was a '*métropole*' with clear domination over Angers (134,000 inhabitants) and Le Mans (142,000). But the unity of grouping which was thus supposed to be welded was in fact broken. Indeed, the eccentric position of Nantes is evident to the most superficial observer." [42] Nantes has practically no relation with Le Mans, which is nearly as close to Paris as to the port city. Angers, on the other hand, is at the center of the region; it is 90 kilometers from Le Mans, 73 from Laval, and 89 from Nantes. It would therefore have been more reasonable to have developed university facilities and regional administrative services at Angers. In addition, Nantes has traditionally been oriented toward the sea, even though its port activity is less than that of Bordeaux. "The same official voices which proclaim it 'growth pole of the West' express concern over the menace of recession which weighs upon its shipbuilding activity." [43] Nantes presents still further difficulties. Banking and insurance are not well represented; it has only two firms in this sector with over one hundred employees, whereas Angers has four and Le Mans has seven such establishments. Nantes is noted for labor difficulties, and book sales statistics indicate that among large provincial cities it is the one where people read the least. In general, it would appear that conditions which characterize Nantes render it "incapable of fulfilling metropolitan functions," whereas Angers "possesses a great deal of what is lacking at Nantes"; the demographic and economic growth which have characterized Angers in recent years, as well as its cultural and intellectual attractiveness, make it the natural "center of gravity for the central West." [44]

Thus, there is considerable evidence to indicate that emphasis on the development of a single *métropole* may not be the best urban policy in regions where growth is rapid and broadly based in geographic terms, as in the case of Rhone-Alps; or else that where a single regional *métropole* would be a valuable polarizing force, a wrong choice has been made with respect to its location, as in the case of Nantes in the West. There also remains the more general difficulty that "there exists no doctrine of urbanism capable of orienting the urbanization" of the *métropoles* which have been selected.[45] It is still not known if this urbanization will continue to take place in a radial-concentric manner, or if it will be oriented along axes. "Moreover, the doctrine concerning the intermediate cities appears equally imprecise. In particular, it has not been specified how these cities will be able to come to terms with their lack of public overhead capital." [46] These difficulties are reflected in the Fifth Plan, which maintains that urbanism must "specify its doctrine" and show how it can be utilized as a discipline for practical action.[47]

Nevertheless, from an economic viewpoint the basic problem with the policy of *métropoles d'équilibre* is not so much one of urbanism as it is understood in the city planning sense as one of promoting development poles which will generate regional economic growth. Present French urban policy is based too exclusively on studies of tertiary equipment and zones of urban influence. What is needed in addition is a thorough study of the nature and intensity of propulsive activities (including, of course, those of an industrial character) in major urban centers and of the technical and geographic linkages which characterize regional economic activity. The Commission on Urban Equipment of the General Planning Commission was established for the purpose of finding specific geographical locations for application of the regionalization of the budget, even though the policy of *métropoles d'équilibre* is concerned more with coordinating diverse activities than with direct budget allocations. However, the hierarchy which it has defined has been based on the consequences of past development rather than the dynamic interdependencies of the economy at the level where propulsive activities induce other activities. Of course, it may be argued, as Aydelot has done, that in the contemporary world a propulsive industry is not so much a cause of polarization as an effect of it, i.e. the presence in relative abundance of a wide range of tertiary activities attracts industries which in turn induce new activities (see page 54). Given this view, emphasizing the development of tertiary activities in a few select places may be the best way to attract industry. Nevertheless, French urban planning needs to take greater account of the specifically economic aspects of the urbanization process. In particular, it needs more systematic study of the mechanisms by which economic growth is transmitted from one sector to another in specific geographical areas, for only in this way can it escape the limitations of a merely functional approach to the urban hierarchy.

Summary and Conclusions

In the past few years French regional policy has given increasing attention to the structure and functions of the nation's urban hierarchy. Deficiencies in previous decentralization measures and the trend toward greater urbanization have combined to create a new emphasis on the basic urban structure to which regional policy measures should be applied in the future. The structure of the urban pyramid has been defined largely in terms of tertiary importance and exterior influence of cities. On the basis of such considerations, the superior level of the hierarchy includes eight agglomerations (excluding Paris). Because financial constraints preclude equipping a large number of scattered cities with a complete range of services and activities, and because these eight agglomerations are considered to have the greatest number of existing external economies, they will be given priority for a wide variety of public investments; as favored *métropoles d'équilibre* these agglomerations will, it is hoped, eventually constitute both zones of attraction to offset the attractiveness of the Paris Region and development poles for their respective regions. In addition to the *métropoles,* the planners have designated a group of cities at the intermediate level whose growth is to be tied to that of the *métropoles.* Special attention will be given to a group of ten "regional centers." Finally, at the base of the urban pyramid are a large number of towns and rural centers whose role is to relay the influence of larger cities to the countryside.

The principal advantages of the *métropoles* stem for the most part from their relatively large populations within the French context. In most respects, the economic and cultural services which they offer are inferior to those found not only in Paris but in other European centers of comparable size or function. In terms of population growth, the *métropoles* taken as a whole are not as dynamic with respect to growth rates as somewhat smaller cities in the intermediate level of the French hierarchy. Moreover, the relatively large size of the *métropoles* does not constitute an advantage in relation to public preferences, since survey data show pronounced hostility to the development of large cities. Thus, the policy of giving priority to the development of a few large agglomerations is basically one of inducement and persuasion: inducement because, taken as a whole, these centers are not characterized by their dynamism, and persuasion because it is hoped that the public can be educated to like life in large cities.

These considerations make it questionable whether the priority given to the *métropoles* is justifiable on opportunity cost grounds. For example, even in the case of Lyon, certainly one of the most progressive of French cities, it would appear that its growth has contributed little to the expansion of other cities in Rhone-Alps. In other words, the expansion of this region has been based on a number of relatively autonomous spatial growth poles. What seems called for in this case is a more balanced allocation of investment credits among the principal centers of growth, rather than priority to one center.

On the other hand, in lagging areas it may be desirable to promote the equipment of single *métropoles* so that they may become regional development poles. Since there is a general lack of external economies in lagging regions it is not financially feasible to attempt to sprinkle investment projects thinly over a large area. Pierre Janrot has pointed out that in the face of increasing competition, French firms will continue to become more and more concentrated. At the same time, however, there is a "spectacular multiplication of small and medium-size firms which manufacture highly elaborated products and which work in large measure as suppliers of large propulsive industries nearby." [48] Although these smaller firms are dependent upon their relations with large buyers, there would seem to be no compelling reason why they could not be located throughout the whole of the urban pyramid in an area the size of one, or even several, of France's program regions. This is especially true since the relatively light and elaborated products produced by the smaller firms, together with improved transportation facilities, greatly reduce the difficulties posed by transportation costs. Thus, if the development of a lagging region calls for emphasis on inducing the location of propulsive industries in a regional *métropole* through the provision of external economies, this does not imply that the economic life of the region as a whole would be drained toward the *métropole.* Once the functions of the cities and towns in the region's urban pyramid are defined, in terms of industrial interdependencies as well as tertiary activities, public investment priorities can be assigned which correspond to the given functions. For example, towns at the base of the hierarchy may be given priority with regard to industrial zones for light industry, while the regional *métropole* may be given priority for an expressway or institutions for higher learning or the teaching of specialized vocational skills.

In any event, it should be emphasized that a policy of *métropoles d'équilibre* need not be applied uniformly over the whole country. Although it might be thought that the promotion of an already relatively well-equipped city such as Lyon would be the most efficient way to provide a balance to the attractiveness of the Paris Region, this is not necessarily the case. It would be more in keeping with public preferences to encourage continuing multipolar growth in a region such as Rhone-Alps than to favor deliberately the growth of a single agglomeration (even though other cities in the region may not be neglected). A policy of *métropoles d'équilibre* applied to an intermediate region where growth is rapid and geographically well balanced may only foster the creation of a congested region in the regional *métropole*. Moreover, there is no reason in the case of Rhone-Alps, or a similar region, why the region as a whole, rather than just its largest city, should not provide an attractive force to offset the weight of the Paris Region. In areas deprived of active development poles, on the other hand, a policy of *métropoles d'équilibre* may indeed be the most feasible path to self-sustained growth. In brief, therefore, the problems and prospects involved in the creation of *métropoles d'équilibre* must be viewed in a specifically regional context, rather than applied in a more or less homogeneous manner to the entire nation. In this respect it is unfortunate that there has been a certain shift of emphasis from the program region framework to that of the urban hierarchy. This issue, however, will receive more detailed treatment in Chapter 11.

11

A Summary View

The preceding chapters have shown how regional planning in France has developed from a postwar concern with decentralizing economic activity into a comprehensive framework wherein local, regional, and national public authorities and representatives of major economic groups cooperate in the preparation of "regional sections," which constitute the spatial counterpart of the national plan by sectors.

In evaluating the evolution of the objectives and means which have characterized French regional planning I have relied in large measure on a general policy model formulated in the light of relevant theoretical and empirical considerations from economic and related social science disciplines. One of the basic attributes of this model is its distinction among three types of analytic regions: congested, intermediate, and lagging. The advantage of these distinctions over the familiar division between "developed" and "underdeveloped" regions is that they come to grips directly with the problem of overconcentra-

250

tion of population and economic activity in some areas, a problem too often neglected in favor of studying the difficulties experienced by relatively underdeveloped regions. Moreover, the concept of an intermediate region helps to clarify the issue of the opportunity costs of investing in lagging regions when there are better alternatives elsewhere from a national and social viewpoint.

French regional planning was initiated largely on the basis of a distinction between an overconcentrated Paris Region and a relatively deprived French "desert," i.e. the provinces. The recognition that Paris is a congested region has continued to be one of the fundamental assumptions of regional policy. Thus, in addition to tax and credit measures and direct controls designed to curtail the growth of the Paris Region and encourage location elsewhere, the Fifth Plan has called for the progressive introduction of pricing and fiscal measures which will compel firms and households to pay the true social cost of their location in the region. However, the new system will take the form of higher *average* charges for services such as public transportation, water, and parking, presumably on the ground of practicality, and will in fact therefore still not force new households and firms to pay the *marginal* cost of their presence. In any event, well-designed surveys of public preferences indicate that Parisians and non-Parisians alike overwhelmingly favor public policy efforts to limit the growth of the Paris Region, largely because of opposition to the external diseconomies which accompany congestion.

On the other hand, the notion of a more or less homogeneous area lying outside of the Paris Region has been replaced by a distinction with regard to intermediate and lagging regions. In the terminology of the Fifth Plan, the French approach maintains that

> the policy of *aménagement du territoire* must find a practical compromise between regions depending on a policy of publicly induced growth (*politique d'entraînement*) and regions depending on a policy of induced public investment (*politique d'accompagnement*). On the one hand, it must give every opportunity, under conditions of lively competition, to "strong" regions whose potential benefits the whole of the country. On the other hand, it must seek to involve the "weak" regions in a process of development at first induced, then autonomous, in a manner which will enable them to participate in the current of modernization and expansion which characterizes our time.[1]

The areas which benefit from government efforts to induce self-sustained economic growth through excess public overhead capital capacity and financial incentives are the lagging regions of the West and Southwest. Policy measures for the intermediate regions of the East, on the other hand, provide for public expenditures just sufficient to meet the needs arising from their relatively rapid natural growth. The Nord and, to a somewhat lesser extent, Lorraine constitute rather special cases; they are characterized by a relatively high degree of industrialization but their dominant sectors are either declining or stagnating. Regional planning for these regions is marked by a mixed policy approach aimed at industrial conversion.

In addition to differentiating three types of region, the policy model presented in Chapter 1 was formulated in terms of three kinds of investment. Private investment and investment in directly productive activities are considered as synonymous. Public investment, however, is divided into two components, social (SOC) and economic (EOC). Investments of the latter type are specifically aimed at supporting directly productive activities and include projects such as roads, harbors, and power supply. SOC investment, on the other hand, is more concerned with the development of human resources and includes education, welfare, health, and similar undertakings. While SOC items obviously contribute to the support of directly productive activities, their impact is less tangible than that of EOC investment. It was argued on the basis of long-run opportunity cost considerations from a national point of view that public investment in intermediate regions should emphasize EOC projects, whereas public investment in lagging regions should be characterized by a greater emphasis on SOC projects. A special situation is represented by intermediate areas near the lagging-region range of the regional spectrum. These areas are industrialized and therefore have external economies not found in lagging regions, but they are dominated by stagnating sectors. Such regions should benefit from balanced SOC and EOC investment to promote industrial conversion.

In Chapter 7 it was shown that the difficulties of France's lagging regions are in large measure a result of a relative lack of benefits accruing from SOC investment. This is not to deny that EOC investment in lagging regions will produce advantages, but the effectiveness of such projects also depends on the degree to which the regions' human resources have been developed by SOC investment.

In Chapter 8 it was shown that in the intermediate regions of the East the greatest relative need with regard to public investment policy is for more EOC. In particular, the development of a Rhine-Rhone transportation axis has been urged by regional authorities and experts in the fields of transportation and regional economics.

Concrete policy objectives and projects have clearly reflected government recognition of the relative importance of EOC investment for the East. While such projects as the Rhine-Rhone axis are viewed as means to induce greater economic expansion in the East, the government nevertheless has decided to expand public investment in this area at a modest rate, in response to immediate needs, so that more funds may be allocated to lagging regions and areas in need of industrial conversion. Policy measures for regions where a major conversion effort is called for, such as the Nord, reflect the need for balanced EOC-SOC investment. For example, EOC undertakings are needed to aid in providing new industrial structures and SOC outlays are required to retrain workers now employed in stagnating activities for employment in expanding sectors. Moreover, both EOC and SOC investment is badly needed to make up for pronounced deficiencies in urban amenities and health and educational standards. It may be said, therefore, that in these regards French regional policy is in accord with the assumptions of the model presented in Chapter 1, as well as with the policy measures derivable from it. Of course, this does not mean that any such model has in fact guided French planners. This is apparent from the approach taken toward the lagging regions of the West and Southwest.

While there is official recognition of the need to provide facilities for training surplus agricultural labor for employment in industry, there has not been adequate emphasis on the general problem of developing the human resources of these areas, despite the multitude of evidence concerning pronounced needs in this regard. The nature of allocations from the Fund for Intervention for *Aménagement du Territoire,* which, it will be recalled, was established to facilitate the execution of regional projects which might otherwise be precluded or delayed for financial reasons, provides a clear illustration of this point. As would be expected, the Fund has favored lagging regions; the ten program regions of the West and Southwest, along with Corsica, account for something over one third of France's total population, yet they have received over two thirds of all the expenditures made from the Fund (cumulated through July 1965). The great bulk of these outlays has been for EOC projects. Thus, expenditures for highway and water transportation alone have accounted for 42.5 per cent of all Fund allocations; these items combined with telecommunications investments make up 46.9 per cent of the total. In contrast, agricultural training, technical training, vocational education for adults, and operations concerning health and social welfare projects all taken together make up only 13.3 per cent of Fund expenditures.[2] Since the Fund is managed by the DATAR, it may be inferred that its activities reflect in some significant manner the priorities held by this key organism.

More generally, the *First Report of the National Committee for Aménagement du Territoire* and subsequent official documents relating to the Fifth Plan have given more attention to EOC measures than to SOC projects in policy discussions concerning the West and Southwest. The First Report states that it is essential to emphasize investments which will permit "rapidly a better utilization of human and material potentialities now badly employed, rather than those which, whatever their spectacular nature, would have only a limited effect at present on the economic and social structures of these regions." [3] Nevertheless, while there is clear recognition of the need for structural change in the broad social as well as economic sense, the concern with rapidity can only tend to favor EOC projects with more superficially obvious relation to industrialization than the less tangible benefits flowing from SOC investment. This is especially true in view of the fact that, according to the First Report, the growth of the economies of the West and Southwest should become self-sustaining by the end of the Fifth Plan.[4] Thus, policy recommendations are primarily concerned with immediate attraction of industries to these areas, whereas discussion of specific measures for the long-run transformation of their structures so as to make them more attractive to industry on comparative cost grounds is notably lacking.

Similarly, both the *Report on the Principal Options* for the preparation of the Fifth Plan and the Fifth Plan itself adopt the industrialization of the West (including the Southwest) as a major goal of regional

policy, yet neither gives systematic attention to the role of SOC investment in development policy. The *Report on the Principal Options* is
especially weak in this regard and is clearly more concerned with
providing highways and other transportation facilities for the West
than with providing investment directed toward human resources.[5] The
Fifth Plan provides for improvement in university facilities for the
three *métropoles d'équilibre* of the West and for increased vocational
training programs, but no attempt is made to define what priority
should be attached to SOC in relation to EOC measures or to clarify
what might be expected concerning the timing and nature of the
results of SOC undertakings.[6] However, the formulation of the Plan
was hampered because of the lag in obtaining priority estimates from
the modernization commissions and the Regional Economic Development Commissions. It may be hoped that greater clarification of the
role of SOC investment in lagging regions will be obtained at the end
of 1967, when the government critically re-examines the totality of
the programs undertaken to realize its main objective for the West,
i.e. the location in the West of from 35 to 40 per cent of all new employment created in France from 1966 to 1970, as provided for in the
Plan.

Largely because the external economies available to private firms
are greater in alternative regions, it seems unlikely that the government's employment goal for the West as a whole will be realized. As
the regression models formulated in Chapter 3 indicate, government-
aided investment has been spatially distributed in close accord with
degree of regional need, yet new industry and commerce have still
strongly tended to locate in regions which already have a high degree
of commercial and industrial importance. The magnitude of the government's efforts to provide external economies for lagging regions—
either through financial aids to private firms, public overhead capital
investment, or decentralization of its own activities—does not seem
sufficient to substantially change this pattern, at least not in so short
a period as that of the Fifth Plan. Nevertheless, some regions of the
West can expect important gains, partly because of favorable regional
policy measures and partly because of an important external economy,
namely, their proximity to Paris. The government points out that industrial growth often takes place along economic axes or in privileged
directions.[7] However, the areas which have grown because of their

participation in a growth axis, i.e. because of cumulative growth of EOC investment and private investment, are found, like the Seine and Rhone Valleys, outside of the lagging regions of the West and Southwest, or else are cities in the West that are relatively close to Paris, which tends to give them the quality of intermediate regions. In general, it is seen that EOC investment is most conducive to economic growth where it is located in intermediate regions, as was argued in Chapter 1. Moreover, intermediate regions tend to generate their own development axes, or poles, partly by inducing government EOC investment. On the other hand, the example of Lacq provides a clear illustration of the difficulties involved in trying to induce self-sustained growth in a lagging region through EOC; in this case, considerations of rational resource allocation from a national viewpoint led to a shift in most of the EOC benefit stream in favor of other regions.

A great deal has been said and written about moving industry and other economic activities to people, but policy-makers generally are more reluctant to urge the movement of people to job sources. Until very recently, official French policy has attempted to maintain a large number of small, individually-owned farms in the face of rapid technological change. This attitude, combined with inadequate SOC investment, has served to perpetuate the social and economic structures characteristic of lagging agricultural regions, including a surplus agricultural labor force. One of the principal arguments in favor of moving industry to lagging regions, even at considerable public expense in the form of subsidies or similar means, has been that the social costs involved in this type of action are less than the social costs which would be entailed by the uprooting of persons seeking employment in other regions and by the increased congestion which would result in industrial agglomerations. However, the latter difficulty is not a necessary one, since migration can be channeled to intermediate, rather than congested, regions.

On the other hand, the issue of uprooting residents of lagging areas is a genuine problem since there is abundant evidence that the number of persons preferring to live in these regions is high in both absolute and relative terms. Moreover, migration is not feasible for many persons because deficiencies in SOC in lagging regions have limited the development of human resources and thus the possibility for their employment in other regions. Nevertheless, these arguments should not be used to discourage migration, since at the margin there are always persons ready and willing to migrate from lagging regions. The regression model developed in Chapter 6 to examine the determinants of interregional migration patterns showed a very strong direct relationship between population change in a region as a result of migration and levels of living standards and economic opportunity.

Since both labor and capital are attracted to already advanced regions, and since such regions have numerous external economies, it would seem rational to concentrate public investment in intermediate regions so as to minimize spatial opportunity costs. However, given present residential preference patterns and the rigidities which they entail, it is no doubt preferable from a social viewpoint to continue the policy of investing just enough in intermediate regions to meet immediate and short-run requirements resulting from natural economic expansion, and just enough in the Paris Region to alleviate difficulties resulting from past neglect in public services, so that funds may be freed for inducing growth in lagging regions. As already suggested, however, a higher proportion of the latter outlays should be devoted to SOC projects. The consequences of expanded SOC for out-migration from lagging regions are complex because two contrary tendencies are involved; one is the attraction of firms seeking qualified labor (and lower wage rates, at least in the short run), and the other is out-migration of persons with skills and training in greater demand in more economically advanced regions. The extent of out-migration therefore will depend on the extent to which industry is in fact attracted and the time lag involved in this process, and on the extent to which residents prefer their own regions despite economic disadvantages. Nevertheless, many adults who benefit from initial emphasis on SOC investment will remain in a lagging region because of attachment to family, friends, and surroundings, whereas persons of school age will necessarily remain, at least until they are ready for employment or more specialized higher education. These persons eventually would constitute a body of qualified labor sufficient to permit greater emphasis on EOC investment. Then external economies from balanced SOC-EOC investment will serve to induce expanded private investment. In any event, SOC investment in lagging regions will not necessarily check out-migration in the short run, and it may possibly even encourage it; from a national opportunity cost point of view, the problems of lagging regions are not amenable to rapid short-run solution, though initial emphasis on investment in human resources still offers the most feasible policy from a long-run standpoint. It should be emphasized in conclusion that rational public investment policy should not be confused with attempts to stabilize regional populations, at least insofar as economic policy is concerned with increasing overall national welfare. In this respect, the Fifth Plan's insistence that it is "indispensable that regional development policy facilitate and orient the mobility of the employed population" [8] marks an important advance over the Fourth Plan, whose principal general objective for the whole of France was to limit migratory movements from regions with a population surplus.

In general, then, it may be said that French regional policy has been facilitated by its distinction among three types of region, and that its over-all division of effort *among* the regions so as to induce growth in lagging regions while limiting the growth of the Paris Region and allowing for the expansion of intermediate regions has been substantially correct. Investment policy *within* regions, however, should place relatively greater stress on SOC for lagging regions. As to population policy, the new emphasis on encouraging interregional labor migration is a positive step away from the more conservative attitudes which have prevailed heretofore.

If in most of these respects the Fifth Plan has been characterized by definite improvements, it is questionable if this has been the case with regard to the geographical framework which forms the concrete field of application for regional policy measures. More specifically, the new emphasis on a policy of *métropoles d'équilibre* has yet to be consistently integrated with the framework of the twenty-one program regions.

It was pointed out in Chapter 10 that the decision to give priority to the development of a few *métropoles* is justifiable in lagging areas where a general lack of external economies makes it unfeasible to scatter public investment projects thinly over a large area. Decentralization projects created in relative isolation in the countryside or in smaller towns will probably have little effect on the long-run growth of a lagging region. In contrast, the grouping of projects around a given geographic development pole permits firms to take maximum advantage of the technical and financial external economies generated by the interaction of mutually interdependent activities. These "agglomeration effects" explain why "in our time, despite progress in transportation and telecommunications, and despite the quasi-ubiquity of various forms of energy, economic activity is much more concentrated than a century ago." [9] Moreover, if public policy can succeed in creating viable development poles in certain agglomerations of lagging regions, there would seem to be no reason to preclude the location throughout the urban pyramid of an area, equivalent to one or several of France's program regions, of smaller firms dependent on large firms located in the regional *métropole*. The chief difficulty to realizing this objective is that although the Fifth Plan explicitly identifies its policy of *métropoles d'équilibre* for the West with the concept of development poles,[10] the approach taken in defining the *métropoles* is by no means equivalent to the economic concept of a development pole, or better, the process of polarization. As was shown in Chapter 5, an economic approach to the process of polarization requires careful analysis of relevant structural interdependencies and of the various ways in which growth may be transmitted or inhibited. As Paelinck has maintained, the notion of development poles is useful primarily as "a *conditional* theory of regional growth; it is valuable, above all, to the extent that it clearly indicates the conditions under which accelerated regional development can occur." [11] The policy of *métropoles d'équilibre,* on the other hand, has been based almost exclusively on study of the tertiary functions performed by cities and of their areas of influence. This functional approach thus has neglected essential economic aspects of development theory. Much of the responsibility for this phenomenon undoubtedly lies in the fact that urbanists and geographers, rather than economists, have had a predominant role in developing *métropole d'équilibre* policy. Indeed, one of the principal objections raised against the Fifth Plan is that economists were not given a great enough role in its preparation. Jules Milhau, for example, has protested that economic research has remained a guarded preserve of government administrations; and "it is quite evident that the administrations are incapable, by their nature, of carrying out true scientific research. This is not their role, and they are not prepared for it." [12]

If *métropole* policy is correct in principle but deficient in the methods of its elaboration with respect to lagging regions, it is questionable whether it is even correct in principle when applied to intermediate regions (such as Rhone-Alps) which already are experiencing relatively rapid and self-sustained expansion based on a number of spatial development poles. To give priority to one center under such circumstances is to run the risk of making it congested, especially in view of French residential preference patterns, which are characterized by dislike for large agglomerations. Moreover, the balanced, multipolar growth of such regions may be unnecessarily complicated by giving priority to one city; thus, objections already have been raised in Rhone-Alps that Lyon would constitute a "false" *métropole* and an unnecessary intermediate stage between other parts of the region and decision centers in Paris. In addition, there is no reason why a region whose growth is rapid and broadly based should not in itself, rather than only one of its cities, provide a force of attraction to help offset that of the Paris Region.

In any event, it is obvious that the value for policy purposes of development pole theory, whether or not it is posed in terms of *métropoles d'équilibre,* is related to the actual context in which it is to be applied. In this respect, the creation of regional organisms to participate in the formulation of regional priorities and in the regionalization of the government budget should be of particular value in the elaboration of policy ends and means. Unfortunately, earlier efforts in this direction were characterized by important defects. The "programs for regional action" which were drawn up as planning guides for the various program regions generally have been plans in name only. They have been for the most part inventories of regional conditions at a given time, and their staggered appearance over the past decade (the first of these documents, that for Brittany, appeared in 1956, while the last, that for Upper Normandy, appeared only in the middle of 1966) means that they have really not been comparable. In addition, they have been deficient in stipulating orders of priority and modes of finance for suggested future projects. Nevertheless, they have served to confront the General Planning Commission with the need for horizontal consultation and coordination in regional terms as a complement to vertical planning by sectors, and they have marked an initial, if not always successful, attempt to encourage cooperation among ministries and departments on common problems.

The basic concrete means for the regionalization of the national Plan are the regional sections. In 1962 the General Planning Commission decided to introduce the sections as an essential part of the Fourth Plan. The sections are parts of the various regional plans, and in their totality they represent the geographic breakdown of the national Plan; they are intended to project to the regional level the objectives specified in the Plan. Like the latter, the sections include a schedule of realizations, an order of priorities, and indications of the corresponding means of finance, all of which were lacking in the initial programs for regional action. The preparation of the regional sections for the Fourth Plan was a frankly experimental undertaking; by the time that the first sections were worked out in 1963, the Fourth Plan already had been in operation for one year and the annual budget for 1963 already had been prepared. The sections, therefore, were relevant only to investments of a residual nature. Other difficulties in elaborating the sections included lack of agreement between methods of preparation proposed by the General Planning Commission and those proposed by certain ministries; lack of real authority for the interdepartmental conferences which were charged with synthesizing the sections at the regional level; lack of coordination at the regional level, especially concerning consultation with the private Regional Expansion Committees; authoritarian attitudes on the part of some Paris ministries; and basic changes in regional planning institutions which occurred during the Fourth Plan.

The principal institutional reforms at the national level have been the creation of the National Commission for *Aménagement du Territoire* and the Délégation à l'aménagement du territoire et à l'action régionale (DATAR). The National Commission was created to replace the *aménagement du territoire* section of the Ministry of Construction; it is directly attached to the General Planning Commission and is responsible for preparing long-term studies on regional planning. The DATAR, which is directly attached to the Prime Minister, is closely associated in the work of the National Commission, since its head also is a vice-president of the commission. However, it also participates directly in the formulation of the annual investment budgets of the government. Its role is primarily one of coordination and impulsion with respect to the realization of regional objectives within the framework of the national Plan. Nevertheless, resistance to change of customary modes of action by the administrations continues to constitute an obstacle to horizontal coordination. Thus, the degree of success which the DATAR will have in realizing its objectives will depend on the pressure which it will be able to bring to bear, despite its lack of real authority, on the administrations, particularly in the Interministerial Committee for problems of regional planning.

Recent institutional reforms in the structure of planning at the regional level also have been far reaching. The role of the regional *préfets,* who are responsible for putting government regional policy into operation in their respective circumscriptions, has been clarified so as to give them a measure of real authority, rather than the nominal distinction of being "first among equals," where the "equals" are all of the departmental *préfets* in any given program region. Moreover, Prime Minister Pompidou indicated in June 1966 that regional *préfets* soon would be relieved of their functions as *préfets* of their respective departments so that they will be able to devote full time to regional duties.[13]

At the time of the creation of the regional *préfets,* in 1964, each program region also was given a Regional Economic Development Commission. Although the function of each commission is purely advisory, consultation is obligatory during the preparation of the regional sections. As of the middle of 1966 the composition of the commissions included, among others, 286 mayors, 202 municipal councilors (some of whom also were mayors), 40 farm representatives, and 119 representatives from labor unions.[14] It should also be noted that although the functions which had been performed by the Regional Expansion Committees were largely accorded to the Regional Economic Development Commissions, about a third of the administrators (regional, departmental, and local) of the Regional Expansion Committees now belong to the Regional Economic Development Commissions, and 80 per cent of the latter groups have presidents taken from the Regional Expansion Committees.[15]

It is, of course, too early to evaluate adequately the structure and methods of the new regional planning system, but as was shown in Chapter 4, it is already clear that both regional participation and coordination of regional policy at the national level have been vastly more effective in the preparation of the Fifth Plan than previous methods were in the elaboration of regional policy. It now remains to be seen to what extent regional considerations will in fact be taken into account in the execution of the Plan. This, in turn, will depend on the extent to which the regional *préfets* and Regional Economic Development ment Commissions actually influence the composition of the annual regional sections of the budget, and on the extent to which the DATAR can induce horizontal coordination at the national level in the light of regional planning objectives.

In any event, there remains the problem of harmonizing the planning framework based on the program regions and the policy of *métropoles d'équilibre,* assuming the latter is maintained despite its weaknesses, or else reformed. There is widespread agreement that the present number of program regions is too great; consolidations resulting in fewer regions, for example, the eight suggested by Beaud (see Chapter 6), would seem to be called for before the present structure acquires the rigidities and resistances to change which have characterized the departmental structure. This would then make it more feasible for the program regions to be structured around viable regional capitals, and for *métropole* policy to be integrated more closely into the institutional structure for planning at the regional level. At present, the relationship of the *métropoles* to the preparation of regional sections is ambiguous because policy measures pertaining to the *métropoles* are geared more toward loose coordination of diverse programs than to coherent integration into the elaboration of the budget at the regional level. Moreover, a more consistent integration of the program regions and the *métropoles* would permit the Regional Economic Development Commissions to consider regional problems and policies in a more comprehensive context. It thus would also facilitate their assuming the functions of regional social and economic councils on the model of the national council, an aim frequently proposed by those who favor both political and economic decentralization as a basis for more widespread participation in French democracy. However, any attempt to harmonize French regional policy will have to deal with the fact that the *métropoles,* as they now exist, tend to be located around the fringe of the national territory, whereas the lagging regions where development problems are most critical, i.e. Limousin and Auvergne, are located in the center of the country.

If activities related to the budget of the government, the Fund for Intervention for *Aménagement du Territoire,* and the Economic and Social Development Fund, which remains the most powerful single instrument for financing specifically regional projects, have increasingly been brought into the sphere of comprehensive regional policy, there are other important institutions whose relationship to regional goals remains to be defined.

For example, investments of local authorities account for a large share of the public investment directly relevant to regional planning. Investments of local governments are financed only to a very small extent by surpluses on the current account; for their share of investment costs [16] they must rely primarily on borrowing from public organisms, particularly the Caisse des dépôts et consignations. Although the regionalization of the budget for 1965 included data by region and by category for loans made by the Caisse to local public authorities, it is not yet possible to evaluate accurately the nature of the consequences of these undertakings. As the government has pointed out, this task requires data for entire regions over a number of years, and not from the Caisse alone but from other public bodies which lend to local governments, such as the Crédit agricole and the Crédit foncier.[17] At this writing such comprehensive data have not yet been published, although the government intends soon to give more detailed consideration to this matter. Nevertheless, there are indications that investment of local authorities has tended primarily to benefit already relatively prosperous regions. For example, local borrowing generally is induced by conditions such as growth of population and economic activity. Thus, in 1964 about two thirds (64.5 per cent) of all local investment financed by the Caisse was linked directly or indirectly to growth in housing construction.[18]

The Caisse also plays a leading role in the Sociétés d'Equipment which have been formed to execute numerous public investment undertakings, such as zones for priority urbanization, urban renewal, and the creation of equipped industrial zones. The partners in these groups generally include local governments, interested private parties, and the establishments responsible for their financing, notably the Caisse. Indeed, of the some one hundred Sociétés d'Equipment now in existence, sixty-four are directly dependent on a branch of the Caisse, the Société Centrale pour l'Equipment du Territoire.[19] The cumulative outlays (through 1964) of the groups dependent on this organism amount alone to 1.811 billion francs. However, they are largely absent in lagging regions,[20] whereas in other areas the existence of a number of such groups "lends itself to a dispersion of efforts which could increase

the over-all cost of operations and which could hinder the coordinated realization of investments anticipated within the planning
framework." [21]

For the immediate future it is questionable whether local governments as a whole can in fact find the means to realize the public
investment projects anticipated by the Fifth Plan. A recent law remov-
ing a number of public and quasi-public bodies from the government
budget and making them dependent on borrowing from the Caisse des
dépôts threatens to deprive local governments of capital funds which
they might otherwise have expected to receive. Thus, despite measures
such as the regrouping and fusion of communes—especially in urban
agglomerations—it is likely that the objectives of the Plan can only be
achieved through greater self-financing on the part of local governments.[22] A new law passed in January 1966 provides for replacing
the present local tax structure—based on property, land, and turnover
taxes—with a new system based on income tax revenues. Whereas
income from the present system increased by 49 per cent from 1955
to 1964, the increase derivable from the income tax would have been
95 per cent. When the new system goes into effect local governments
are expected to receive 400 million francs more in revenue than would
have been obtained under the present system. Unfortunately, the
changeover will not take place until 1968.

The over-all difficulties of local governments in raising investment
funds, as well as the tendency for their investments to be of most
benefit to relatively advanced regions, have their counterpart in the
activities of the Regional Development Societies. Although the societies
were founded for the express purpose of financing industrial enterprises in lagging regions, and although the government gives them
financial advantages on this ground, they have not, as was shown in
Chapter 3, been able to raise the amounts of capital which had been
hoped; moreover, it also was shown that their activities have actually
been of greater benefit to intermediate regions.

Thus, regional policy must somehow come to terms with the problem of integrating decentralized public and quasi-public investment
programs into the nation's general regional development framework.
In many respects this task should be easier in France than in a nation
such as the United States because of the higher degree of central influence that characterizes the structure of French public finance. Local

governments are highly dependent on central government grants or on borrowing from bodies subject to the authority of the central government. Moreover, even the Regional Development Societies must submit to certain controls exercised by a government commissioner. All of these factors create the possibility for increased central government influence on behalf of the goals of regional policy, even if such action is characterized more by its indicative than its coercive nature.

Finally, as the recent decline in decentralization operations accompanying emphasis on price stability has shown, the favorable execution of comprehensive regional policy is in large measure linked to the pace of aggregate economic expansion. Indeed, aggregate growth is an important precondition for the realization of the structural changes required to assure more rational spatial resource allocation in terms of public preferences.

12

Some Implications
for
American Regional Policy

The Case
of Appalachia

The Appalachian Regional Development Act of 1965 represents a unique attempt on the part of the federal government to provide substantial outlays for the explicit purpose of dealing with the economic development problems of a large, lagging region of the nation.

The ARD Act stipulates four principal areas of public investment: access both to and within the region; improved natural-resource utilization; water control; and improvements in human resources. The judgment of the President's Appalachian Regional Commission that Appalachia's "penetration by an adequate transportation network is the first requisite of its full participation in industrial America" [1] is reflected in the ARD Act data presented in Table 12.1. Expenditures authorized for economic development highways, to be constructed over a six-year period, account for $840 million, or over three fourths of total outlays authorized. The only other specific program receiving over 5 per cent of total outlays is that for demonstration health facilities (6.3 per cent). The explicit purpose of these outlays is to stimulate growth rather than to ameliorate problems arising from growth, as is the case with most domestic public investment.[2]

Table 12.1

Federal funds appropriated under
the Appalachian Regional
Development Act of 1965

Item	*Amount (millions)*	*Per cent of total*
Economic development highways and local access roads.......	$ 840.0	76.9
Demonstration health facilities.............................	69.0	6.3
Land stabilization, conservation, and erosion control.........	17.0	1.6
Timber development organizations.........................	5.0	0.5
Mining area restoration...................................	36.5	3.3
Water resource survey....................................	5.0	0.5
Vocational education facilities.............................	16.0	1.5
Sewage treatment works..................................	6.0	0.5
Supplements to federal grant-in-aid programs...............	90.0	8.2
Administrative costs......................................	7.9	0.7
Total...	$1,092.4	100.0

Source: Appalachian Regional Development Act of 1965.

The methods and aims of the regional development program embodied in the ARD Act are based on two major assumptions, (1) that the region is rich in potential attractiveness to private enterprise; and (2) that provision of large-scale infrastructure investment, primarily in the form of regional development highways, constitutes the most feasible means for assuring that private investment will in fact be drawn to the region on a scale sufficient to generate self-sustained growth. Although neither of these assumptions were targets of Congressional criticism, even among those most opposed to the program, both are highly questionable.[3]

Growth Prospects of Present Dominant Sectors. It is not likely that permanent growth of the Appalachian economy will result from expansion of industries presently dominant in the region. Between 1951 and 1961, production of coal, Appalachia's leading material resource, declined by 32 per cent while employment in coal dropped by 66 per cent; despite output increases since 1961, employment has continued to fall as a result of increased mechanization.[4] Thus, even if coal output continues to increase, it is not to be expected that this will significantly effect employment opportunities. Nevertheless, the ARD Act gives "special preference to the use of mineral resource materials indigenous to the Appalachian region" in constructing highways authorized by the act.[5] An amendment that use of such materials should not increase the cost of highway construction was voted down in committee in the House. Such preferential treatment, in addition to being a disincentive to short-run cost minimization, serves no useful long-run development purpose since this particular demand will cease after six years.

Timber is another major Appalachian resource, but "within the past one-half century, demand for Appalachian hardwood has declined. Much of this decline can be traced to the development of new materials which provide economical substitutes for Appalachian timber." [6] Since 80 per cent of timber volume in the region is hardwood, it therefore is not surprising that at present "timber growth is about double the volume harvested . . . and the volume added is generally low in quality." [7] In Senate testimony Professor J. G. Yoho strongly urged an increase in public funds for basic research on hardwood utilization in view of the forest-product industry's "notoriously poor record with regard to investment in research." [8] The question of whether basic research funds for alternative industries (even within Appalachia) might yield greater returns was not raised. Yoho further maintained that increased efficiency would mean that "the more capital intensive firms that will result may offer somewhat fewer jobs in the short run. However, they are likely to be able to provide better paying and more stable jobs in the long run." [9] Thus, as in the case of the coal industry, there is no promise of more jobs.

Assistance to agriculture is provided by the ARD Act in the form of a program of land stabilization, conservation, and erosion control.[10] Both cropland and pastureland will be eligible for improvements through a system of grants to landowners. However, as the House Minority Report points out, this program is inconsistent with national agricultural objectives. Whereas the President's budget for fiscal year 1966 states that some 2.5 million families now living on marginal farms will have to seek alternative employment as a result of increasing mechanization, the Appalachian program "would have the effect of subsidizing these marginal units and thus prolonging the inevitable closing of uneconomic farm units." [11] Whatever the merit of the conservation measures embodied in the act, it remains apparent that it provides no long-run solution for the region's declining agricultural sector.

In general, then, it is not to be expected that Appalachia's economy will be transformed on the basis of sectors which are now dominant. Future growth of the region therefore must be posited on significant attraction of other industries, preferably those characterized by relatively high labor intensity and/or relatively high backward and forward linkage effects.

Attraction of New Industry. The ARD Act assumes that regional development will take place through a process of unbalanced growth, initiated by excess public overhead capital capacity, and with the preponderance of public investment in the form of EOC rather than SOC. Unfortunately, the heavy emphasis which the ARD Act gives to providing greater access to the resources of Appalachia, including those which may be developed under other provisions of the act, cannot be expected to attract enough firms to the area to assure self-sustained growth.

Private firms tend to be attracted to areas which already are relatively well developed because of the variety and importance of the external economies found in such areas. These include, in addition to transportation and natural resources—on which the ARD Act focuses —proximity to suppliers and markets, skilled labor, social and cultural amenities, auxiliary business services, and relatively well-developed education and health facilities. It is difficult to imagine that the public overhead investment envisaged by the act will provide, on balance, sufficient external economies to overcome the relative advantages of more developed areas. In fact, the mining area restoration program, third most important in terms of funds authorized, is designed solely to overcome glaring diseconomies in the region. Furthermore, difficulties of lagging regions in these regards are not merely conjectural, as French experience clearly has shown. Indeed, French regional policy favors location of private economic activity in lagging regions in three important ways beyond those provided for in the ARD Act;

in addition to public overhead investment, French policy includes (1) a "push" effect resulting from decongestion measures; (2) deliberate decentralization of government agencies; and (3) direct financial incentives to private entrepreneurs. Yet commercial and industrial growth is directly related to existing degree of commercial and industrial importance. Thus, despite government efforts to develop lagging regions, firms continue to locate primarily in regions which offer external economies not available in less-developed areas.

While the ARD Act's preponderant emphasis on providing access through highway construction assumes that industry will thereby be drawn to Appalachia, the possibility of out-migration of the region's residents has been either ignored or decried in the various reports and hearings concerning the act.[12] What this approach ignores is that, although highways will open Appalachia to the nation, the rest of the nation will also be opened to Appalachia. Consequently, out-migration may increase rather than decrease. In any event, comprehensive regional policy should take account of population mobility and the effects on it of alternative public investment programs.

The SOC-EOC Composition of Regional Investment: The National Viewpoint. It has been argued that the greatest relative need in areas lacking industry and commerce is for SOC facilities. In contrast, less than 10 per cent of ARD Act funds are specified for education, health, and other SOC activities.

It might be argued, of course, that the mountainous terrain of Appalachia poses special problems with regard to EOC. John Sweeney, in fact, argued that "present highway formulas discriminate against Appalachia" since "a million dollars of highway construction money in Appalachia will buy about a third of what it will bring generally in the rest of the country."[13] However, it is a peculiar economic argument which maintains that a given EOC program should be undertaken in region A rather than in region B because costs are three times greater in A.

On the other hand, there are no persuasive reasons for believing that provision of given SOC facilities should be more costly in less-developed regions. Moreover, the benefit side of investment in human resources has been stressed in a great deal of recent literature. In the present context, Caudill has effectively argued that Appalachia's foremost need is "a comprehensive and effective system of public education," a need which has been "robbed of adequate financing." [14] Thus, consideration of relevant marginal benefit to cost ratios would favor emphasis on SOC, rather than EOC, investment in lagging regions such as Appalachia.

In conclusion, whenever a political consensus favors giving special aid to a lagging region, presumably on the grounds of social justice, it is fitting that economic analysis should aid in determining the nature of specific policy measures, given the relevant budget constraint. In the Appalachian case neglect of opportunity cost and labor-mobility considerations has resulted in too great an emphasis on expenditures for EOC, primarily in the form of highways. Instead, policy measures should have favored initial emphasis on SOC (though not, of course, to the exclusion of EOC), with a longer-run shift in SOC-EOC composition in favor of the latter. In any event, investment in either SOC or EOC would result in economically beneficial out-migration, whatever its political desirability.

Growth and Congestion

Study of regional economic development problems in the United States has centered primarily on ways and means to stimulate growth in lagging regions, but more recently there has been greater awareness of the difficulties associated with the opposite end of the regional spectrum, that is, with large, highly concentrated metropolitan areas. Nevertheless, economists still have neglected to analyze the issue of congestion within a specifically *regional* context. Rather, attention has been focused on relieving isolated symptoms of congestion, for example by improving existing transportation systems. Unfortunately, the contribution which such projects represent to already existing agglomeration economies will serve to attract new population and economic activity to the congested area. Thus, the long-run effect will be to increase congestion and associated social costs; more people will live in the state of congestion that the original project was intended to relieve. This situation sets the stage for yet another round of public investment, increased external economies, further influx of firms and residents, and increased external diseconomies of congestion.

It has been argued that this cumulative process will tend to choke itself off because rising external diseconomies will cause firms to locate new activities in alternative regions. For example, Myrdal states with respect to external diseconomies in expanding regions that they

> tend to retard or, when it has reached a certain level of development, even to reverse the cumulative process by causing an increase in public expenditure and, perhaps, in private costs because industry and population become too concentrated. Once again this can be stated in the more homely terms of folk wisdom: "Trees can never grow as high as heaven." [15]

Unfortunately, however, many of the most important social costs of overconcentration are not reflected in firms' cost functions; therefore private and social patterns of optimal spatial resource allocation diverge.

Moreover, recent evidence concerning greater equality in geographical distribution of manufacturing industries does not indicate any corresponding diminution of regional income disparities or any relatively greater attractiveness of small towns. In recent years growth of total national employment has been accounted for primarily by expanding tertiary activities, which have been located for the most part in metropolitan areas.[16] In addition, those industries, such as textiles, which have tended to leave metropolitan areas have been characterized by relative stagnation or decline; they have been seeking cheap labor in areas with surplus agricultural populations. Rapidly expanding industrial sectors such as chemicals and service activities have favored already concentrated regions primarily because of the external economies of agglomeration to be found in these areas.[17]

While social costs of congestion have not gone unnoticed, American policy suggestions have concentrated on piecemeal devices to help equate social and private costs. It has been suggested, for example, that firms in large agglomerations be charged an amount equivalent to the estimated gap between private and social costs. However desirable this may be from a theoretical viewpoint it is not operationally possible to measure all of the social costs attributable to a given firm; if public policy is to be based on our ability to evaluate these costs in relation to particular firms then there will be no public action.

Another approach to relieving congestion problems emphasizes pricing as it affects public, rather than private, facilities. In this regard particular attention has been given to surtaxes on vehicles using congested routes; the tax would cause some drivers to use less congested roads, some to shift to public transportation, some to shift away from peak-hour use of taxed roads, and others to abandon unimportant trips altogether.

The justification for such a tax is that gains to those who continue to use the road would exceed losses to those who stop using the road because of the increased tax. However, as Sharp recently has emphasized, a congestion tax of this nature would involve marginal cost pricing only "in a very special and limited sense," [18] since it leaves many important questions unanswered. For example, persons using the road for work journeys may have highly inelastic demand over certain price ranges so that the tax might remove too many or too few vehicles from the road. The demand for road space by commercial vehicles also is likely to be inelastic. These problems would be aggravated to the extent that no convenient alternatives to the taxed road exist. Willingness or ability to pay constitutes another difficulty; the relatively wealthy and expense-account motorists are not necessarily those who would receive the greatest benefits. These and other related issues [19] throw considerable doubt on the feasibility of a congestion tax. It is not surprising, therefore, that the chief of the National Highway Planning Division of the Bureau of Public Roads finds that congestion tax proposals "do not offer great promise as a means of improving the conditions of urban transportation." [20]

If isolated efforts to deal with problems of metropolitan congestion are either unfeasible or ineffectual in the long run, what alternative courses of action are open? One, of course, would be to limit expansion of economic activities and population in large metropolitan areas by tax and credit policy and direct controls. This approach, however, would be precluded in the United States for institutional reasons. In any event, measures of this nature would tend to promote congestion in areas immediately surrounding the restricted agglomerations, as French experience has shown.

The unfeasibility of purely negative measures to check the growth of congested metropolitan areas suggests that positive steps should be taken to promote growth in alternative regions. This does not imply a policy of "decentralization" which would attempt to spread economic activity more or less evenly over the entire country; nor does it imply utopian measures designed to enable workers to live in the countryside. Whatever the merits of such proposals they have yet to find economic justification. Conversely, opportunity cost considerations would justify the use of public investment to induce expansion in intermediate regions. There is no question here of artificial force feeding of economic activity in lagging regions. What is at issue, on the other hand, is our ability to identify growth centers whose future expansion would be capable of relieving the pressures now responsible for rapidly rising external diseconomies in large agglomerations.

Conclusion

In general, the foregoing discussion implies that the development of intermediate regions should be the pivotal attribute of regional policy from a national viewpoint. In addition to providing benefits to their resident populations, such regions serve the double external function of providing economic opportunity for residents of lagging regions, of which a most prominent characteristic is high rates of out-migration, and of relieving growth pressures on congested regions. Yet American regional policy continues to be almost exclusively related to lagging and congested regions, largely because it has lacked national perspective. Moreover, even within regions which have received attention there has been a marked deficiency in comprehensive planning. Indeed, the Economic Development Administration of the Department of Commerce has pointed out that "The last Congress alone produced 21 new health programs, 17 new educational programs, 15 new economic development programs, 12 new programs to meet the problems of our cities, 4 new programs for manpower training, and 17 new resource development programs." [21] Yet the task remains of harmonizing these diverse measures, of finding "a way or ways of identifying and relating the variety of available Federal programs so they will provide the maximum benefit at the State and local levels," [22] as well as in more specifically regional terms.

The Economic Development Regions which have been designated under provisions of the Public Works and Economic Development Act of 1965 mark an advance in coordinating multistate area planning.[23] Nevertheless, the orientation of this effort is much the same as that of the Appalachian Regional Development Act, namely, it places almost exclusive emphasis on attracting economic activity to lagging areas. Federally assisted projects which are to be undertaken in the Economic Development Regions are supposed to be located, so far as possible, "in an area determined by the state to have a significant potential for growth"; [24] yet rapidly growing intermediate areas immediately adjacent to the Economic Development Regions are deliberately left outside of the regional planning framework. As in the case of Appalachia there is reluctance to explore the possibilities which nearby intermediate regions might offer in relation to out-migration from areas of low family income and stagnant or declining job opportunities. Here again, public policy is deficient in the kind of comprehensive spatial approach that alone promotes rational decision-making in terms of opportunity costs. What kind of research is necessary, then, if policy formulation is more closely to approximate this objective?

John Meyer has argued that "a more nearly optimal allocation of research resources within regional economics would seem to involve less relative effort on income accounting and interregional trade-flow coefficient estimation and more attention to developing and testing hypotheses." [25] Insofar as regional economic policy is directed toward satisfying public preferences it should seem obvious that one of the first tasks of policy-oriented research should be to formulate and test hypotheses concerning these preferences. French opinion surveys have proven useful not only in formulating economic objectives but in pointing up areas where opinion tends to be ill-informed or inconsistent, and therefore in need of education concerning alternative choices. There is a definite need to establish the extent to which residents of large American metropolitan areas feel that population and economic activity have become too concentrated in their regions, and the extent to which the various consequences of congestion—noise, air pollution, traffic problems—are felt. We also need to know the extent to which residents of congested regions would favor policy measures designed to lessen growth pressures on their regions, as well as the extent to which and conditions under which they would prefer to live in less congested regions. Similarly, residents of lagging regions should be surveyed concerning their knowledge of and participation in programs designed to stimulate their regions' growth, the degree to which lack of local employment opportunities inhibits participation in human resource development projects, and the degree of willingness to migrate if this were the only way to find employment for increased skill and training. It should be emphasized that questions designed to obtain responses to these issues should be formulated within a community rather than a market context. As Arthur Maass recently has emphasized, an individual's response is highly dependent "on the institutional environment in which the question is asked. Since the relevant response for public investment analysis is a community, not privately, oriented one, the great challenge for welfare economics is to frame questions in such a way as to elicit from individuals community oriented answers." [26]

Once relevant public preference patterns are established, it is necessary to evaluate the magnitude and composition of present public investment patterns in terms of regional resources and growth prospects. For example, present American policy for lagging regions emphasizes investment in economic rather than social overhead capital. This already has been shown with respect to the ARD Act, and over 94 per cent of public works projects approved by the Economic Development Administration at this writing have been for various economic overhead activities, chiefly utilities.[27] It is evident, therefore, that a major re-evaluation of the consequences of the structure and composition of public investment by type of region is in order. It would also seem advisable to devote relatively less attention to the effects of public investment and other external economies on industrial location, and relatively more attention to their interaction with tertiary activities, which account for the great bulk of increasing employment opportunities.

Although these issues are amenable to empirical investigation, the operational relevance of research findings pertaining to them and related subjects depends on the degree to which policy formulation takes place within a comprehensive regional framework. Efforts to achieve spatially optimal resource allocation should involve not only opportunity cost considerations within lagging, intermediate, and congested regions, but also among regions. Thus, the progress being made with respect to intraregional coordination will probably not be matched at the interregional level without a comprehensive system of planning regions.

Insofar as possible, an attempt also should be made to disaggregate the Federal budget along regional as well as project lines. The recent regionalization of the French budget already has proven useful both in providing information for analyzing regional needs and in controlling the implementation of regional objectives. Although this experience is too new to permit definitive evaluation, American planners should benefit by careful investigation of the successes and shortcomings which mark its development.

The question of whether or not the Federal government ought to influence the location of economic activity has long been bypassed by government participation in our mixed economy on a scale which inevitably has important regional consequences. It is undoubtedly in recognition of this phenomenon that important efforts already have been made to give the government a creative role in the solution of regional problems. Nevertheless, these efforts are not yet commensurate with the difficulties posed by lagging regions and congested metropolitan areas. A number of operationally feasible approaches to some of the tasks which remain in the quest for optimal spatial resource allocation from a social point of view have been suggested by French experience. While they do not pretend to indicate final solutions they are at least conceived on a scale consistent with the issues involved.

I
Appendix: French Departments by Program Region

II
List and Abbreviations of Official French Publications

III
List and Abbreviations of Periodicals

IV
Selected Bibliography

V
Notes

VI
Subject Index

VII
Index of Names

Appendix: French Departments by Program Region

PARIS REGION
Seine*
Seine-et-Oise*
Seine-et-Marne

Regions of the West

AQUITAINE
Dordogne
Gironde
Landes
Lot-et-Garonne
Pyrénées (Basses)

AUVERGNE
Allier
Cantal
Haute Loire
Puy de Dôme

BRITTANY
Côtes-du-Nord
Finistère
Ille-et-Vilaine
Morbihan

CENTER
Cher
Eure-et-Loire
Indre
Indre-et-Loire
Loire-et-Cher
Loiret

LANGUEDOC
Aude
Gard
Hérault
Lozère
Pyrénées Orientales

LIMOUSIN
Creuse
Corrèze
Haute Vienne

LOWER NORMANDY
Calvados
Manche
Orne

MIDI-PYRENEES
Ariège
Aveyron
Garonne Haute
Gers
Lot
Pyrénées (Hautes)
Tarn
Tarn-et-Garonne

PAYS DE LA LOIRE
Loire-Atlantique
Maine-et-Loire
Mayenne
Sarthe
Vendée

POITOU-CHARENTES
Charente
Charente-Maritime
Sèvres (Deux)
Vienne

* The departments of Seine and Seine-et-Oise recently have been divided into six new departments.

Regions of the East

ALSACE
Bas Rhin
Haut Rhin

BURGUNDY
Côte-d'Or
Nièvre
Saône-et-Loire
Yonne

CHAMPAGNE
Ardennes
Aube
Marne
Marne (Haute)

FRANCHE-COMTE
Belfort
Doubs
Haute Saône
Jura

LORRAINE
Meuse
Meurthe-et-Moselle
Moselle
Vosges

NORD
Nord
Pas-de-Calais

PICARDY
Aisne
Oise
Somme

PROVENCE-RIVIERA
Alpes (Basses)
Alpes (Hautes)
Alpes-Maritime
Bouches-du-Rhône
Var
Vaucluse

RHONE-ALPS
Ain
Ardèche
Drôme
Isère
Loire
Rhône
Savoie
Savoie (Haute)

UPPER NORMANDY
Eure
Seine-Maritime

List and Abbreviations
of Official French Publications

Activité du District	*18 mois d'activité du District de Paris.* Paris: District de la Région de Paris, 1964.
L'aide financière, 1962–1965	*L'aide financière du District aux collectivités de la Région de Paris pendant les quatres années du IVᵉ Plan, 1962–1965.* Paris: Imprimerie Municipale, 1965.
Aides au développement	*Aides au développement régional.* Paris: Délégation à l'aménagement du territoire et à l'action régionale, 1966.
L'aménagement de la région parisienne	*L'aménagement de la région parisienne.* Paris: La Documentation Française, October 20, 1960.
Aménagement du territoire	*Aménagement du territoire et action régionale.* Textes d'intérêt général, No. 63–27. Paris: Journaux officiels, February, 1963.
Annuaire statistique	*Annuaire statistique de la France.* Paris: Institut National de la Statistique et des Etudes Economiques.
Avant-projet	Délégation Générale au District de la Région de Paris. *Avant-project de programme duodécennal pour la Région de Paris.* Paris: Imprimerie Municipale, 1963.
Avis et rapports	*Avis et rapports du Conseil Economique et Social.* Published in the *Journal officiel.*
Avis et rapports, Vᵉ Plan	Conseil Economique et Social. *Avis et rapports sur le projet de Vᵉ Plan.* Paris: Imprimerie des Journaux officiels, 1965.

Avis, Lemaire

Avis présenté au Nom de la Commission de la Production et des Echanges sur le Projet de Loi portant Approbation du Plan de Développement Economique et Social, M. Lemaire, No. 1637. Paris: Imprimerie de l'Assemblée Nationale, 1ère Session ordinaire de 1965–66.

L'axe de transport

L'axe de transport par voie d'eau entre le Nord-Est de la France et la Méditerranée. Rapport du Groupe de travail au Premier Ministre. Paris: La Documentation Française, 1962.

Claudius-Petit, *Pour un Plan*

Claudius-Petit, Eugène. *Pour un Plan d'aménagement du territoire.* Paris: Ministère de la Réconstruction et de l'Urbanisme, 1950.

CREDOC, *Essai*

CREDOC. *Essai de classement hiérarchique des principales villes. Le niveau supérieur de l'armature urbaine française*, complément No. 1. Paris: Commissariat Général du Plan, 1963.

Décentralisation

Décentralisation industrielle. Paris: Journaux officiels, 1963.

Documents, Ve Plan

Documents concernant le Ve Plan destinés à l'information des parlementaires, No. 1638 (annexè). Paris: Imprimerie de l'Assemblée Nationale, 1ère Session ordinaire de 1965–66.

Environment Planning

France: Town and Country Environment Planning. New York: Ambassade de France Service de Presse et d'Information, 1965.

L'exécution du Plan

Projet de loi de finances pour 1966, Rapport sur l'exécution du Plan en 1964 et 1965 et sur la régionalisation du budget d'équipment de 1966, Volume I, *L'exécution du Plan en 1964 et 1965.* Paris: Imprimerie Nationale, 1965.

Ve Plan

Cinquième Plan de développement économique et social (1966–1970). Volume I. Paris: Imprimerie des Journaux officiels, 1965.

IVe Plan

Quatrième Plan de développement économique et social (1962–1965). Paris: Imprimerie des Journaux officiels, 1962.

France and Agriculture

France and Agriculture. New York: Ambassade de France Service de Presse et d'Information, 1963.

France and Economic Planning   *France and Economic Planning.* New York: Ambassade de France Service de Presse et d'Information, 1963.

Hautreux and Rochefort, *La fonction*   Hautreux, J., and M. Rochefort, *La fonction régionale dans l'armature urbaine française.* Paris: Commissariat Général du Plan, 1964.

Hautreux, Lecourt, and Rochefort, *Le niveau supérieur*   Hautreux J., M. Lecourt, and M. Rochefort. *Le niveau supérieur de l'armature urbaine française.* Paris: Commissariat Général du Plan, 1963.

LeFillatre, *Le pouvoir*   LeFillatre, P. *Le pouvoir de commandement des villes françaises sur des salariés d'établissements situés en dehors d'elles. Le niveau supérieur de l'armature urbaine française,* complément No. 2. Paris: Commissariat Général du Plan, 1963.

Nungesser, *Contre Paris*   Nungesser, Roland. *L'aménagement du territoire ne peut se faire contre Paris.* Extrait du *Journal officiel,* No. 132, November 28, 1963.

Organisation, circonscriptions   *Organisation des services de l'état dans les circonscriptions d'action régionale.* Textes d'intérêt général, No. 64–65. Paris: Journaux officiels, April, 1964.

Organisation, départements   *Organisation des services de l'état dans les départements et les circonscriptions d'action régionale et déconcentration administrative.* Textes d'intérêt général, No. 64–40. Paris: Journaux officiels, March, 1964.

Paris en question   District de la Région de Paris. *Paris en question.* Paris: Presses Universitaires de France, 1965.

Plan quadriennal   *Plan quadriennal d'aménagement et d'équipment.* Paris: Imprimerie Municipale, 1963.

Premier rapport   Commissariat Général du Plan. *Premier rapport de la Commission nationale de l'aménagement du territoire.* Paris: Imprimerie de l'Assemblée Nationale, 1964.

Principales options   *Préparation du Ve Plan: rapport sur les principales options.* Paris: Journaux officiels, 1964.

Provence-Côte d'Azur   *Plan régional de développement et d'aménagement de la Provence-Côte d'Azur.* Paris: Imprimerie des Journaux officiels, 1961.

Rapport, Vallon	*Rapport fait au Nom de la Commission des Finances, de l'Economie générale et du Plan sur le Projet de Loi portant Approbation du Plan de Développement Economique et Social, M. Louis Vallon,* No. 1638. Imprimerie de l'Assemblée Nationale, 1ère Session ordinaire de 1965–66.
Réflexions pour 1985	*Réflexions pour 1985.* Paris: La Documentation Française, 1964.
Régionalisation du budget, 1964	Projet de loi de finances pour 1964. *Régionalisation du budget d'équipment pour l'année 1964 et coordination des investissements publics au regard des objectifs de l'aménagement du territoire,* tome I. Paris: Imprimerie Nationale, 1963.
Régionalisation du budget, 1966	Projet de loi de finances pour 1966, Rapport sur l'exécution du Plan en 1964 et 1965 et sur la régionalisation du budget d'équipment de 1966, Volume II, *Régionalisation du budget d'équipment pour l'année 1966,* tome II. Paris: Imprimerie Nationale, 1965.
Régionalisation en 1964	Délégation à l'aménagement du territoire et à l'action régionale. *La régionalisation du budget d'équipment en 1964.* Paris: La Documentation Française, 1964.
Région d'Alsace	*Région d'Alsace, programme d'action régionale.* Paris: Journaux officiels, 1959.
Région de Bretagne	*Région de Bretagne, programme d'action régionale.* Paris: Journaux officiels, 1964.
Région de Poitou-Charentes	*Région de Poitou-Charentes, programme d'action régionale.* Paris: Journaux officiels, 1964.
Région du Nord	*Région du Nord, programme d'action régionale.* Paris: Journaux officiels, 1959.
The Region of Paris	*The District of the Region of Paris.* Paris: District de la Région de Paris, no date. Mimeographed.
Rhône-Alpes	*Rhône-Alpes, plan régional de développement et d'aménagement.* Paris: Journaux officiels, 1960.
Schéma directeur	*Schéma directeur d'aménagement et d'urbanisme de la Région de Paris.* Paris: Société Parisienne d'Imprimerie, 1965.
Un grand débat	*Un grand débat parlementaire: l'aménagement du territoire.* Paris: Délégation à l'aménagement du territoire et à l'action régionale, 1964.

List and Abbreviations
of Periodicals

French

B.S.	Bulletin statistique (Ministère de la Construction)
C.I.S.E.A.	Cahiers de l'Institut de Science Economique Appliquée
C.R.	Cahiers de la République
E.A.	Economie appliquée
Entreprise	Entreprise
E.P.	Economie et politique
E.R.	Expansion régionale
J.O.	Journal officiel
Le Monde	Le Monde
M.T.	Moniteur des travaux publics et du bâtiment
N.E.D.	Notes et études documentaires
Population	Population
R.A.P.	Revue de l'action populaire
R.E.	Revue économique
Réalités	Réalités
R.E.M.	Revue de l'économie méridionale
R.E.P.	Revue d'économie politique
R.F.S.P.	Revue française de science politique
S.E.F.	Statistiques et études financières
Sondages	Sondages
T.M.	Tiers-monde
Urbanisme	Urbanisme

United States

A.E.R.	American Economic Review
A.E.R.P.P.	American Economic Review Papers and Proceedings
E.D.	Economic Development (Department of Commerce)
E.D.C.C.	Economic Development and Cultural Change
F.A.	France Actuelle

J.P.E.	*Journal of Political Economy*
L.E.	*Land Economics*
P.P.R.S.A.	*Papers and Proceedings of the Regional Science Association*
Q.J.E.	*Quarterly Journal of Economics*
R.E.S.	*Review of Economics and Statistics*
S.E.J.	*Southern Economic Journal*
S.R.	*Social Research*

Other

C.B.	*Cahiers de Bruges*
C.J.E.	*Canadian Journal of Economics and Political Science*
E.J.	*Economic Journal*
N.T.	*Nationalφkonomisk Tidsskrift*
Z.N.	*Zeitschrift für Nationalökonomie*

Selected Bibliography

Augé-Laribé, M. *La Politique agricole de la France de 1880 à 1940.* Paris: Presses Universitaires de France, 1950.

L'avenir économique du Sud-Ouest. Paris: Centre Economique et Social de Perfectionnement de Cadres, 1961.

Bauchet, Pierre. *Les tableaux économiques, analyse de la région lorraine.* Paris: Génin, 1955.

Boudeville, Jacques. *Les espaces économiques.* Paris: Presses Universitaires de France, 1961.

_____. *Les programmes économiques.* Paris: Presses Universitaires de France, 1963.

_____. *Problems of Regional Economic Planning.* Edinburgh: Edinburgh University Press, 1966.

Capronnier-Spielhagen, Janine. *Comptes nationaux et régionaux de l'énergie.* Paris: Colin, 1962.

Carillon, Robert. *La politique de développement régional.* Paris: Expansion régionale, 1965.

Caudill, Harry M. *Night Comes to the Cumberlands.* Boston: Houghton-Mifflin, 1963.

Chinitz, Benjamin, ed. *City and Suburb.* Englewood Cliffs, N.J.: Prentice-Hall, Inc., 1964.

Conseil Economique, *Etude sur une politique des économies régionales.* Paris: Presses Universitaires de France, 1957.

Coront-Ducluzeau, François. *La formation de l'espace économique national.* Paris: Colin, 1964.

Davin, L. E., L. Deeger, and J. Paelinck. *Dynamique économique de la région liégeoise.* Paris: Presses Universitaires de France, 1959.

Debré, Michel. *Au service de la Nation.* Paris: Stock, 1963.

Delmas, Claude. *L'aménagement du territoire.* Paris: Presses Universitaires de France, 1963.

Denison, Edward F. *The Sources of Economic Growth in the United States and the Alternatives Before Us.* New York: Committee for Economic Development, 1962.

Documents de la Conférence sur les économies régionales, Brussels, December, 1961. Brussels: Communauté Economique Européenne, 1963.

Economic Aspects of Higher Education. Paris: Organization for Economic Cooperation and Development, 1964.

Economic Survey of Europe, 1954. Geneva: United Nations Department of Economic and Social Affairs, 1955.

Economie et Humanisme. *Démocratie, planification, aménagement.* Paris: Les Editions Ouvrières, 1964.

Enke, Stephen. *Economics for Development.* Englewood Cliffs, N.J.: Prentice-Hall, Inc., 1963.

The European Markets. New York: Chase Manhattan Bank, 1964.

Faucheux, Jean. *La décentralisation industrielle.* Paris: Editions Berger-Levrault, 1959.

Friedmann, John, and William Alonso, eds. *Regional Development and Planning.* Cambridge: The Massachusetts Institute of Technology Press, 1964.

Fuchs, Victor. *Changes in the Location of Manufacturing Since 1929.* New Haven: Yale University Press, 1962.

Gravier, J.-F. *L'aménagement du territoire et l'avenir des régions françaises.* Paris: Flammarion, 1964.

―――. *Paris et le désert français.* Paris: Le Portulan, 1947.

Hackett, John and Anne-Marie. *Economic Planning in France.* Cambridge: Harvard University Press, 1963.

Higbee, Edward. *The Squeeze: Cities Without Space.* New York: William Morrow, 1960.

Hirschman, Albert O. *The Strategy of Economic Development.* New Haven: Yale University Press, 1958.

Hoover, Edgar M. *The Location of Economic Activity.* New York: McGraw-Hill, 1948.

Institut d'Etudes Politiques de l'Université de Grenoble. *Administration traditionelle et planification régionale.* Paris: Colin, 1964.

Institut de Science Economique de Liège. *Problèmes de conversion économique.* Paris: Editions Génin, 1965.

Isard, Walter. *Location and Space Economy.* New York: M.I.T. Press and Wiley, 1956.

Jouandet-Bernadat, R. *Comptabilité économique et espaces régionaux.* Paris: Gauthier-Villars, 1964.

―――. *Les comptes du département de la Gironde.* Bordeaux: Imprimerie Bière, 1963.

Kapp, K. William. *The Social Costs of Private Enterprise.* Cambridge: Harvard University Press, 1950.

Kayser, Bernard, and Pierre George. *La géographie active.* Paris: Presses Universitaires de France, 1964.

Kendrick, J. W. *Productivity Trends in the United States.* Princeton: Princeton University Press, 1961.

Kindleberger, Charles P. *Economic Growth in France and Britain, 1851–1950.* Cambridge: Harvard University Press, 1965.

Lamour, Philippe. *L'aménagement du territoire.* Paris: Editions de l'Epargne, 1964.

Lanversin, Jacques de. *L'aménagement du territoire.* Paris: Librairies Techniques, 1965.

Leroy, Louis. *Le ruralisme.* Paris: Les Editions Ouvrières, 1960.

Liebhafsky, H. H. *The Nature of Price Theory.* Homewood, Ill.: The Dorsey Press, 1963.

Lösch, August. *The Economics of Location.* Trans. William Wolgom and W. F. Stolper. New Haven: Yale University Press, 1954.

Maillet, Pierre. *La structure économique de la France.* Paris: Presses Universitaires de France, 1964.

Massé, Pierre. *Le Plan ou l'anti-hasard.* Paris: Editions Gallimard, 1965.

Mendès-France, Pierre. *A Modern French Republic.* Trans. Anne Carter. New York: Hill and Wang, 1963.

Myrdal, Gunnar. *Rich Lands and Poor.* New York: Harper and Brothers, 1957.

National Bureau of Economic Research Studies in Income and Wealth. *Regional Income,* Vol. 21. Princeton: Princeton University Press, 1957.

Nurkse, Ragnar. *Problems of Capital Formation in the Underdeveloped Economies.* Oxford: Oxford University Press, 1953.

Oxenfeldt, Alfred, and Vsevolod Holubnychy. *Economic Systems in Action,* 3rd ed. New York: Holt, Rinehart and Winston, 1965.

Pautard, Jean. *Les disparités régionales dans la croissance de l'agriculture française.* Paris: Gauthier-Villars, 1965.

Perloff, H. S., E. S. Dunn, E. E. Lampard, and R. E. Muth. *Regions, Resources and Economic Growth.* Baltimore: The Johns Hopkins Press, 1960.

Perroux, François. *L'économie du XXᵉ siècle,* 2d ed. Paris: Presses Universitaires de France, 1964.

Planification française et démocratie. Lyon: Economie et Humanisme, 1961.

La politique régionale dans la Communauté Economique Européenne. Brussels: Communauté Economique Européenne, 1964.

President's Appalachian Regional Commission. *Appalachia.* Washington, D.C.: Government Printing Office, 1964.

Problèmes du développement régional, travaux du Congrès des économistes de langue française, 1959. Paris: Editions Cujas, 1960.

Prost, Marie-Andrée. *La hiérarchie des villes en fonction de leurs activités de commerce et de service.* Paris: Gauthier-Villars, 1965.

Regional Development in the European Economic Community. London: Political and Economic Planning, 1962.

The Residual Factor and Economic Growth. Paris: Organization for Economic Cooperation and Development, 1964.

Riotte, A., and Robert Carillon. *Comment concevoir le regroupement communal.* Paris: Expansion régionale, 1964.

Rudel, Christian. *Mon village à l'heure de l'expansion.* Paris: Les Editions Ouvrières, 1965.

Le Sud-Ouest construit son avenir. Paris: Centre Economique et Social de Perfectionnement des Cadres, 1962.

Thünen, Johann H. von. *Der isolierte Staat in Beziehung auf Landwirtschaft und Nationalökonomie.* Hamburg: Fr. Derthes, 1826.

Trintignac, André. *Aménager l'hexagone.* Paris: Editions du Centurion, 1964.

United States Bureau of the Census. *Compendium of State Government Finances in 1962.* Washington, D.C.: Government Printing Office, 1963.

Vernon, Raymond. *The Changing Economic Function of the Central City.* New York: Committee for Economic Development, 1959.

Notes

*Definitions of abbreviations used in the notes will be found
in the List and Abbreviations of Official French Publications
and List and Abbreviations of Periodicals.*

1. Resource Allocation in a Regional Context

1. John Friedmann and William Alonso, "Introduction," *Regional Development and Planning*, ed. John Friedmann and William Alonso (Cambridge: The Massachusetts Institute of Technology Press, 1964), p. 1.

2. Ibid.

3. John Friedmann, "The Concept of a Planning Region," *L. E.*, XXXII (February, 1956), pp. 2–3.

4. John and Anne-Marie Hackett, *Economic Planning in France* (Cambridge: Harvard University Press, 1963), p. 17.

5. Alfred Oxenfeldt and Vsevolod Holubnychy, *Economic Systems in Action* (3rd ed.; New York: Holt, Rinehart and Winston, 1965), p. 167.

6. J.-F. Gravier, *L'aménagement du territoire et l'avenir des régions françaises* (Paris: Flammarion, 1964), p. 127.

7. Philippe Lamour, *L'aménagement du territoire* (Paris: Editions de l'Epargne, 1964), p. 7.

8. Philippe Laurent, "Aménager l'espace de l'homme," *R. A. P.*, No. 145 (February, 1961), p. 197.

9. *Rapport, Vallon*, p. 9.

10. Economie et Humanisme, *Démocratie, planification, aménagement* (Paris: Les Editions Ouvrières, 1964), p. 161.

11. Claudius-Petit, *Pour un plan*, p. 3.

12. See Joseph Lajugie, "Qu'est-ce que l'aménagement du territoire?" *C. B.*, No. 2 (1958), pp. 6–11; and Jacques de Lanversin, *L'aménagement du territoire* (Paris: Librairies Techniques, 1965), pp. 8–10.

13. P. N. Rosenstein-Rodan, *Notes on the Theory of the "Big Push"* (M.I.T. Center for International Studies, March, 1957), p. 1.

14. Ragnar Nurkse, "Some International Aspects of the Problem of Economic Development," *A. E. R.*, XLII (May, 1952), p. 572; and Nurkse, *Problems of Capital Formation in the Underdeveloped Economies* (Oxford: Oxford University Press, 1953), Chap. 1.

15. For detailed discussion of various aspects of this approach see also

P. N. Rosenstein-Rodan, "Problems of Industrialization in Eastern and Southeastern Europe," *E. J.,* LIII (June-September, 1943), pp. 202–211; and Tibor Scitovsky, "Two Concepts of External Economies," *J. P. E.,* LXII (April, 1954), pp. 143–152.

16. See, for example, Albert O. Hirschman, *The Strategy of Economic Development* (New Haven: Yale University Press, 1958), Chap. 3; H. W. Singer, "Economic Progress in Underdeveloped Countries," *S. R.,* XVI (March, 1949), pp. 1–11; Stephen Enke, *Economics for Development* (Englewood Cliffs, N.J.: Prentice-Hall, Inc., 1963), Chap. 16; and Marcus Fleming, "External Economies and the Doctrine of Balanced Growth," *E. J.,* LXVI (June, 1955), pp. 241–256.

17. Enke, p. 316.

18. Ibid., p. 314.

19. Singer, p. 10.

20. These effects refer, respectively, to induced supply of inputs and induced use of outputs. See Hirschman, pp. 100–117.

21. François Perroux, "La notion de pôle de croissance," *L'économie du XXe siècle* (2d ed.; Paris: Presses Universitaires de France, 1964), pp. 142–153; originally published in *E. A.,* Nos. 1–2 (1955).

22. Hirschman, p. 184.

23. EOC-SOC distinctions are elaborated further in Niles M. Hansen, "The Structure and Determinants of Local Public Investment Expenditures," *R. E. S.,* XLVII (May, 1965), pp. 150–162; and "Municipal Investment Requirements in a Growing Agglomeration," *L. E.,* XLI (February, 1965), pp. 49–56. It also should be noted that government subsidies to induce firms to locate in less-developed regions are clearly a form of EOC investment. Indeed, the induced effects of such EOC investment are more easily identifiable than those resulting from, say, the construction of a highway.

24. Hirschman, pp. 83–84. See also *La politique régionale dans la Communauté Economique Européenne* (Brussels: Communauté Economique Européenne, 1964), p. 28.

25. For a discussion of American experience in this regard see Chester Rapkin, "Some Effects of Economic Growth on the Character of Cities," *A. E. R. P. P.,* XLVI (May, 1956), p. 297.

26. Institut de Science Economique de Liège, *Problèmes de conversion économique* (Paris: Editions Génin, 1965), pp. 183–184.

27. Hirschman, pp. 192–193.

28. Ibid., pp. 190, 194–195.

29. Douglass C. North, "Location Theory and Regional Economic Growth," *J. P. E.,* LXIII (June, 1955), pp. 243–258.

30. Edward Higbee, *The Squeeze: Cities Without Space* (New York: William Morrow, 1960), pp. 9–10.

31. "Stress is Called Population Curb," *New York Times,* September 22, 1963, p. 79.

32. Concerning these external economies, see, for example, Raymond

Vernon, *The Changing Economic Function of the Central City* (New York: Committee for Economic Development, 1959), pp. 28–37; Edgar M. Hoover, *The Location of Economic Activity* (New York: McGraw-Hill, 1948); Louis Reboud, "Progrès technique et décentralisation," *R. E. P.,* No. 2 (March–April, 1964), pp. 497–525, and No. 3 (May–June, 1964), pp. 730–754; and Eric E. Lampard, "The History of Cities in the Economically Advanced Areas," *E. D. C. C.,* III (January, 1955), pp. 95–102.

33. Benjamin Chinitz, "City and Suburb," in *City and Suburb,* ed. B. Chinitz (Englewood Cliffs, N.J.: Prentice-Hall, Inc., 1964), pp. 9–10.

34. George H. Borts, "The Equalization of Returns and Regional Economic Growth," *A. E. R.,* L (June, 1960), pp. 319–345.

35. An elaborate treatment of the social costs of industrial and commercial concentration is given in K. William Kapp, *The Social Costs of Private Enterprise* (Cambridge: Harvard University Press, 1950).

36. The reasons for a shift to relatively high per capita SOC outlays are complex. For some activities, for example police protection, there is a definite need for higher expenditures. Other activities, such as education, involve both increased "need" for various skills and increased "wants" resulting from higher incomes and other socioeconomic factors.

37. See my articles cited in Note 23 above.

38. Unfortunately, the Census of Governments data are not available in a form to permit analysis along SOC-EOC lines.

39. The source of the data used in this analysis is *Compendium of State Government Finances in 1962* (Washington, D. C.: United States Bureau of the Census, 1963), p. 52.

40. For the sake of simplicity all external effects are subsumed under the second bracketed term, even though *D*-induced *P* may in turn induce further *D*. A more detailed examination of intersectoral relations would require a system of equations based on input-output data. See H. H. Liebhafsky, *The Nature of Price Theory* (Homewood, Ill.: The Dorsey Press, 1963), p. 177.

41. See, for example, *Regional Development in the European Economic Community* (London: Political and Economic Planning, 1962), p. 39; H. S. Perloff, E. S. Dunn, E. E. Lampard, and R. E. Muth, *Regions, Resources and Economic Growth* (Baltimore: The Johns Hopkins Press, 1960), pp. 606–607; and *La politique régionale dans la Communauté Economique Européenne,* pp. 28–30.

42. Direct benefits include reduction in vehicle operating costs and gains in time per unit of distance traveled, reduction in number and severity of accidents per vehicle-mile, and increase in vehicle capacity. Indirect benefits include greater mobility, the growth of the automobile industry, and possibly increased tax revenue. The last two examples would be benefits of a more specifically national character. For further discussion of these and related points see Claude Abraham, "L'étude économique des investissements routiers," *R. E.,* XII (September, 1961), pp. 762.–780.

43. All external effects are subsumed under the second bracketed term

even if initially induced D in turn induces further D (or P). See Note 40.

44. See, for example, Rufus B. Hughes, Jr., "Interregional Income Differences: Self Perpetuation," *S. E. J.*, XXVIII (July, 1961), pp. 41–45; E. J. R. Booth, "Interregional Income Differences," *S. E. J.*, XXXI (July, 1964), pp. 44–51; H. S. Perloff, *et al.*, pp. 600–607; and Borts, *op. cit.*

45. See, for example, Moses Abramovitz, "Resource and Output Trends in the U.S. Since 1870," *A. E. R. P. P.*, XLVI (May, 1956), pp. 1–23; J. W. Kendrick, *Productivity Trends in the United States* (Princeton: Princeton University Press, 1961); E. D. Domar, "Total Productivity and the Quality of Capital," *J. P. E.*, LXXI (December, 1963), pp. 586–588; Robert W. Solow, "Technical Change and the Aggregate Production Function," *R. E. S.*, IL (August, 1957), pp. 312–320.

46. Theodore W. Schultz, "Investment in Human Capital," *A. E. R.*, LI (March, 1961), p. 1. See also the series of articles on "Investment in Human Beings" in the special supplement to *J. P. E.*, LXX (October, 1962).

47. Edward F. Denison, *The Sources of Economic Growth in the United States and the Alternatives Before Us* (New York: Committee for Economic Development, 1962), pp. 148, 266. See also Chap. 7. An excellent critique of Denison's study is given in Moses Abramovitz, "Economic Growth in the United States: A Review Article," *A. E. R.*, LII (September, 1962), pp. 762–782.

48. Edward F. Denison, "Measuring the Contribution of Education (and the Residual) to Economic Growth," in *The Residual Factor and Economic Growth* (Paris: Organization for Economic Cooperation and Development, 1964), p. 37.

49. Denison, *The Sources of Economic Growth*, p. 74.

50. R. S. Eckaus, "Economic Criteria for Education and Training," *R. E. S.*, XLVI (May, 1964), pp. 181–190.

51. *Economic Survey of Europe, 1954* (Geneva: United Nations Department of Economic and Social Affairs, 1955), p. 151.

52. Hansen, "The Structure and Determinants of Local Public Investment Expenditures."

53. Edgar M. Hoover, "Pittsburgh Takes Stock of Itself," in Chinitz, ed., pp. 63–64.

54. Seymour E. Harris, "Higher Education: Resources and Finance (U.S.A.)," in *Economic Aspects of Higher Education* (Paris: Organization for Economic Cooperation and Development, 1964), p. 113.

55. This formulation is similar to that given in H. B. Chenery, "The Application of Investment Criteria," *Q. J. E.*, LXVII (February, 1953), pp. 76–96.

2. Urban Concentration and Individual Preferences: The Case of Paris

1. Charles P. Kindleberger, *Economic Growth in France and Britain, 1851–1950* (Cambridge: Harvard University Press, 1964), p. 255.

2. André Trintignac, *Aménager l'hexagone* (Paris: Editions du Centurion, 1964), p. 174.

3. Ibid., pp. 176–177.

4. Ibid., pp. 179–180; and *L'aménagement de la région parisienne*, première partie, pp. 10–11.

5. Trintignac, pp. 178–180; *L'aménagement de la région parisienne*, première partie, pp. 10–11.

6. J.-F. Gravier, *Paris et le désert français* (Paris: Le Portulan, 1947). A revised edition was published in 1958 by Flammarion.

7. *Régionalisation du budget, 1966*, p. 165.

8. "Paris—1975 and Beyond," *France actuelle*, XII (October 15, 1963), p. 1.

9. *Régionalisation du budget, 1966*, pp. 212, 258, 259, 268, 320, 321.

10. *B. S.*, Nos. 7–8 (July–August, 1965), p. 101.

11. *Régionalisation du budget, 1964*, pp. 32–33.

12. *Régionalisation du budget, 1966*, pp. 329–334.

13. Michel Drancourt, "Plaidoyer pour Paris," *Réalités*, No. 222 (July, 1964), p. 76.

14. "Paris—1975 and Beyond," pp. 1–7.

15. Ibid., p. 2.

16. *Paris en question*, p. 133.

17. Ibid., p. 84.

18. George Jouve, "Paris qui grogne," *Réalités*, No. 222 (July, 1964), p. 71.

19. *Paris en question*, p. 131.

20. Ibid., p. 15. See also Christian Rudel, *Mon village à l'heure de l'expansion* (Paris: Les Editions Ouvrières, 1965), pp. 18–19.

21. *L'aménagement de la région parisienne*, première partie, p. 24; and Stanislaw Wellisz, "Economic Planning in the Netherlands, France, and Italy," *J. P. E.*, LXVIII (June, 1960), p. 280. Wellisz erroneously gives these values as cost per marginal inhabitant rather than per marginal household.

22. *L'aménagement de la région parisienne*, premièr partie, p. 24.

23. Claude Delmas, *L'aménagement du territoire* (Paris: Presses Universitaires de France, 1963), p. 60.

24. Wellisz, pp. 279–280.

25. Alain Girard and Henri Bastide, "Les problèmes démographiques devant l'opinion," *Population*, XV (April-May, 1960), pp. 246–287.

26. Ibid., p. 287.

27. "La Région de Paris: perspectives de développement et d'aménagement," *Sondages*, No. 4 (1963), p. 26.

28. Ibid., p. 38.

29. Wellisz, p. 282.

30. "A French-American 'Forward Look,'" *France actuelle*, XII (July 1, 1963), p. 6.

31. Wellisz, p. 280.

32. *Paris en question,* p. 29.

33. Ibid.

34. Ibid.

35. Nungesser, *Contre Paris,* p. 16.

36. *Documents de la conférence sur les économies régionales,* volume II, Brussels, December, 1961 (Brussels: Communauté Economique Européenne, 1963), p. 195.

37. Michel Debré, *Au service de la nation* (Paris: Stock, 1963), p. 237.

38. Jean-Louis Quermonne, "Planification régionale et réforme administrative," in Institut d'Etudes Politiques de l'Université de Grenoble, *Administration traditionnelle et planification régionale* (Paris: Colin, 1964), p. 109. See also Quermonne, "Ver un régionalisme 'fonctionnel'?" *R. F. S. P.,* XIII (November–December, 1963), pp. 849–876.

39. *Avant-projet,* p. 71.

40. Ibid., pp. 69–70.

41. *Principales options,* p. 33.

42. Ibid., p. 173. A similar position is taken in a preliminary document in the preparation of the Fifth Plan. *Réflexions pour 1985,* p. 75.

43. Ibid., p. 181.

44. *Vᵉ Plan* pp. 129–131.

45. *Premier rapport,* p. 47.

46. Ibid., p. 17.

47. *Regional Development in the European Economic Comunity* (London: Political and Economic Planning, 1962), pp. 55–56.

48. Ibid., p. 56.

49. Quermonne, p. 111.

50. *L'aménagement de la région parisienne,* première partie, pp. 5–6.

51. Ibid., p. 6.

52. Ibid., deuxième partie.

53. *Le Monde,* September 30, 1965, p. 24.

54. The publications of the District include *Avant-projet; L'aide financière, 1962–1965; Plan quadriennal;* and *Schéma directeur.* See also the following documents: *Activité du District* and *The Region of Paris.*

55. For further expenditure data see *L'aide financière, 1962–1965.*

56. *Le Monde,* September 19–20, 1965, p. 8.

57. *Le Monde,* January 14, 1966, p. 18.

58. See, for example, *Paris en question,* pp. 178–180; *Le Monde,* September 15, 1965, p. 16; J.-F. Gravier, *L'aménagement du territoire et l'avenir des régions françaises* (Paris: Flammarion, 1964), pp. 108–112; and Jean Maze, "Visage de la ville axiale," *E.R.,* V (March, 1965), pp. 17–20.

59. *Le Monde,* September 15, 1965, p. 16; Maze, p. 20.

60. Maze, p. 20.

61. *Le Monde,* September 15, 1965, p. 20.

62. *Paris en question,* pp. 179–180. See also *Vᵉ Plan,* pp. 130–131.

63. The Economic and Social Council is a consultative body created to advise the government on economic and social matters and to foster collaboration among diverse social and professional groups. It is composed of 205 members, two thirds of whom are designated by business associations, trade unions, farm organizations, and other similar organisms, and one third of whom are appointed by the government on the basis of their competence in special areas. Consultation with the council is obligatory during the preparations of the national Plan.

64. *Avis et rapports, Ve Plan*, pp. 55–57. To compensate for the existence of the Paris Region's Strategic Plan, the Fifth Plan provides for the creation of similar plans for other major agglomerations. Concrete steps toward the creation of agglomeration-wide urban planning agencies were implemented in 1966 for the *métropoles d'équilibre* which will receive priority in French urban development planning (see Chap. 10). *Ve Plan*, pp. 133; *Le Monde*, May 10, 1966, p. 22.

65. *Avis et rapports, Ve Plan*, p. 57.

66. *Ve Plan*, p. 130.

67. Marcel Boiteux, "The Green Tariff of the Electricité de France," trans. W. E. and L. C. Clemens, *L. E.*, XL (May, 1964), pp. 185–197.

3. French Decentralization Policy

1. Claudius-Petit, *Pour un plan*.

2. Joseph Lajugie, "Aménagement du territoire et développement économique régionale en France (1945–1964)," *R. E. P.*, LXXIV (January–February, 1964), p. 290.

3. Jean Faucheux, *La décentralisation industrielle* (Paris: Editions Berger-Levrault, 1959), pp. 86–87.

4. Ibid., pp. 203–206.

5. Ibid., pp. 206–207.

6. *Décentralisation*, pp. 97–101, 111–115, 145–163.

7. "Insuffisance de la politique de décentralisation industrielle," *E. R.*, V (March, 1965), p. 13.

8. *Avis, Lemaire*, pp. 62–66. The figures given here concern declarations of intent on the part of entrepreneurs; they may not necessarily have been followed in each case. In addition, the various values reported are not always mutually consistent. However, despite these qualifications the values presented here give a reasonable indication of the relevant changes which have taken place.

9. Faucheux, pp. 231–232.

10. Ibid.

11. "Inventaire et bilan de l'action des sociétés de développement régional," *Avis et rapports*, May 26, 1963, pp. 370–371.

12. Ibid., p. 377.

13. Ibid.

14. Ibid., p. 378.

15. Jules Milhau, "Le financement de l'expansion régionale," *R. E. P.,* LXXIV (January-February, 1964), p. 132. See also P. Bauchet, "L'échelon régional," in *Planification française et démocratie* (Lyon: Economie et Humanisme, 1961), p. 63.

16. "Inventaire et bilan de l'action des sociétés de développement régional," p. 378.

17. "Problèmes de l'élaboration et de l'exécution des plans régionaux," *Avis et rapports,* May 15, 1960, p. 368.

18. Milhau, p. 131.

19. Ibid. See also *IVᵉ Plan,* p. 190.

20. "Inventaire et bilan de l'action des sociétés de développement régional," p. 378.

21. M. Byé, "Rapport sur les moyens d'une politique des économies régionale," in Consil Economique, *Etude sur une politique des économies régionales* (Paris: Presses Universitaires de France, 1957), p. 57.

22. "Inventaire et bilan de l'action des sociétés de développement régional," p. 376.

23. Byé, p. 52.

24. *Décentralisation,* p. 9.

25. Ibid., pp. 19–21.

26. Ibid., pp. 23–24.

27. "Septième rapport du Conseil de Direction du Fonds de développement économique et social," *S. E. F.,* No. 157 (January, 1962), pp. 133 ff.

28. Ibid., p. 136.

29. Ibid.

30. *Décentralisation,* pp. 35–37.

31. See Ibid., pp. 53–55. This text includes revisions which were made by decrees of 1960 and 1962. For details of prior relevant decrees see Faucheux, pp. 215–216.

32. *Décentralisation,* p. 53.

33. Ibid., p. 54.

34. "Dixième rapport du Conseil de Direction du Fonds de développement économique et social," *S. E. F.,* No. 198 (June, 1965), pp. 968–969.

35. Ibid., pp. 969–974.

36. Jacqueline Claudet, "Les organismes de l'aménagement du territoire en France," *C. B.,* No. 2 (1958), pp. 83–84.

37. Milhau, p. 118.

38. Data for observations on Y are taken from *S. E. F.,* No. 190 (October, 1964), pp. 1442–1444. For X_2, see *The European Markets* (New York: Chase Manhattan Bank, 1964), pp. 51–52. For X_1 and X_3, see *Annuaire statistique, 1963,* pp. 155 and 306.

39. For data on the first of these independent variables see *Annuaire statistique, 1963,* p. 414. For migration data see *Ibid.,* p. xiii. These variables were not included in the above regression equations because of problems arising from intercorrelated independent variables.

40. Data for variable Y is taken from *Annuaire statistique, 1962,* p. 242,

and *Annuaire statistique, 1963,* p. 254. For variable *X,* see Note 39. Variable *Y* includes only projects involving over 500 square meters of floor space.

41. *Décentralisation,* pp. 15–18.

42. John and Anne-Marie Hackett, *Economic Planning in France* (Cambridge: Harvard University Press, 1963), pp. 247–248.

43. Pierre Mendès-France, *A Modern French Republic,* trans. Anne Carter (New York: Hill and Wang, 1963), pp. 111–112.

44. *IVe Plan,* pp. 150–151. *France and Economic Planning,* p. 34.

45. *Avant-projet,* pp. 108–109.

46. Mendès-France, p. 112. See also "Problèmes de la décentralisation des établissements relevant de l'état ou soumis à son controle," *Avis et rapports,* December 30, 1960.

47. *IVe Plan,* p. 120.

4. The Institutional Framework for Regional Planning

1. Joseph Lajugie, "Aménagement du territoire et développement économique régionale en France," *R. E. P.,* LXXIV (January-February, 1964), pp. 305–306.

2. *Problèmes du développement régional, travaux du Congrès des économistes de langue française, 1959* (Paris: Editions Cujas, 1960), p. 27.

3. *Rhône-Alpes,* p. 3.

4. *Journal officiel,* December 6, 1956.

5. *Rhône-Alpes,* pp. 13–15.

6. J.-F. Gravier, *L'aménagement du territoire et l'avenir des régions françaises* (Paris: Flammarion, 1964), pp. 162–163. See also "Problèmes administratifs posés par la mise en oeuvre des plans régionaux," *Avis et rapports,* April 14, 1960, p. 296.

7. Jacques Boudeville, *Les programmes économiques* (Paris: Presses Universitaires de France, 1963), p. 81. See also Pierre Bauchet, "La comptabilité économique régionale et son usage," *E. A.,* XIV (January, 1961), p. 80.

8. "Etude des statistiques régionales et des moyens d'observation de la conjoncture économique régionale," *Avis et rapports,* August 5, 1961, p. 741. See also "Méthodes d'élaboration du Ve Plan," *Avis et rapports,* December 7, 1963, pp. 713–714; Pierre Massé, *Le Plan ou l'anti-hasard* (Paris: Editions Gallimard, 1965), p. 112; and Bernard Kayser and Pierre George, "La région comme objet d'intervention," in *La géographie active* (Paris: Presses Universitaires de France, 1964), p. 387.

9. "Méthodes d'élaboration du Ve Plan," p. 714.

10. *Le Monde,* November 17, 1965, p. 20.

11. *Rhône-Alpes,* p. 5.

12. Ibid., pp. 7–9.

13. "Problèmes de l'élaboration et d'exécution des plans régionaux," *Avis et rapports,* May 15, 1960, pp. 358–361.

14. Bernard Pouyet and Patrice de Monbrison-Fouchère, "La régionalisation dans le IVᵉ Plan: l'expérience des tranches opératoires," in Institut d'Etudes Politiques de l'Université de Grenoble, *Administration traditionelle et planification régionale* (Paris: Colin, 1964), p. 156.

15. Jacques de Lanversin, *L'aménagement du territoire* (Paris: Librairies Techniques, 1965), p. 104.

16. Philippe Bernard, "La planification régionale en France," *R. E. P.,* No. 145 (February, 1961), p. 188.

17. M. Bloch-Lainé, "L'adaptation des administrations aux problèmes régionaux en France," in *La politique régionale dans la Communauté Economique Européenne* (Brussels: Communauté Economique Européenne, 1964), p. 375.

18. *Rhône-Alpes,* pp. 11–12.

19. Lajugie, p. 315.

20. "Problèmes de l'élaboration et de l'exécution des plans régionaux," p. 360.

21. *Rhône-Alpes,* pp. 13–15.

22. Lajugie, pp. 315–316.

23. *Organisation, départements,* pp. 11–16.

24. *Organisation, circonscriptions,* p. 6.

25. *Organisation, départements,* pp. 6–8, 15.

26. *Journal officiel,* April 26, 1964, p. 3707.

27. *Organisation, départements,* pp. 17–19.

28. *Aménagement du territoire,* pp. 3–5.

29. Ibid., pp. 5–13.

30. Ibid.

31. Ibid.

32. "Le dossier de l'aménagement du territoire," *Entreprise,* XXVII (December, 1963), p. 12.

33. Lajugie, pp. 313–314.

34. Pouyet and Monbrison-Fouchère, p. 200.

35. Ibid., p. 161.

36. *IVᵉ Plan,* p. 121.

37. Jean Fuchs, "Les tranches opératoire du IVᵉ Plan," *M. T.,* No. 50 (December 16, 1962), p. 19. See also Jules Milhau, "La régionalisation du Plan en France," *R. E. M.,* XXXVIII (April–June, 1962), pp. 115–122, and A. Jourlin, "La politique régionale au service des monopoles," *E. P.,* X (September, 1963), pp. 25–39.

38. Pouyet and Monbrison-Fouchère, p. 163; Claude Vimont, "Methods of Forecasting Employment in France," in *Economic Aspects of Higher Education* (Paris: Organization for Economic Cooperation and Development, 1964), pp. 223–246.

39. *Organisation, circonscriptions,* pp. 8–12.

40. Pouyet and Monbrison-Fouchère, pp. 166–167.

41. Ibid., pp. 189, 199.

42. Ibid., pp. 174–175.

43. Ibid., pp. 184–185, 190, 205.
44. Ibid., pp. 180, 197, 210, 214.
45. Lanversin, p. 110.
46. *Régionalisation en 1964*, p. 10.
47. Ibid., p. 11. See also *Régionalisation du budget, 1964*, pp. 9–10.
48. *Régionalisation en 1964*, p. 9.
49. *Régionalisation du budget, 1964*, p. 30, and the corresponding volumes for 1965 and 1966.
50. *Journal officiel*, July 25, 1965, p. 6491.
51. *Documents, Vᵉ Plan*, pp. 385–387.
52. Ibid., pp. 385–402.
53. Ibid., pp. 402–404.
54. Ibid., pp. 402–408.

5. Regional Economic Theory: The French Approach

1. See, for example, Johann H. von Thünen, *Der isolierte Staat in Beziehung auf Landwirtschaft und Nationalökonomie* (Hamburg: Fr. Derthes, 1826), and August Lösch, *The Economics of Location*, trans. William Wolgom and W. F. Stolper (New Haven: Yale University Press, 1954).

2. Lloyd Rodwin, "Choosing Regions for Development," in Carl J. Freidrich and Seymour E. Harris, eds., *Public Policy*, XII (Cambridge: Harvard University Press, 1963), pp. 149–150.

3. Charles M. Tiebout, "Intra-Urban Location Problems: An Evaluation," *A. E. R. P. P.*, LI (May, 1961), pp. 271–278.

4. Pierre Bauchet, "La comptabilité économique régional et son usage," *E. A.*, XIV (January, 1961), pp. 69, 80.

5. See, for example, his "An Operational Model of Regional Trade in France," *P. P. R. S. A.*, VII (1961), pp. 177–187, and *Problems of Regional Economic Planning* (Edinburgh: Edinburgh University Press, 1966).

6. Bauchet, p. 69.

7. Ibid., p. 70.

8. See Claude Zarka, "Un exemple de pôle de croissance: l'industrie textile du Nord de la France, 1830–1870," *R. E.*, IX (January, 1958), pp. 65–106. A more recent study which emphasizes this point is Charles P. Kindleberger, *Economic Growth in France and Britain, 1851–1950* (Cambridge: Harvard University Press, 1963).

9. François Perroux, "Note sur la notion de pôle de croissance," in François Perroux, *L'économie du XXᵉ siècle* (2d ed.; Paris: Presses Universitaires de France, 1964), pp. 142–153.

10. Jules Milhau, "La théorie de la croissance et l'expansion régionale," *E. A.*, No. 3 (July–September, 1956), p. 361.

11. P. Pottier, "Axes de comunication et théorie de développement," *R. E.*, XIV (January, 1963), pp. 113–114.

12. Ibid., pp. 70–113. Although Pottier's analysis is based on French

experience, he points out that development axes are usually interregional or international in nature.

13. Ibid., p. 128.

14. Perroux, p. 143.

15. Jean Paelinck, "La théorie du développement régional polarisé," *C. I. S. E. A.*, Series L, No. 15 (March, 1965), pp. 10–11.

16. François Perroux, "Economic Space: Theory and Applications," *Q. J. E.*, LXIV (February, 1950), p. 90.

17. Ibid., p. 91. The emphasis is Perroux's.

18. Ibid.

19. Ibid., pp. 94–97. See also Perroux, "Les espaces économiques," *E. A.*, No. 1 (January, 1950).

20. Jacques Boudeville, *Les espaces économiques* (Paris: Presses Universitaires de France, 1961), p. 8.

21. Ibid., p. 10.

22. Ibid., pp. 11–13.

23. Jacques Boudeville, "Un modèle des mouvements commerciaux interrégionaux en France," *C. I. S. E. A.*, Series L, No. 9 (October, 1961), pp. 5–78. See also *Les espaces économiques*, pp. 14–15, and Boudeville, "La région plan," *C. I. S. E. A.*, Series L, No. 6 (January, 1960).

24. Boudeville, *Les espaces économiques*, p. 16.

25. Ibid.

26. Ibid. The emphasis is mine.

27. Ibid., pp. 16–17.

28. Jacques Boudeville, "Les notions d'espace et d'intégration," Paper given at the International Conference on Town and Regional Planning, Basle, September 22–25, 1965, p. 2.

29. François Perroux, *L'économie du XXᵉ siècle*, p. 85.

30. Ibid., p. 40.

31. Ibid., pp. 142–153.

32. H. Aujac, "La hiérarchy des industries dans un tableau des échanges interindustriels, et ses conséquences dans la mise en oeuvre d'un plan national décentralisé," *R. E.*, XI (May, 1960), pp. 169–238.

33. Rodwin, pp. 150–151.

34. See, for example, Pierre Bauchet, *Les tableaux économiques, analyse de la région lorraine* (Paris: Génin, 1955); Janine Capronnier-Spielhagen, *Comptes nationaux et régionaux de l'énergie* (Paris: Colin, 1962), R. Jouandet-Bernadat, *Les comptes du département de la Gironde* (Bordeaux: Imprimerie Bière, 1963); and R. Jouandet-Bernadat, *Comptabilité économique et espaces régionaux* (Paris: Gauthier-Villars, 1964).

35. Sylvan Wickham, "French Planning: Retrospect and Prospect," *R. E. S.*, XLV (November, 1963), p. 340.

36. André Trintignac, *Aménager l'hexagone* (Paris: Editions du Centurion, 1964), pp. 218–219.

37. Paelinck, p. 8.

38. Philippe Aydalot, "Note sur les économies externes et quelques notions connexes," *R. E.,* XVI (November, 1965), p. 962.

39. For a fuller discussion of these phenomena, see, for example, Paelinck, "La théorie du développement régional polarisé"; J. Boudeville, "La région plan"; F. Perroux, "La firme motrice dans une région, et la région motrice," *C. I. S. E. A.,* Series AD, No. 1 (March, 1961); and L. E. Davin, *Economie régionale et croissance* (Paris: Génin, 1964), pp. 54–72.

40. Paelinck, pp. 34–37.

41. Bauchet, *Les tableaux économiques,* p. 10.

42. Davin, p. 56.

43. Ibid., p. 64.

44. Aydalot, p. 963.

45. Ibid., p. 964.

46. Ibid.

47. Ibid., pp. 964–965.

48. Ibid., p. 967.

49. Ibid.

50. Paelinck, pp. 10–13.

51. Ibid., p. 13.

52. Albert O. Hirschman, *The Strategy of Economic Development* (New Haven: Yale University Press, 1958), pp. 194–195.

53. Aydalot, pp. 967–968.

54. Raymond Vernon, *The Changing Economic Function of the Central City* (New York: Committee for Economic Development, 1959), pp. 28–37.

55. Davin, p. 57.

56. Niles M. Hansen, "The Structure and Determinants of Local Public Investment Expenditures," *R. E. S.,* XLVII (May, 1965), pp. 150–162.

57. Davin, p. 56.

58. Paelinck, pp. 10–11.

59. Ibid., p. 47. The emphasis is Paelinck's.

6. The Regional Structure of the French Economy

1. *IVe Plan,* p. 131.

2. *Annuaire statistique, 1963,* p. 46.

3. Ibid., p. xviii.

4. Ibid., p. 155.

5. *Régionalisation du budget, 1966,* pp. 244–245.

6. *Le Monde,* January 26, 1966, p. 22.

7. See O. Guichard, *Aménager la France* (Paris: Laffont-Gonthier, 1965), p. 210, and *Le Monde,* October 28, 1965, p. 14.

8. *Premier rapport,* p. 38. See also *Principales options,* pp. 172–173, and *Réflexions pour 1985,* pp. 152–155.

9. *Ve Plan,* pp. 124–131.

10. *Premier rapport,* p. 38.

11. Michel Beaud, "Une analyse des disparités régionales de croissance," *R. E.,* XVII (January, 1966), pp. 55–91. Another somewhat similar study is F. Coront-Ducluzeau, *La formation de l'espace économique national* (Paris: Colin, 1964). However, this work is less interesting because the data which it utilizes are from 1954 or earlier, it is not presented in terms of the program regions, and its method is for the most part based on location coefficients.

12. H. S. Perloff, *et al., Regions, Resources and Economic Growth* (Baltimore: The Johns Hopkins Press, 1960), pp. 70–74. See also E. S. Dunn, Jr., "Une technique statistique et analytique d'analyse régionale, description et projection," *E. A.,* No. 4 (October, 1959), pp. 521–530, and Frank H. Hanna, "Analysis of Interstate Income Differentials: Theory and Practice," in *Regional Income,* National Bureau of Economic Research Studies in Income and Wealth, Vol. 21 (Princeton: Princeton University Press, 1957), pp. 113–160.

13. Let $e_{\beta\alpha}^{\theta}$ represent employment in branch β of region α at time θ. Then:

$$E_{\alpha}^{(\theta_1-\theta)} = \frac{\sum\limits_{\beta} e_{\beta\alpha}^{\theta_1}}{\sum\limits_{\beta} e_{\beta\alpha}^{\theta_0}} - \frac{\sum\limits_{\beta}\sum\limits_{\alpha} e_{\beta\alpha}^{\theta_1}}{\sum\limits_{\beta}\sum\limits_{\alpha} e_{\beta\alpha}^{\theta_0}},$$

$$S_{\alpha}^{(\theta_1-\theta_0)} = \frac{\sum\limits_{\beta}\left[e_{\beta\alpha}^{\theta_0}\dfrac{\sum\limits_{\alpha} e_{\beta\alpha}^{\theta_1}}{\sum\limits_{\alpha} e_{\beta\alpha}^{\theta_0}}\right]}{\sum\limits_{\beta} e_{\beta\alpha}^{\theta_0}} - \frac{\sum\limits_{\beta}\sum\limits_{\alpha} e_{\beta\alpha}^{\theta_1}}{\sum\limits_{\beta}\sum\limits_{\alpha} e_{\beta\alpha}^{\theta_0}}, \text{ and}$$

$$R_{\alpha}^{(\theta_1-\theta_0)} = \frac{\sum\limits_{\beta} e_{\beta\alpha}^{\theta_1}}{\sum\limits_{\beta} e_{\beta\alpha}^{\theta_0}} - \frac{\sum\limits_{\beta}\left[e_{\beta\alpha}^{\theta_0}\dfrac{\sum\limits_{\alpha} e_{\beta\alpha}^{\theta_1}}{\sum\limits_{\alpha} e_{\beta\alpha}^{\theta_0}}\right]}{\sum\limits_{\beta} e_{\beta\alpha}^{\theta_0}}.$$

14. *Provence-Côte d'Azur,* p. 214.

15. Beaud, pp. 75–76.

16. Ibid., p. 76.

17. Ibid., pp. 79–80.

18. Ibid.

19. *Documents de la conference sur les économies régionales* (Brussels: Communauté Economique Européenne, 1963).

20. *Avis. Lemaire,* pp. 50–71.

21. Michel Beaud, "Analyse régionale-structurale et planification régionale," *R. E.*, XVII (March, 1966), pp. 264–287.

22. Ibid., p. 272.

23. Ibid., p. 274.

24. Ibid.

25. Ibid., p. 275.

26. See also David B. Houston, "The Shift and Share Analysis of Regional Growth: A Critique," *S. E. J.*, XXXIII (April, 1967), pp. 577–581.

7. The Need for Social Overhead Capital in Lagging Regions

1. Claude Delmas, *L'aménagement du territoire* (Paris: Presses Universitaires de France, 1963), pp. 113–114.

2. Ibid., p. 123. See also J. Boudeville, *Les programmes économiques* (Paris: Presses Universitaires de France, 1963), p. 69.

3. André Aumonier, "Mesures à prendre pour le développement de la promotion sociale," *Avis et rapports,* March 1, 1962, p. 432.

4. Milhau, "Rapport présenté au nom du Conseil Economique," in *Etude sur une politique des économies régionales* (Paris: Presses Universitaires de France, 1957), p. 17. See also F. Perroux, *L'économie du XXᵉ siècle* (2d ed.; Paris: Presses Universitaires de France, 1964), p. 135.

5. Jean Faucheux, *La décentralisation industrielle* (Paris: Editions Berger-Levrault, 1959), pp. 46–47.

6. J.-F. Gravier, *L'ámenagement du territoire et l'avenir des régions françaises* (Paris: Flammarion, 1964), pp. 156–157.

7. Charles Roig, "L'administration locale et les changements sociaux," in Institut d'Etudes Politiques de l'Université de Grenoble, *Administration traditionelle et planification régionale* (Paris: Colin, 1964), p. 28.

8. Niles M. Hansen, "On the Sources of Economic Rationality," *Z. N.*, XXIV (Winter, 1964), pp. 445–455, and "The Protestant Ethic as a General Precondition for Economic Development," *C. J. E.*, XXIX (November, 1963), pp. 462–474.

9. Jean Pautard, *Les disparités régionales dans la croissance de l'agriculture française* (Paris: Gauthier-Villars, 1965), pp. 139–140.

10. Ibid., pp. 58, 119–146. See also M. Augé-Laribé, *La politique agricole de la France de 1880 à 1940* (Paris: Presses Universitaires de France, 1950), pp. 45, 86.

11. Pautard, pp. 141–143.

12. Ibid., p. 143.

13. Ibid.

14. Edward Higbee, "The French Paysan is Angry," *New York Times Magazine*, October 27, 1963, p. 20. Higbee cites as evidence of inefficiencies in French agriculture and marketing that "the average French family has to spend about 35 per cent of its income on food, compared with 20 per cent in the U.S." However, this fact is not necessarily an indication of inefficiency; it reflects low income elasticity of demand for food.

15. *France and Agriculture*, p. 8. See also *France actuelle*, XIII (June 1, 1964) p. 6.

16. *Régionalisation du budget, 1966*, p. 195.

17. Ibid., p. 205.

18. Ibid., p. 186.

19. R. Livet, *L'avenir des régions agricoles* (Paris: Les Editions Ouvrières, 1965), p. 207.

20. Ibid. The emphasis is Livet's.

21. Ibid., p. 208.

22. Gravier, pp. 33–35.

23. Ibid., p. 35. The emphasis is mine.

24. Livet, p. 212.

25. Ibid.

26. *Régionalisation du budget, 1966*, p. 186.

27. Ibid., p. 195.

28. *Région de Bretagne*, p. 17.

29. *Le Monde*, October 28, 1965, p. 20. See also *Le Monde*, September 30, 1965, p. 22.

30. *IVe Plan*, p. 131.

31. *Rapport, Vallon*, p. 9.

32. Milhau, p. 10.

33. A. Prate, "Marché commun et politique régionale," *R. E. P.*, LXXIV (January-February, 1964), p. 172.

34. Alain Girard and Henri Bastide, "Les problèmes démographiques devant l'opinion," *Population*, XV (April-May, 1960), p. 273.

35. *France actuelle*, XIII (October 1, 1964), p. 7.

36. "L'aménagement du territoire et l'action régionale," *Sondages*, No. 1, 1965, pp. 61–62.

37. Maurice Halff, "Problèmes posés par l'exécution du IVe Plan," *Avis et rapports*, January 11, 1963, p. 14.

38. *Région de Poitou-Charentes*, pp. 58–59.

39. Faucheux, p. 46.

40. See "Les présidents des C. O. D. E. R. vous parlent," *E. R.*, V (June, 1965), pp. 10–15.

41. Niles M. Hansen, "The Structure and Determinants of Local Public Investment Expenditures," *R. E. S.*, XLVII (May, 1965), pp. 150–162, and Hansen, "Municipal Investment Requirements in a Growing Agglomeration," *L. E.*, XLI (February, 1965), pp. 49–56.

42. *Documents, Ve Plan*, p. 400.

43. "L'aménagement du territoire et l'action régionale," p. 48.

44. Ibid., p. 50.

45. Ibid., p. 48.

46. "Paradoxically, 45 per cent of the French believe that agriculture lacks workers, and indeed the regions where the exodus has been most marked and where it is necessary in order to modernize operations are those where people find that there are not enough farmers!" Ibid., pp. 78–80.

47. Ibid., p. 50.

48. Philippe Aydalot, "Etude sur le processus de polarisation et sur les réactions des industries anciennes à la lumière de l'expérience de Lacq," *C. I. S. E. A.*, Series L, No. 15 (March, 1965), pp. 116–118.

49. Gravier, p. 39. See also Aydalot, p. 119.

50. Aydalot, p. 118.

51. Ibid., p. 119.

52. Ibid., p. 111. See also F. Coront-Ducluzeau, *La Formation de l'espace économique* (Paris: Colin, 1964), p. 220.

53. *Région de Poitou-Charentes*, p. 47.

54. *Regional Development in the European Economic Community* (London: Political and Economic Planning, 1962), p. 51.

55. Ibid., p. 15.

56. Gravier, pp. 39–40.

57. Raymond Guglielmo, "Géographie active de l'industrie," in *La géographie active* (Paris: Presses Universitaires de France, 1964), pp. 223–224.

58. Coront-Ducluzeau, p. 220.

59. *Problèmes du développement régional, travaux du Congrès des économistes de langue française, 1959* (Paris: Cujas, 1960), p. 32.

60. Louis Leroy, *Le ruralisme* (Paris: Les Editions Ouvrières, 1960), p. 97.

61. Michel Beaud, "Une analyse des disparités régionales de croissance," *R. E.*, XVII (January, 1966), p. 90.

62. Aydalot, pp. 112–113.

63. Ibid., p. 113.

64. Ibid., pp. 121–122. Somewhat different proportions are given in this regard by Pierre Maillet in *La structure économique de la France* (Paris: Presses Universitaires de France, 1964), p. 35.

65. Aydalot, p. 122.

66. François Robin, "Possibilités de décentralisation des laboratoires de recherche scientifique et technique," *Avis et rapports*, February 2, 1962, p. 36.

67. Antoine de Tavernost, "Les investissements et l'économie du Sud-Ouest," in *L'avenir économique du Sud-Ouest* (Paris: Centre Economique et Social de Perfectionnement de Cadres, 1961), p. 30.

68. Aydalot, pp. 127–128.

69. Ibid., p. 128.

70. Ibid., pp. 139–144.

71. Ibid., pp. 163–164.

8. Public Investment in Intermediate Regions: The Need for Economic Overhead Capital

1. Jacques de Lanversin, *L'aménagement du territoire* (Paris: Libraires Techniques, 1965), p. 173.

2. Claude Delmas, *L'aménagement du territoire* (Paris: Presses Universitaires de France, 1963), pp. 72–75.

3. Ibid., pp. 75–76.

4. *France and Agriculture,* pp. 12–14. See also Jacques Boudeville, "Aménagement des grands bassins fluviaux au Brésil et en France," *T. M.,* II (October-December, 1961), p. 493.

5. André Trintignac, *Aménager l'hexagone* (Paris: Editions du Centurion, 1964), p. 260.

6. Boudeville, pp. 498–499. See also Boudeville, *Les espaces économiques* (Paris: Presses Universitaires de France, 1961), pp. 112–113.

7. Philippe Lamour, *L'aménagement du territoire* (Paris: Editions de l'Epargne, 1964), p. 33.

8. *Rhône-Alpes,* p. 55. See also M.-A. Prost, "Structure et croissance des communes du département du Rhône," *C. I. S. E. A.,* Series L, No. 7 (September, 1960), pp. 1–17, and Prost, "Rayonnement commercial des pôles satellites du département du Rhône," *Ibid.,* pp. 19–32.

9. *Rhône-Alpes,* p. 55.

10. M.-A. Prost, *La hiérarchie des villes en fonction de leurs activités de commerce et de service* (Paris: Gauthier-Villars, 1965), pp. 223–230.

11. J.-F. Gravier, *L'aménagement du territoire et l'avenir des régions françaises* (Paris: Flammarion, 1964), p. 164.

12. Robert Butheau, "Paris est-il la véritable capitale de la région Rhône-Alpes?" *Le Monde,* April 20, 1966, p. 11.

13. Jean Maze, "Le dossier de l'axe Nord-Sud," *E. R.,* IV (November-December, 1964), p. 52.

14. Ibid.

15. Ibid., p. 51.

16. Ibid., p. 52. See also Gravier, p. 222.

17. Jacques Boudeville, "Les instruments de la région de programme," *C. I. S. E. A.,* Series L, No. 14 (September, 1964), p. 15.

18. *Principales options,* p. 179. See also *Premier rapport,* pp. 45–46.

19. *Vᵉ Plan,* p. 127.

20. Ibid., pp. 126–129.

21. *Le Monde,* November 7–8, 1965, p. 9.

22. *Région d'Alsace,* p. 97.

23. Ibid., p. 96. See also Jean-Paul Courthéoux, "Groupes de pression face à l'innovation économique: la canalisation de la Moselle," *R. E.,* XVI (November, 1965), p. 932.

24. Jean-Claude Hahn, "La foire européenne de Strasbourg," *Le Monde,* September 17, 1965, p. 19.

25. *L'axe de transport,* p. 57.

26. Gravier, pp. 221–222.

27. P. Pottier, "Axes de comunication et théorie de développement," *R. E.,* XIV (January, 1963), pp. 58–132.

28. Claude Zarka, "Un exemple de pôle de croissance: l'industrie textile du Nord de la France, 1830–1870," *R. E.,* IX (January, 1958), pp. 65–106;

René Gendarme, "Les problèmes actuels du développement régional dans le Nord," *R. E.,* VII (November, 1956), p. 897.

29. Charles P. Kindleberger, *Economic Growth in France and Britain 1851–1950* (Cambridge: Harvard University Press, 1965), pp. 261–262.

30. *Région du Nord,* p. 21.

31. *Avis, Lemaire,* p. 50.

32. Ibid., p. 58.

33. Michel Beaud, "Analyse régionale-structurale et planification régionale," *R. E.,* XVII (March, 1966), pp. 264–287.

34. Henri Deligny, "Une région-pilote qui s'essouffle," *Le Monde,* April 23, 1966, p. 5.

35. Guy Debeyre, "Les problèmes du Nord," *E. R.,* No. 31 (December, 1963), p. 11.

36. Ibid. See also Prost, pp. 199–200.

37. *La politique régionale dans la Communauté Economique Européenne* (Brussels: Communauté Economique Européenne, 1964), p. 201.

38. *Région du Nord,* p. 100.

39. Debeyre, p. 11.

40. *IVe Plan,* p. 133.

41. *Premier rapport,* p. 45.

42. *Ve Plan,* p. 127.

43. Beaud, p. 286.

44. Pottier, *op. cit.* See also Jean Pautard, *Les disparités régionales dans la croissance de l'agriculture française* (Paris: Gauthiers-Villars, 1965), pp. 108–118, 147–175.

45. Gendarme, p. 901.

46. Gravier, p. 38.

47. "Dunkirk Serves the New Europe," *France actuelle,* XII (April 15, 1963), pp. 1–7.

48. *IVe Plan,* p. 133.

49. Ibid.

50. Delmas, p. 107.

51. *IVe Plan,* p. 133.

52. *Ve Plan,* p. 127.

9. French Regional Policy in the Fourth and Fifth Plans

1. John and Anne-Marie Hackett, *Economic Planning in France* (Cambridge: Harvard University Press, 1963), p. 89.

2. *IVe Plan,* p. 26.

3. Sylvan Wickham, "French Planning: Retrospect and Prospect," *R. E. S.,* XLV (November, 1963), p. 338.

4. *IVe Plan,* p. 39.

5. Ibid.

6. Ibid.

7. Ibid.

8. Ibid., p. 40. See also p. 131.

9. Ibid., pp. 40, 130–131, 134–136.

10. Ibid., p. 130.

11. Maurice Halff, "Méthodes d'élaboration du Ve Plan," *Avis et rapports,* December 7, 1963, p. 713.

12. Ibid.

13. *IVe Plan,* p. 121.

14. *L'exécution du Plan,* p. 25, and *Le Monde,* November 24, 1965, p. 3.

15. *L'exécution du Plan,* p. 168.

16. Ibid.

17. "Principales options du Ve Plan," *Avis et rapports,* November 13, 1964, p. 886. See also *Avis et rapports, Ve Plan,* p. 22.

18. *L'exécution du Plan,* p. 168.

19. *Le Monde,* October 31, 1965, p. 9.

20. Michel Beaud, "Analyse régionale-structurale et planification régionale," *R. E.,* XVII (March, 1966), p. 287.

21. Maurice Benoit, "Une angoissante contradiction," *E. R.,* IV (Summer, 1964), p. 9.

22. *Premier rapport,* p. 41.

23. Ibid., pp. 19–24.

24. Ibid., p. 20.

25. Ibid., pp. 25–29.

26. Ibid., pp. 29–33.

27. Ibid., pp. 40–44.

28. Ibid., pp. 44–46.

29. Ibid., pp. 114–115.

30. *Principales options,* p. 13.

31. Ibid., pp. 30–31.

32. Ibid., pp. 174–175.

33. Ibid., pp. 178–180.

34. Ibid., pp. 180–181.

35. Ibid., pp. 181–182.

36. Ibid., pp. 184–185.

37. Ibid., p. 185.

38. Roger Millot, "Rapport pour avis présenté au nom de la section des économies régionales," *Avis et rapports,* November 13, 1964, p. 907.

39. Ibid.

40. *Ve Plan,* pp. 17, 117–118.

41. Ibid., p. 119.

42. Ibid.

43. Ibid., pp. 119–121.

44. Ibid., pp. 121–123.

45. Ibid., pp. 124–126.

46. Ibid., pp. 126–129.

47. Ibid., pp. 129–134.

48. Ibid., pp. 134–135.
49. Ibid., pp. 135–137.
50. Ibid., pp. 137–138.
51. *Régionalisation du budget, 1966*, pp. 12–15.
52. Ibid., p. 21.
53. Ibid.
54. Ibid., p. 23.
55. Ibid., pp. 28–33.
56. *Avis et rapports, Ve Plan*, p. 3.
57. Ibid., p. 21.
58. Ibid., pp. 23, 57–58.
59. Ibid., pp. 22–23. See also René Chouteau, "L'éducation nationale sans dot," *Le Monde*, October 17–18, 1965, p. 16.
60. *Avis et rapports, Ve Plan*, p. 55.

10. The Urban Hierarchy and the Policy of *Métropoles d'Equilibre*

1. François Bloch-Lainé, "Justification des choix," *Urbanisme*, No. 89 (1965), p. 6.
2. P. Bauchet, "La comptabilité économique régionale et son usage," *E. A.*, XIV (January, 1961), p. 74. See also M. Roncayolo, "Inégalité géographique en France," *C. R.*, No. 51 (January, 1963), pp. 65–66.
3. Yvon Chotard, "Evolution des fonctions et des structures urbains et rurales dans le cadre d'une politique d'aménagement du territoire," *Avis et rapports*, March 16, 1966, p. 213.
4. Bloch-Lainé, p. 6.
5. Hautreux, Lecourt, and Rochefort, *Le niveau supérieur*. See also Hautreux and Rochefort, *La fonction*, and CREDOC, *Essai*.
6. LeFillatre, *Le pouvoir*.
7. J. Hautreux, "Les principales villes attractives et leur ressort d'influence," *Urbanisme*, No. 78 (1963), pp. 57–64.
8. *Premier rapport*, p. 82.
9. Ibid., pp. 83–84.
10. Ibid., p. 84.
11. Ibid., pp. 85–87.
12. Ibid., pp. 87–89. See also Chotard, p. 216.
13. *Premier rapport*, pp. 89–90.
14. Ibid., pp. 90–91.
15. *Principales options*, p. 183.
16. Ibid., p. 184.
17. *Ve Plan*, p. 131.
18. Ibid., p. 132.
19. Ibid., pp. 132–133.
20. Ibid., p. 133.
21. Ibid.

22. Serge Antoine and Gérard Weill, "Les métropoles et leur région," *Urbanisme*, No. 89 (1965), p. 11.

23. *Régionalisation du budget, 1966,* pp. 55–61; La Documentation Française, "La régionalisation du budget de l'état et l'aménagement du territoire, 1966," *N. E. D.,* December 7, 1965, pp. 22–25.

24. Chotard, p. 227.

25. Ibid., p. 207.

26. A. Lewin, "Caractères originaux des métropoles d'équilibre," *Urbanisme*, No. 89 (1965), p. 29.

27. Ibid., p. 31.

28. Ibid., p. 32.

29. Hautreux, Lecourt, and Rochefort, *Le niveau supérieur.*

30. Pierre Bauchet, "Perspectives de développement de la Lorraine," *R. E.,* VII (November, 1956), pp. 926–927.

31. J.-F. Gravier, *L'aménagement du territoire et l'avenir des régions françaises* (Paris: Flammarion, 1964), p. 57.

32. *Le Monde,* October 15, 1965, p. 22.

33. *Avis, Lemaire,* p. 39.

34. Ibid.

35. Ibid., p. 49.

36. Olivier Guichard, *Aménager la France* (Paris: Laffont-Gonthier, 1965), p. 69.

37. See, for example, A. Riotte and R. Carillon, *Comment concevoir le regroupement communal* (Paris: Expansion régionale, 1964), pp. 11–15; and François Mitterand, "L'aménagement rural et urbain est mal appliquée," *Un grand débat,* pp. 11–14.

38. "L'aménagement du territoire et l'action régionale," *Sondages,* No. 1 (1965), pp. 64–65.

39. Ibid., p. 66.

40. Ibid., p. 81.

41. Robert Butheau, "Paris est-il la véritable capitale de la région Rhône-Alpes?" *Le Monde,* April 20, 1966, p. 11.

42. Gravier, p. 321.

43. Ibid., p. 322.

44. Ibid., pp. 322–323.

45. Robert Carillon, *La politique de développement régional* (Paris: Expansion régionale, 1965), p. 58.

46. Ibid.

47. *Ve Plan,* p. 133.

48. Pierre Janrot, "Du village-centre à la métropole d'équilibre," *E. R.,* IV (November–December, 1964), p. 14.

11. A Summary View

1. *Ve Plan,* p. 118.

2. *Régionalisation du budget, 1966,* pp. 131–133.

3. *Premier rapport*, p. 44.

4. Ibid., p. 41.

5. *Principales options*, pp. 176–177, 184–185.

6. *Vᵉ Plan*, pp. 124–126.

7. *Régionalisation du budget, 1966*, tome I, p. 21.

8. *Vᵉ Plan*, p. 119.

9. M. Flamant, "Concept et usages des 'économies externes,'" *R. E. P.*, LXXIV (January-February, 1964), pp. 108–109.

10. *Vᵉ Plan*, p. 125.

11. J. Paelinck, "La théorie du développement régional polarisé," C. I. S. E. A., Series L, No. 15 (March, 1965), p. 47.

12. Jules Milhau, "La recherche économique doit-elle rester une 'chasse gardée' de l'administration," *Le Monde*, October 10–11, 1965, p. 11.

13. *Le Monde*, June 21, 1966, p. 22.

14. *Le Monde*, June 12–13, 1966, p. 10.

15. Alphonse Thelier, "Les comités d'expansion régionaux sont-ils condamnés à disparaître?" *Le Monde*, June 19–20, 1966, p. 11.

16. "Normal budget subsidies are written each year into the Finance Act under the relevant Ministry. The basic rate is 30 per cent of total cost but the maximum rate is not always reached. Examples are the Ministry of the Interior for roads, drainage, water and housing in urban centres where the average participation rate is 16 per cent, and the Ministries of Education and Health whose participation can reach 80 per cent of total cost." John and Anne-Marie Hackett, *Economic Planning in France* (Cambridge: Harvard University Press, 1963), p. 250.

17. *Régionalisation du budget, 1966*, tome I, p. 54.

18. Ibid.

19. *Régionalisation en 1964*, p. 10.

20. *Régionalisation du budget, 1966*, tome I, p. 38.

21. Ibid.

22. Guy Muller, "Communes et départements pourront-ils faire face aux lourdes charges d'équipment prévues?" *Le Monde*, May 4, 1966, p. 15.

12. Some Implications for American Regional Policy

1. President's Appalachian Regional Commission, *Appalachia* (Washington, D.C.: United States Government Printing Office, 1964), p. 32.

2. Ibid., p. 23.

3. United States House of Representatives, Committee on Public Works, Appalachian Regional Development Act of 1965, House Report No. 51, 89th Cong., 1st. sess. (cited hereafter as "House Report No. 51"), pp. 33–58.

4. President's Appalachian Regional Commission, p. 42.

5. Appalachian Regional Development Act of 1965, 79 Stat. 5 (1965), sec. 201(d).

6. House Report No. 51, p. 16.

7. President's Appalachian Regional Commission, p. 40.

8. United States Senate, Committee on Public Works, Hearings on Appalachian Regional Development Act of 1965, 89th Cong., 1st sess. (cited hereafter as "Senate Hearings"), p. 54.

9. Ibid., pp. 53–54.

10. Appalachian Regional Development Act of 1965, sec. 203.

11. House Report No. 51, p. 50.

12. See, for example, Senate Hearings, p. 158, and House Report No. 51, p. 4.

13. United States House of Representatives, Committee on Public Works, Hearings on Appalachian Regional Development Act of 1965, 89th Cong., 1st sess., p. 42.

14. Harry M. Caudill, *Night Comes to the Cumberlands* (Boston: Houghton-Mifflin, 1963), p. 136; see also pp. 374–375.

15. Gunnar Myrdal, *Rich Lands and Poor* (New York: Harper and Brothers, 1957), p. 35.

16. Victor Fuchs, *The Growing Importance of the Service Industries,* National Bureau of Economic Research Occasional Paper No. 96 (New York: National Bureau of Economic Research, 1965), pp. 1–2, 17–19, and Raymond Vernon, *The Changing Economic Function of the Central City* (New York: Committee for Economic Development, 1959), p. 35.

17. Victor Fuchs, *Changes in the Location of Manufacturing Since 1929* (New Haven: Yale University Press, 1962); Erling Olsen, "Erhvervslivets Lokalisering," *N. T.,* Nos. 1–2 (1965), pp. 18–30.

18. Clifford Sharp, "Congestion and Welfare—An Examination of the Case for a Congestion Tax," *E. J.,* LXXVI (December, 1966), p. 807.

19. Ibid., pp. 806–817.

20. G. P. St. Clair, "Congestion Tolls—An Engineer's Viewpoint," *Highway Research Record,* No. 47 (1964), p. 110.

21. Ross Davis, "New EDA Lineup to Link Aid Programs," *E. D.,* IV (January, 1967), p. 1.

22. Ibid.

23. Public Works and Economic Development Act of 1965, 79 Stat. 552 (1965), Title V.

24. Ibid., sec. 504.

25. John Meyer, "Regional Economics: A Survey," *A. E. R.,* LIII (March, 1963), p. 47.

26. Arthur Maass, "Benefit-Cost Analysis: Its Relevance to Public Investment Decisions," *Q. J. E.,* LXXX (May, 1966), pp. 216–217.

27. This information is based on Economic Development Administration data for 245 projects.

Subject Index

VII

Index of Names

319